Able Assistants for the Professional Minister

BROADMAN & HOLMAN PROFESSIONAL DEVELOPMENT BOOKS recognize church ministry as a distinct profession and encourage the professional growth of church ministers by providing information to help them:

- Learn new ministry methods
- Enrich their skills as preachers, teachers, and counselors
- Enhance their administrative abilities, particularly in the area of strategic planning, accounting, and human resources management
- Improve their abilities to manage church growth
- Stay abreast of trends in ministry

THE PROFESSIONAL DEVELOPMENT BOOKS SERIES:
- The Issachar Factor: *Understanding Trends that Confront Your Church and Designing a Strategy for Success*
- Power House: *A Step-by-Step Guide to Building a Church that Prays*
- Eating the Elephant: *Bite-Sized Steps to Achieve Long-Term Growth in Your Church*
- The 12 Essential Skills for Great Preaching
- The Antioch Effect: *8 Characteristics of Highly Effective Churches*
- The Empowered Communicator: *7 Keys to Unlocking an Audience*
- The Empowered Leader: *10 Keys to Servant Leadership*
- Giant Awakenings: *Making the Most of 9 Surprising Trends that Can Benefit Your Church*
- The Exodus Principle: *A 5-Part Strategy to Free Your People for Ministry*
- The Word for the Wise: *Making Scripture the Heart of Your Counseling Ministry*

Some books I enjoy. But Thom Rainer's *Effective Evangelistic Churches* is a book for which I give gratitude to God. Out of all the wonderful books on church growth and evangelism, I have always had the distinct impression that each of them suffered from a certain imbalance. This book captures not only what is happening but also what ought to happen.

Paige Patterson, President
Southeastern Baptist Theological Seminary, Wake Forest, North Carolina

This book is packed with helpful insights on how effective churches *really* reach out to their communities. Based on a well-conceived study of 576 churches, it gives us facts, not theory. Save yourself some time and read this book!

Rick Warren, Senior Pastor
Saddleback Valley Community Church, Mission Viejo, California

In this important book, evangelistic churches tell their own story—and Thom Rainer has asked the right questions. Clearly, this is one of the most important books any preacher seeking to lead an evangelistic church should read.

R. Albert Mohler Jr., President, The Southern Baptist Theological Seminary

Rainer's emphasis on prayer is a key to a reawakening of conversion growth through the church. Every discouraged pastor, staff member, or church leader should read this book about churches that are winning the lost.

Nell P. Bruce, Minister of Prayer
Highview Baptist Church, Louisville, Kentucky

Get it, read it, implement its insights and its many varied, multifaceted experiences, and any pastor of any church in any part of the kingdom will be visited with glorious results from heaven itself.

W. A. Criswell, Pastor Emeritus
First Baptist Church, Dallas, Texas

Thom Rainer has, once again, produced a first-of-a-kind book. This time it is a hard, objective, factual look at the nuts and bolts that make a successful soul-winning church tick. *Effective Evangelistic Churches* is a powerful beacon light which will steer God's people to join the master in seeking and saving the lost.

C. Peter Wagner
Donald A. McGavran Professor of Church Growth,
Fuller Theological Seminary

In his book, *Effective Evangelistic Churches,* Thom Rainer does a great job in cutting through contemporary stereotypes to explain, statistics in hand, what really causes a church to be effective in outreach. For many of us, Thom has confirmed what we have been suspecting for a long time. There is no substitute for making evangelism a priority.

Jerry Sutton, Senior Pastor
Two Rivers Baptist Church, Nashville, Tennessee

The thoroughness of the study, involving nearly 600 churches of varied sizes, makes its conclusions unusually beneficial and usable by churches of virtually any size, and in virtually any setting.

Morris H. Chapman, President and Chief Executive Officer
Executive Committee of the Southern Baptist Convention

Thom Rainer has taken us beyond theory of church growth. He has taken us into growing churches to document the principles of why they grew. Some sacred cows about growth don't stand up under the scrutiny of examination. At other places, we see new reasons why churches grow.

Elmer L. Towns, Dean
School of Religion, Liberty University

This book is truly a seminary course in evangelism and church growth.

T. W. Wilson, Executive Assistant to Billy Graham

Thom Rainer moves the focus of church growth back where it belongs—to conversion growth of the church. By researching churches that are effectively reaching the lost, he finds out what really works, which brings both insight and encouragement to the task of intentional evangelism.

Robert E. Coleman, Director of the School of World Mission and
Evangelism, Trinity Evangelical Divinity School

Rainer has done an excellent job in differentiating between "church growth" and "evangelistic churches." They obviously should go together, but the renewed emphasis upon soul-winning and church building through leading people to Christ is a needed emphasis in our day of broad market-based schemes of promotion. The bottom line for the New Testament Church must be confronting people with the Gospel and leading them to faith in Jesus Christ.

James T. Draper Jr., President
Sunday School Board, SBC

Fishers of men need this volume to enhance methods of evangelism. Keepers of the aquarium need it to demonstrate that the message is still as effectual as it was on Pentecost.

Stephen Drake, Pastor
First Baptist Church, Ashville, Alabama

A wonderful antidote to a certain silliness in the land that declares traditional evangelistic methods dead.

Mark Coppenger, President
Midwestern Baptist Theological Seminary

This work is needed and worthwhile because of its broad scope, because of its penetrating analysis, and because it does not quibble about the basic need of evangelistic churches. I commend it fully and enthusiastically.

Adrian Rogers, Pastor
Bellevue Baptist Church, Memphis, Tennessee

What Dean Kelly did for the seventies, Thom Rainer has done for the nineties. Among his most surprising and encouraging findings is the fact that genuine church growth correlates more with solid biblical preaching and authentic pastoral ministry than with the trendy peddling of the gospel so highly touted in recent years.

Timothy George, Dean
Beeson Divinity School, Samford University

I recommend Thom Rainer's book, *Effective Evangelistic Churches,* to anyone who honestly wants to look at solid principles of church growth for changing times. In days like this when paradigms of growth and effectiveness for churches seem to change with the wind, Rainer has once again provided an outstanding resource to help churches, pastors, and church leaders stay focused in their Great Commission task. It is a must to read for anyone building an evangelistic church.

Gene Mims, Vice-President
Church Growth Group, Sunday School Board, SBC

Thom Rainer's book turns the current wisdom about church growth on its head. His research shows us that the old ways still work in growing an evangelistic church.

Al Jackson, Pastor
Lakeview Baptist Church, Auburn, Alabama

Too many books on church growth give excuses to fail rather than ways to succeed. "You must have a good location," "you must have a certain worship style," and so on, they say. *Effective Evangelistic Churches* gives reasons to succeed rather than excuses to fail. It is the story of evangelistic growth by practitioners, not theorists. Read it! You will be affirmed and surprised.

Alvin L. Reid, Associate Professor
of Evangelism and Church Growth/Bailey Smith Chair of Evangelism
Southeastern Baptist Theological Seminary

Before reading this valuable and "hard-to-stop-reading" book, get ready to discover some facts that even Thom Rainer admits contradict some of his own presuppositions.

Larry Gilbert, Chairman and Founder
Ephesians Four Ministries, the parent company of Church Growth Institute
and Sunday School Dynamics

Effective Evangelistic Churches is a fascinating practical look at "What makes evangelistic churches tick." A modern-day pastor is faced with a plethora of church growth fads and church growth fables. This book is a clarion call to get back to the basics which God has used for 2000 years in building his church. I commend it heartily.

James Merritt, Pastor
First Baptist Church, Snellville, Georgia

The book bears the marks of competent professional statistical research and a style that is interesting and readable. It is a "must read" book for every pastor and church leader who has a commitment to the mission of Christ for their church.

Darrell W. Robinson, Vice President, Evangelism
Home Mission Board, SBC

When you read this book you are in for some startling surprises. And here is the biggest: it is not necessarily all of those "new ideas" or innovative methodologies that constitutes an effective evangelistic ministry, but doing the more traditional ministries very well. Rainer's well-documented investigation will help you in building a healthy, quality congregation.

Lewis A. Drummond, Billy Graham Professor of Evangelism and
Church Growth, Beeson Divinity School, Samford University

The insights are practical. Many of them are surprising—in some instances because they confirm evangelistic practices that churches once employed but have abandoned amid the profusion of more recent theory. The research-based hard data in this book demand that we rethink our assumptions about how we go about the principal task of the church.

Joe S. Ellis, Distinguished Professor of Church Growth
Cincinnati Bible Seminary

A book that carries so many references to prayer has my personal endorsement. The brother's quote in chapter six says it all: "If you desire to see the engine that provides power for our church, visit our upper room during the worship service. . . .You will see ten or more people pleading to God for a service of power and conviction. . . . We never cease to be amazed at the miraculous answers to prayer each Sunday."

Don Miller, Director, Bible Based Ministries

Effective Evangelistic Churches is one of the most exciting and encouraging publications in recent years. Church leaders in every size congregation will here find guidance to motivate God's people to renewed efforts in outreach. Those expecting to read just another book on evangelism will be surprised, informed, and challenged.

David S. Dockery, President
Union University

Finally! A research study on evangelism that looks at conversion growth rather than transfer growth. Thom S. Rainer has unlocked the doors of evangelistic churches in the United States to let us see precisely what works and what doesn't.

Gary L. McIntosh, Professor
Talbot School of Theology, LaMirada, California

The chapter on preaching alone is worth the price of the book. This is valuable information that is rarely found in church growth and evangelism literature—but desperately needed.

Kent R. Hunter, Church Growth Center

Every pastor and evangelist needs to read this book. As a vocational evangelist for 21 years, I am constantly encouraging ministers to stick to the basics—preaching the Word, powerful prayer, practical Sunday School and personal evangelism. As Thom Rainer has so well documented in this book, it's the basics that result in conversion growth.

Jerry Drace, Jerry Drace Evangelistic Association

Meticulously detailing every step in this investigation, Dr. Rainer has established what is truly bringing results to churches, especially, in evangelism. Without a preset agenda, he describes ten surprises, and then captures the real reasons churches are being effective in reaching people.

Bill L. Taylor, Director
Bible Teaching-Reaching Division, Sunday School Board, SBC

EFFECTIVE
EVANGELISTIC
CHURCHES

Published by Broadman & Holman Publishers, Nashville, Tennessee
Acquisitions & Development Editor: John Landers
Typography and Page Design: TF Designs, Mt. Juliet, Tennessee
Printed in the United States of America

4254-02
0-8054-5402-0

Dewey Decimal Classification: 269.2
Subject Heading: EVANGELISTIC WORK / CHURCH GROWTH
Library of Congress Card Catalog Number: 96-14454

Unless otherwise noted, Scripture quotations are from the Holy Bible, New International Version, copyright © 1973, 1978, 1984 by International Bible Society.

Library of Congress Cataloging-in-Publication Data
Rainer, Thom S.
    Effective evangelistic churches : successful churches reveal what works, and what doesn't / Thom Rainer.
        p. cm.
    ISBN 0-8054-5402-0
    1. Evangelistic work—United States. 2. Southern Baptist Convention—Membership. 3. Baptists—United States—Membership. I. Title.
    BX6462.3.R35   1996
    269'.2—dc20

96-14454
CIP

96 97 98 99 00 5 4 3 2 1

EFFECTIVE
EVANGELISTIC
CHURCHES

SUCCESSFUL CHURCHES

REVEAL WHAT WORKS

AND WHAT DOESN'T

THOM RAINER

BROADMAN
& HOLMAN
PUBLISHERS

Nashville, Tennessee

To:
Jess Keller,
my uncle, but like a father;
Arthur Clyde King and Nell King,
in-laws summa cum laude;
and always to
Jo
for eighteen years of joy and love

Contents

Map of 576 of the Most Effective Evangelistic Churches in America

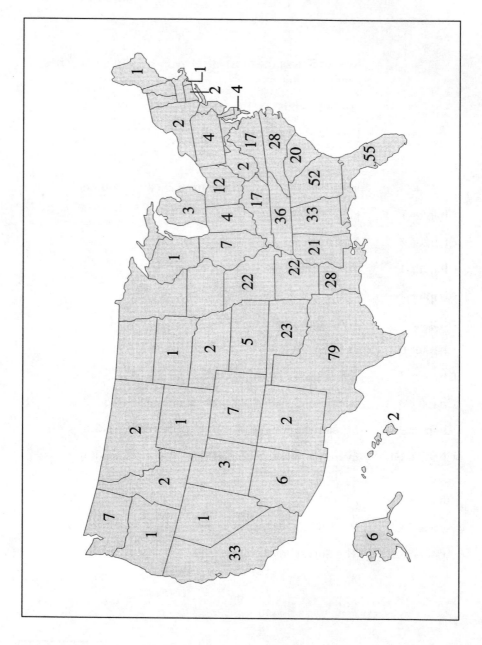

List of Exhibits

Foreword

Truly and verily, I do not exaggerate in the avowal that a reader of this volume, *Effective Evangelistic Churches,* will have a whole library of information before him and will be introduced to the marvelous achievement of reaching the lost and building up the congregation of the Lord. This professor-preacher, Thom Rainer, has done an unbelievably effective work in looking at these churches who are carrying out the Great Commission of our Savior, the Lord Jesus.

There are literally thousands of churches who do not have any burden for the lost. There are other thousands who would do the work of evangelism if they knew how to implement the effective methods of reaching lost souls. This book by Thom Rainer is an answer to every spiritual and homiletical and evangelistic assignment of the church of Christ.

Get it, read it, implement its insights and its many varied, multifaceted experiences, and any pastor of any church in any part of the kingdom will be visited with glorious results from heaven itself.

W. A. Criswell, Pastor Emeritus
First Baptist Church, Dallas

Acknowledgments

Two years of data gathering and research. . . . In some ways I feel as though I have been involved with this project for a lifetime. This work was truly a team effort. Though I am the author of the book, numerous persons contributed to make this work a reality.

My deepest appreciation is extended to my colleague in the Christian Education School of Southern Seminary, Jon Rainbow, for designing the survey instrument. Jon, you took a lot of suggestions and made it work. Thanks.

Though I will not name all of the contributors, thirty-two persons from diverse fields provided input into the survey. I hope this project helped in your areas of interest.

A special thanks goes to my colleagues in the Graham School: Hal Poe, Mark Terry, and Bob Hughes. Thank you, friends, for all the help you gave me on this project. You are a joy to have on the team!

Six Ph.D. students in evangelism and church growth at Southern Seminary deserve recognition for their hours of labor: Ron McLain, Chuck Lawless, Don Cox, Tommy Ferrell, Scott Guffin, and Rob Jackson. Ron McLain especially deserves accolades and honor for the hours he spent in interviews and data tabulations. Thanks, Ron, your work is evident throughout the book.

One day in the near future a child will be told of his or her last days in Mama's womb as she worked countless hours on this project. The mom and my secretary, Robin Ebeyer, worked weeks and months on this project, virtually up to her delivery date. As I write these words, Robin has not yet given birth, but the time is imminent. Thank you, Robin, for your great work and great attitude. Your patience with my poor planning is exemplary.

My gratitude is also expressed to the Dehoney Institute for funding this project. The Dehoney Institute is part of the Billy Graham School of Missions, Evangelism, and Church Growth at Southern Seminary.

To John Landers and the Broadman & Holman team, once again it has been a joy to work with you. This work is my fourth book with B & H. My appreciation for you has grown with each new project. I hope the feeling is mutual!

The best is always saved for last. Sam, Art, and Jess, you always pray for me. You always pray for my books. You are always patient with me. I thank God for you, boys. The book is done! Get out the basketballs and footballs again. Watch your old man humiliate you! Seriously, boys, you are the best sons a dad could have. I love you so much.

And now *the* best. Jo, as I write these words, we are just a few days away from our eighteenth anniversary. I am so thankful that my writing is complete so I can give you the time you deserve. You have been so patient with me on this book, my most tedious work yet. Now we can go for a walk, sip a diet cola, and just talk. You are God's gift of love to me, and I love you with all my heart. Here's to the next eighteen years!

Introduction:
New Insights from Exciting Churches

When we began this study, I sensed that we would discover some new and exciting insights. I must admit, however, that my expectations were surpassed many times over. Like any researcher, I came to this study with my own biases. Undoubtedly, I am far from being bias-free even at its conclusion.

But this project made me reevaluate some assumptions and "truths" I thought were unalterable. It helped me appreciate more the men and women, ordained and laypersons, who pour out their lives in sacrificial service to their local churches. It also helped me realize more clearly who the true "experts" of church growth are. They are not the academicians and researchers such as myself, but those people who are on the front line of spiritual warfare in their local churches.

Please remember that you are reading neither another church growth book nor another book based on the empirical research of a few dozen churches. I appreciate the keen insights from those authors and researchers who have done such works in recent years.

This book, however, is a work on *evangelistic* growth, not just church growth. As I read again through my rather extensive church growth library, I realized that none of the works had devoted themselves to the study of leading *conversion* growth churches. I am first a student of evangelism before church growth because the biblical priority is the new life in Christ rather than the relative size of a church.

This book also is not another research work on a few dozen growing churches. It is one of the most challenging evangelistic research projects ever attempted: to study in great detail 576 of the most evangelistic churches in America. The churches' attendance ranged from sixty to six thousand, but they were all reaching people for Christ. When I shared with my friend, Elmer Towns, the scope, breadth, and depth of this project, he saw its potential as one of the most comprehensive studies ever done in evangelism. Whether we met those high expectations remains to be seen. You will be the judge.

A Tale of Two Churches

Before we delve into some further introductory matters, I want you, the reader, to get a taste of the excitement I experienced in leading this study. You will probably run into surprises in this book (such as the amazing fact that almost *no* church leader attributes the evangelistic growth of his church to its location). But first, please meet two churches with two exciting stories. You've probably never heard of them, nor do their names appear in any church growth books, but their churches are making a difference for the kingdom.

Emmanuel Baptist Church

Travel with me some twenty-five miles south of Fort Worth on Interstate 35W. We take U.S. Highway 67 west for another thirty-five miles to the town of Glen Rose, Texas, population around two thousand. The location is not bad, but we have learned it really has no impact on the evangelistic effectiveness of Emmanuel Baptist Church.

Why are we interested in this church? After all, its membership is 202 and attendance averages about 160. The town is small. What can we learn from this church?

Our interest was piqued when we learned that this mid-sized church baptized fifty people in one year. That is one person reached for Christ for every four members! In the Southern Baptist Convention, the average is one baptism yearly for every *forty* members.

To put it into perspective, if a megachurch of four thousand members baptized one person for every four members, it would reach one thousand people for Christ in one year! Or if every church in the Southern Baptist Convention was that evangelistically effective, the denomination would reach 3.75 million people per year for Christ. The actual number is under four hundred thousand. That is why we are interested in Emmanuel Baptist Church.

We could share with you a great deal about this church. Please keep in mind that Emmanuel reached 2 percent of its population for Christ in one year. A church in a metropolitan area of one million would have to reach twenty-five thousand per year to have a comparable ratio. Listen to the evangelistic story of this church.

- The church uses both *Evangelism Explosion* and *Continuous Witness Training* for evangelistic visitation. Many of the seeds for evangelism are planted through personal relationships.
- All new Christians must attend a pastor's class for three weeks. The class includes doctrinal studies, stewardship, Christian living, and church polity.
- The church is conservative theologically.
- The worship service is traditional but sometimes blended. The Sunday morning service typically has some evangelistic emphasis.
- Prayer plays a major role in the church's evangelistic effectiveness. The church has a 9:00 A.M. intercessory time on Sunday morning for the lost. Wednesday evening is designated as the time for corporate prayer for the lost. The women's missions group prays for the lost on Monday mornings. The church is asked to focus on the lost in their prayer times on Tuesday evening.
- Preaching is a priority for evangelistic emphasis.
- The Sunday School uses the *Growth Spiral* (a Southern Baptist growth plan). In the teachers' meetings, the teachers are encouraged to present the plan of salvation in their classes.
- The church has a strong missions emphasis.

First Southern Baptist Church

Garden City, Kansas, is about forty-five miles west of Dodge City on U.S. Highway 50. Population: 24,097. Garden City is the home of First Southern Baptist Church where Randy Caddell has been the pastor for nine years.

In one year this church of 488 members (370 in attendance) baptized 55 persons, or more than one person for every nine members. Once again we discovered a church where evangelism was prominent in almost every ministry and program. Listed below are some of Pastor Caddell's insights.

- A lay evangelism seminar has been presented five times in the last eight years. The focus of the seminar is to build witnessing relationships modeled after Paul's and Timothy's relationships.

- Outreach is intentional and sometimes confrontational. Sunday School is the outreach arm of the church. In Sunday School, the plan of salvation is presented on a regular basis.
- Assimilation takes place through the Sunday School. "Encouragers" are assigned to lead new converts through the *Survival Kit* (a discipleship manual for new Christians).
- Worship services are traditional and sometimes blended. Evangelistic sermons are preached twice a month.
- A twenty-four-hour prayer ministry includes the names of known non-believers.
- A Vietnamese mission meets at the church's facility while the church's worship service is in progress. An Anglo mission is also supported by the church.
- Evangelistic training is best learned on the job.
- The church enjoys a good location in a highly visible, fast-growing section. This location, however, has not been important in the church's evangelistic outreach.

When we asked Pastor Caddell what we could learn from his church, he responded, "There is no wrong way to share Christ as long as we don't compromise the gospel. We encourage one another in evangelism. And we must continue in our own spiritual growth."

The Uniqueness of This Study

You will be reminded throughout this book that we are investigating *evangelistic* growth, not total growth. The total growth of churches has been the subject of numerous books and studies. Though I am grateful for the insights of these works, the primary concern of this study is conversion growth.

A second uniqueness of the study we conducted is the massive amount of data gathered from 576 churches. Even this book could not communicate everything we received from these evangelistic churches.

Also, this research project focuses on churches of all sizes, something most other church growth books have not done. Larger churches have received a significant amount of attention. While we are grateful for the contribution of megachurches and other large churches, we also must recognize the exciting work of God in smaller and medium-sized congregations. The sizes of the churches in the study were:

Average Attendance	Number of Churches	Percent of Total
Less than 100	5	0.9
100–299	220	38.2
300–499	172	29.9
500–699	72	12.5
700–999	51	8.8
1,000–1,499	29	5.0
More than 1,500	27	4.7
Total	576	100

The small number of churches less than one hundred in attendance is not representative of the actual number of small evangelistic churches. Because many of these pastors are part time or bivocational, they had difficulty finding the time to complete the extensive surveys we sent to the churches.

Nearly 40 percent of the churches had an average attendance of 100 to 299, the largest single category. Our research also showed that churches of this size had the best baptismal ratios. More on this issue later.

Finally, remember that much of this study reflects the insights of the leaders of these churches. Often we hear their subjective perspectives. Unlike some other good studies, we did not focus on listening to new believers or new church members.

The Churches Selected

All churches selected for this study are Southern Baptist churches. Undoubtedly some will question the value of a study that is limited to one denomination. We decided to use the data from Southern Baptists for two reasons.

First, as we looked at other denominational statistics, we realized several incongruencies in the types of data gathered. We were interested in determining conversion growth relative to the membership of churches. For Southern Baptists that data is easy to measure and easy to gather. We simply needed total baptisms for one year and resident membership. The inclusion of data from other denominations did not always match easily with our Southern Baptist statistics. Simply stated, we were comparing "apples and oranges."

Second, Southern Baptists are the largest Protestant denomination in the United States. Though their churches are still concentrated in the South, the denomination has experienced significant growth in other areas. We are thus not focusing on one region or even one people group, but a diverse body geographically, racially, and culturally.

At the time we began this study the most recent data available was for the year ending September 30, 1993. We somewhat arbitrarily decided to examine only those churches whose annual baptismal total exceeded twenty-five for that year. We then determined that a church must have a baptismal ratio (resident members/baptisms) of less than 20:1. In other words, the church was reaching at least one person for Christ for every twenty members.

Of the nearly 40,000 Southern Baptist churches, approximately 1,400 met both parameters of at least twenty-six baptisms and a baptismal ratio of less than 20:1. To these churches we sent an extensive ten-page survey.

We were pleasantly surprised to have almost 700 surveys returned, nearly 50 percent, after just one request. And we were able to use the data from 576 of the surveys.

We recognized that, despite the reasons for using the statistics from only one denomination, such an approach had its weaknesses. Generally speaking, Southern Baptists are considered conservative evangelicals on the theological spectrum. Thus this study is not necessarily a good indicator for theologically liberal churches.

Also, Southern Baptists are strong Sunday School based churches. They believe in Sunday School as a primary instrument for teaching, reaching, ministering, and discipling. The Sunday School bias, one which I claim proudly, will be evident in this study.

Yet in the final analysis, we felt that using data from the largest Protestant denomination in America had more strengths than weaknesses. I believe that even if you are not a Southern Baptist, you will still find the results of this study to be a fascinating venture into the hearts of evangelistic churches.

The Methodology Used

Our first task was to design an instrument that asked all of the questions we needed to ask. We thus inquired of dozens of leaders in churches, denominational work, theological education, family ministries, music ministries, and a number of other categories what they would like to see included in this study. Many of their suggestions were taken. The instrument asked the leaders of evangelistic churches for information in eight different categories:

1. Evangelistic methods. Over twenty methods were included in the study, including types of ministries in the churches.

2. Attitudes toward evangelism. Over thirty different attitudinal questions were asked.

3. Worship style. We described seven types: liturgical, traditional, revivalist, contemporary, seeker-sensitive, blended, and other. Because of the similarities in categories, traditional and revivalist were combined for statistical purposes, as were contemporary and seeker-sensitive.

4. Type of congregation. We asked the church leaders to describe their churches as activist, civic, outreach, or fellowship.

5. Theological beliefs. About God, Scripture, sin, and salvation.

6. Preaching type. Expository, textual, topical, thematic, narrative, or other.

7. Other helpful information. Retention rate; discipleship programs or models, attendance, church setting, church age, tenure of pastor, education level of pastor, composition or membership (racial, ethnic, and socioeconomic), missions giving and support, leadership style of pastor, staff composition, and evangelism training programs.

8. Any other helpful information that was not included in the survey.

After the ten-page survey was designed and drafted, it was sent to nearly 1,400 churches that met the minimum parameters described earlier. As stated before, nearly one-half were returned for this study.

One problem we acknowledged from the onset was that churches were selected from one year's data only. It was possible that some churches would have a significant number of baptisms for one year only, an aberration from their normal conversion growth pattern. Such churches should not be classified as "evangelistically-effective" based on one year alone. We discovered, however, that the leaders of such churches usually wrote to let us know that their high baptismal experience was not an ongoing pattern, thereby excluding themselves from the study. Thus we determined that most of the churches which did participate in the study had experienced consistent conversion growth for several years.

After consolidating and tabulating the large amount of data, we interviewed extensively the leaders in more than 100 churches. Some interviews were conducted at the site of the churches; many others were by telephone. These church leaders helped us better understand the data we had received.

Please note that I shift between first-person plural and first-person singular throughout this book. "We" typically refers to the entire research team, while "I" means that I am speaking of an aspect of the study in which I was personally involved. Many times a person's name is given. All names are real; none are fictitious. Where names are mentioned, permission was given to publish them. Otherwise, a generic term, such as "a pastor" or "a staff member," is used.

The Path of This Book

Prepare for an exciting journey to 576 churches in forty-one states. Come with a prayerful heart and an open mind. Some of your presuppositions will be affirmed; others may be challenged.

We begin in the first chapter with the most significant findings about methodologies in these evangelistic churches. Chapter 2 reveals several major "surprises" that were discovered in this study. The next three chapters examine in detail the three major methodologies in evangelistic churches, which were mentioned briefly in chapter 1.

The study then turns its attention to the issue of worship and evangelistic growth. Does style of worship have any relationship to evangelistic growth of the church?

Pastors and other church leaders shared with us openly about their beliefs and attitudes. In chapter 7 we learn how these factors affect the evangelistic priority of the church. Chapter 8 describes the role of such areas as counseling, family ministries, and other social ministries in the church's evangelistic outreach.

Can a church experience evangelistic growth while "giving away" people and funds for mission efforts? We look at the correlation between these two factors in chapter 9.

In chapter 10 we see that evangelistic churches are also strong in discipleship. What this part of the study reveals is the *type* of effective discipleship that truly closes the "back door."

The final chapter provides a profile of evangelistic churches and lessons we can learn from them. You will hear some amazing insights from some of the most outstanding Christian leaders in America.

Conclusion

God is at work in marvelous ways in numerous churches across our nation. I feel privileged and honored to listen to those who serve our Lord in these fellowships. They have taught me many new lessons and affirmed for me many of the basics of growing an evangelistic church. Perhaps even more, I have caught the evangelistic spirit of these leaders. Thank you reader, for joining me on this journey. I pray that you too will learn from these insights and, above all, that you will catch the spirit of evangelism.

CHAPTER ONE

How They Evangelize

> If there is one God, Creator, Redeemer, Judge, as the early Church passionately asserted, then those who have been brought back from their rebellion against him into fellowship with him cannot but pass on the knowledge of that rescue to others; the new life cries out to be shared.
>
> Michael Green, *Evangelism in the Early Church*

Imagine this scenario. You have gathered before you the leaders of nearly six hundred of the most evangelistic churches in America. The churches they represent can be found in almost every state, and their average attendance ranges from sixty to six thousand. Demographically the churches are white-collar, blue-collar, rural, urban, suburban, white, Hispanic, black, Asian, lower-income, middle-income, and upper-income, to name a few. The worship services in these churches are traditional, contemporary, liturgical, blended, country-gospel, and "the blues." (That is what one church leader said anyway!) The pastors in these churches have served from four months to nearly forty years. They are seminary-trained, Bible school-trained, or have no formal theological training. Some have Ph.Ds., while others have high school diplomas only.

The group before you is diverse in many ways. Yet these leaders have one common bond: they are *passionate* about evangelism and leading new believers to discipleship in the local church. Now, not all of these leaders consider themselves "natural" evangelistic leaders. One pastor shared with me: "I am scared to death every time I witness one-on-one. But I know Jesus commanded us to do just that, so I must be obedient. And I must lead my church to lead others to Christ."

Yet another pastor told me: "I don't have the gift of evangelism, but I have discovered the joy of evangelism. But evangelism sure is hard work. There are no shortcuts. You just have to work at it every day."

As you approach this unique group of evangelistic leaders, you are allowed to ask them a few questions. One question is foremost on your mind: you simply desire to know *how*. So you ask, "How has your church been so effective in evangelism?"

The answers gush forth like a roaring waterfall. One after another, each leader gives responses without interruption. There is so much noise that you can barely hear the words. But you focus all of your auditory skills and begin to hear some answers:

- "We normally conduct three revivals a year. That is the key to an evangelistic harvest."
- "Revivals no longer work in our church for evangelism. They are for the renewal of Christians only."
- "The main factor is that we are a contemporary, innovative church."
- "The main factor is that we have refused to abandon the traditions of the church."
- "The pastor must go door-to-door witnessing."
- "We are no longer able to get into homes to share the gospel."
- "The pastor must have a welcome class for people interested in the gospel and the church."
- "The pastor must lead in evangelism."
- "The church must have an attitude of intentional evangelism."
- "Our Sunday School is our most effective tool for outreach."
- "Our Sunday School has been ineffective in evangelism."
- "Counseling has proved to be a wonderful setting for evangelism."
- "I wish our counseling ministries could be more effective in evangelism."
- "Prayer ministries are vital."
- "It begins with prayer."
- "We pray for lost people by name."
- "We are not traditional but led by the Holy Spirit."
- "We are traditional and led by the Holy Spirit."
- "New churches reach people faster! Double the emphasis on church planting."

Hundreds of other comments continue, but you are now more confused than ever. You were looking for some simple answers, but the responses were numerous and often conflicting. Can we really discover how these churches are reaching people for Christ? The answer is yes, but it might take an entire book to answer the question completely! In this chapter we attempt to answer the pragmatic "How?" question. Some of the material might not surprise you. But, for many of you, get ready to discover some surprising insights from churches that reach the lost.

The Methodology Issue

Primarily because of the plethora of material available about church growth methodologies, many church leaders today resist information that tells them "how-to." They have discovered over the years that growing an evangelistic church has no quick-fix solution. Yet we must not move to the other extreme and disregard *any* methodologies as unimportant. Methodologies are important when we see them as tools to be used by God, rather than *the* perfect solution to our church needs.

In our written survey to these churches we asked numerous methodological questions. As we tabulated hundreds of pages of data and followed up with telephone and on-site interviews, we made three general conclusions about evangelistic methodologies.

First, the types of methodologies are as numerous as the churches themselves. God is using a variety of methods in a variety of churches to draw people to Himself. Inevitably, the sheer number of responses meant that some of the methodologies conflict with others. That which works in a traditional church in Anniston, Alabama, may not work in a contemporary church in Fresno, California.

Second, though the methodologies are diverse, the number of evangelistic principles are few. Before you finish reading this book you will be able to discern the major principles guiding these churches.

Finally, in the midst of the many voices which responded to our questions of methodologies, some major trends did emerge. We begin by looking at the "big three" methodologies in evangelistic churches.

The "Big Three" Methodologies

Perhaps one of the most surprising conclusions we reached about evangelistic methodologies is that three factors were consistently important in most churches of all sizes. Because of the importance of these issues, an entire chapter will be devoted to each of them. For now let us take a brief look at the "big three" evangelistic methodologies.

The Pulpit and Evangelism

Repeatedly the leaders of these evangelistic churches told us that preaching is one of the most effective means of reaching people for Christ. (In chap. 3 we will examine the types of preaching models used by these pastors). It cannot be overstated, however, that the spoken word from the written Word is critically important in evangelism. The pulpit is powerful! In our infatuation with church growth methodologies over the past three decades, the role of preaching for evangelistic growth has been sorely neglected.

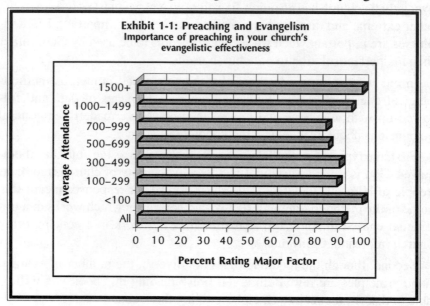

Exhibit 1-1: Preaching and Evangelism
Importance of preaching in your church's
evangelistic effectiveness

When we asked church leaders to rate the evangelistic methodologies, preaching consistently received the highest response. Additionally, the responses varied little with the size of the church. Churches whose average attendance was more than one thousand rated preaching slightly higher than most other churches as a contributing factor to evangelistic effectiveness. Such a response is not surprising, given the high profile of megachurch pastors. What is surprising is that leaders of churches whose average attendance is less than three hundred ranked preaching almost as important as the megachurch pastors.

Remember, we are hearing the views of church leaders whose churches are already evangelistically effective. They are not giving us unsubstantiated opinions. They truly believe preaching is primary in their successful outreach. Second, these pastors see the pulpit as the focus for evangelism in both the messages they preach and the emphases they make in this speaking forum. They not only see the sermon itself as a vehicle for evangelism, but everything that is said from the pulpit provides the church leadership and direction. As one pastor commented, "God's Word is powerful. Faithfully proclaiming from the Bible is absolutely necessary for evangelism. But a pastor can preach faithfully from God's Word every Sunday, yet have little or no evangelistic thrust." He then concluded, "It's not either/or. The preacher must believe and preach God's Word with power, *and* he must keep evangelism as a priority in everything he says."

Prayer Ministries and Evangelism

Across our nation a powerful movement of God's Spirit is transforming many churches from near-death to new life with evangelistic zeal. Though one must be careful about explaining the work of a sovereign God, we see a clearly discernible pattern in many of these newly-awakened churches. Prior to the visible manifestations of God's Spirit through repentance, brokenness, and people coming to Christ, a new emphasis on prayer and prayer ministries touches the church. Often the prayer emphasis takes the form of organized times for intercessory prayer or days of prayer and fasting. Rarely are a majority of the church members involved, but the minority who do participate see their lives radically changed.

This core of Christians provides the spark in the church that ignites an unprecedented evangelistic emphasis. Excitement builds as more and more people accept Christ.

Though the forms of prayer ministries vary, the leaders of these evangelistic churches stress that their personal prayer lives and the prayer ministries of the church are inevitably tied to the winning of souls to Christ. One pastor shared, "We have had a three-year revival which seems to have come from the beginning of PrayerLife, a Southern Baptist prayer ministry. I have never seen anything in my life like this."

Our survey results ranked prayer ministries second only to preaching as the most important methodology in evangelistic effectiveness. Again, responses varied little with church size. We will examine this critical relationship between prayer and evangelism further in chapter 4.

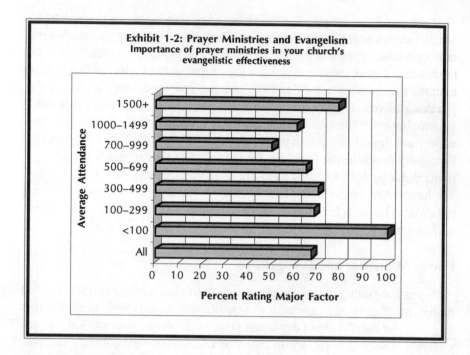

Exhibit 1-2: Prayer Ministries and Evangelism
Importance of prayer ministries in your church's evangelistic effectiveness

Sunday School and Evangelism

If any program-based methodology proved to be a dynamic tool for these evangelistic churches, it was the Sunday School program. Most of the leaders of these churches were amused at the prophesies of the decline or death of Sunday School. When we asked them why such predictions were being made, they had a unified response: The problem with non-evangelistic Sunday Schools is not the program itself; the problem is failure to use the program as an intentional evangelistic tool. Here are a few of their comments.

- "Our Sunday School is the most effective tool for evangelism."
- "We require all our Sunday School teachers to have evangelism training."
- "Our Sunday School teachers are encouraged to minister to those in need in our small community. Many have come to Christ as a result."
- "We evangelize through the Sunday School."
- "A majority of our baptisms come as a result of evangelistic teaching in the youth Sunday School classes."

Sunday School was the third highest response when we asked these churches about the reasons for their evangelistic effectiveness. Though we will look at the specifics of this methodology in chapter 5, for now we see that evangelistic churches of all sizes valued the role of Sunday School as a methodology for reaching people.

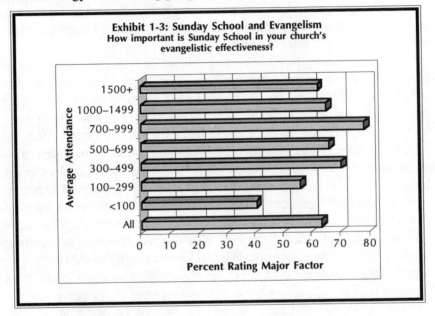

Exhibit 1-3: Sunday School and Evangelism
How important is Sunday School in your church's evangelistic effectiveness?

Other Methodologies in Evangelistic Churches

While three methodologies emerged as significant evangelistic tools, the number of additional methods reported was incredible. God is certainly not limited in how He chooses to draw the lost to Himself! Statistically speaking, however, seven methodologies emerged as major instruments of evangelism. You have heard about the first three. As we examine four other methodologies, you may be as surprised as we were!

Relationship Evangelism

It is difficult to distinguish between Sunday School and relationship building as methodologies for evangelism, because so much of the relationship building takes place in Sunday School classes. According to one pastor nearly 90 percent of his church's baptisms were adults and youth who had developed significant relationships with Christians in their

Sunday School classes. Nevertheless, we separated relationship evangelism from Sunday School as a methodology since some of the relationships develop in the workplace, schools, and homes, apart from the Sunday School environment.

Relationship evangelism responses showed significant statistical variance at different church sizes. Stated more clearly, the larger the church, the more likely it was to consider relationship evangelism a significant factor in its evangelistic effectiveness.

As we interviewed further about the different responses according to church size, we discovered some important insights. First, most pastors considered their own personal evangelistic efforts to be important to their churches and to their own spiritual growth. Often fifteen to twenty baptisms per year were the result of one pastor's own soul-winning efforts.

Members of smaller churches perceived that number of baptisms to be a significant evangelistic harvest. Unless the pastor was persistent in his attempts to train and recruit others for witnessing, the responsibility of soul winning remained primarily with him. The congregational attitude of "that's what we pay him for" often resulted in little churchwide enthusiasm to develop relationships with the lost. After all, "our church is evangelistic enough with our pastor's efforts. We can focus on other ministries."

In the larger churches the pastor, again, was often used of God to bring fifteen to twenty people to Christ. Yet that number of baptisms was not perceived to be a significant evangelistic harvest for the total church. There seemed to be greater motivation on the part of the congregation to "do my part." No one person, not even the pastor, could carry the evangelistic responsibility alone. Thus the larger churches tended to emphasize all church members developing relationships with the lost. Chapter 5 will examine *how* church members develop relationships with these unchurched and lost people.

Traditional Outreach

Students of church growth have heard for years that traditional outreach is declining as an effective growth tool. The arguments are well-known. People resent their homes and privacy being invaded by religious fanatics. You cannot motivate church members to gather every week to go visiting and share the gospel; cold-call visitation is dead.

I recently read some literature by a supposed church growth authority who made similar remarks. Interestingly, almost everything he said about traditional outreach was contradicted by the data we received. Much to my chagrin, *I* was that writer!

But what about other studies of growing churches which made the conclusion that traditional outreach is on the decline? When I read again those studies of recent years, I discovered something significantly different from this study. The other research was based on growing churches, but not necessarily churches that were increasing in size by *conversion* growth. In fact, many of the churches were hardly growing at all through new converts, but by Christians who were leaving one church to join another. Additionally, the other studies rarely looked at more than forty to fifty churches.

We have heard from the leaders of nearly six hundred evangelistic churches. Over one-half (50.2 percent) of these leaders ranked weekly outreach as one of their most effective evangelistic tools. Only four other methodologies fared better.

Why is the traditional method of outreach still effective evangelistically? Why is it important in many of these churches to gather the people once a week to visit the lost, to visit those who visited the church, and to visit those who may not have a church home? Several themes emerged from our conversation with the church leaders.

1. The Great Commission is a mandate to go. Many of these pastors shared that the true spirit of the Great Commission is a spirit of going. While developing relationships with the lost is critically important, the church is still mandated to leave the comfort of their homes and places of work to seek the lost. Relationship building alone is not sufficient to evangelize in the spirit of the New Testament church.

Sammie Daniels is pastor of Park City Baptist Church in Park City, Montana. In one year Park City Baptist baptized forty-two people, but their membership is only 104 (though their worship attendance is 185). For its size, Park City Baptist is one of the most evangelistic churches in America.

Pastor Daniels shared with us that they have door-to-door visitation by the members. Sunday School teachers must visit the prospects for their classes. And Pastor Daniels himself has a daily visitation schedule.

Bill Hohenstreet is another one of many pastors who feels that traditional outreach is critical. His church is Post Falls Baptist Church in Post Falls, Idaho. The two-hundred-member church baptized forty-eight. Pastor Hohenstreet speaks of his primary outreach methodologies as "door-to-door, cold-call visitation, and Tuesday night visitation using a prospect list. Of the 130 in average Sunday School attendance, an average of 40 people participate in Tuesday night visitation!"

2. *The best evangelism training takes place "on the job."* Evangelism is modeled by church leaders who take other members with them on visitation. Gary Kirkendoll, pastor of First Baptist Church, Greenbrier, Arkansas, said, "Formal training is important, but nothing can replace the actual visitation experience." One pastor in Texas takes a different person with him each time he visits someone.

3. *Traditional outreach is a visible manifestation of the church's commitment to evangelism.* A designated time of the week for visitation reminds the church members of their commitment to outreach and evangelism. One pastor commented that the spirit of the church seems to wane if the traditional time of outreach is canceled in a given week. The church, he said, must have a designated day to say "This is our time to emphasize evangelism."

When we asked these church leaders about church growth studies that said such visitation was no longer effective, their responses were very similar. They agreed that people often resist receiving church members who knock on their doors, yet the attitude of the lost should not hinder the obedience of the church to the Great Commission. An associate pastor of a medium-sized southwestern church responded, "People have been resistant to the gospel for two thousand years. It's not a new phenomenon. But the responses of the lost should not determine the obedience or lack of obedience of the saved."

Youth Ministry

One pastor was rather frank about the declining evangelistic effectiveness of Southern Baptists to the youth in America. He said that we must reach out to those who are most receptive to the gospel. "Ninety-five percent of [all] those who get saved are below the age of eighteen. It's time to get busy in the business of evangelism that works! We need quality youth pastors! We have dropped the ball too long."

This pastor reflects the sentiment of a large number (50.1 percent) of leaders who use intentional youth evangelism as one of their primary evangelistic methodologies. A key principle of the church growth movement is one of receptivity. C. Peter Wagner explains "that at a given point in time, certain people groups, families, and individuals will be more receptive to the message of the gospel than others."[1] George Hunter calls church growth's awareness and evangelization of receptive peoples "the Church Growth Movement's greatest contribution to this generation's world evangelization."[2]

Many church leaders fail to recognize that adolescence is a critical time of receptivity to the gospel. The teenage years are a time when a large segment of our population will receive Christ and be discipled in a local church. Resistance to the gospel typically increases once one leaves adolescence.

Many evangelistic churches in this study place a significant emphasis on youth evangelism, not just youth programs. Both staff and lay leaders seek ways to reach teenagers for Christ in everything they do. A youth lock-in, then, becomes more than a fun evening for the teenagers. The Christian youth are encouraged and motivated to bring their unchurched friends with them. Open invitations are given to public schools. And a motivational speaker will present clearly a plan of salvation before the evening concludes. Youth evangelism is highly intentional in many evangelistic churches.

Emphasis on youth evangelism is high in churches of all sizes. However, larger churches generally place a higher value on this method of evangelism than smaller churches. They are more likely to have a staff member who devotes a significant amount of time to the evangelization of the youth. Leaders of smaller churches, however, should not despair. We received numerous testimonies about lay leaders who took up the call to reach the youth for Christ. When one or more lay persons exemplified that passion, baptisms among youth increased at an astounding pace. Perhaps one role of the pastor in a smaller church should be the vocalizing of this needed leadership.

Many leaders in these evangelistic churches shared that adult conversions also increased when youth evangelism was emphasized. Some of the adults were parents of the youth; other converts came to Christ because of the testimonies of the youth who had become Christians.

We in theological education should take our cue from this study as well. We often train ministers for youth or evangelism ministries as though they are separate and distinct fields. From what we have gleaned from these evangelistic churches, we educators should offer numerous opportunities to learn about the evangelization of youth. Courses in youth ministry should prepare men and women to evangelize this age segment. Courses in evangelism and church growth should teach students about this receptive field. We have sorely neglected this group too long. It is time to reconsider youth ministry.

Music Ministry

Our study lead us to two significant conclusions about music ministry. First, music *can* be an effective evangelistic tool. Pastor Steve Thompson of Crown Point Baptist Church in Jacksonville, Florida, shares his philosophy of music for evangelistic results: "Our music is high energy with significant congregational involvement. We tend to use that music which encourages people toward commitment to salvation or to evangelism."

A second significant conclusion is that no single music or worship style predominates in these evangelistic churches. About the only consistency we noted was that a formal, liturgical style was unlikely in most of these churches. Around 40 percent of the church leaders described their services as "traditional," 30 percent as "contemporary," and 30 percent as "blended," with the latter category being the fastest growing. Surprisingly there was general aversion to services designed explicitly for seekers. We will examine all of these findings further in chapter 6.

An Overview of the Seven Most Effective Methodologies

Before we look at other evangelistic methodologies, let us review those tools deemed most effective. We first recognized the "big three": preaching, prayer ministries, and Sunday School. We then looked at four less-mentioned, but still effective, methodologies: relational evangelism, weekly outreach ministry, youth ministry, and music ministry. All seven methodologies were consistently mentioned by many churches as effective tools for evangelism.

It is worth noting at this point the importance of doing the basics well: biblical preaching, prayer, Sunday School, outreach, and others. Yet it is not enough *only* to do the basics well; evangelism must be *intentional*. Emphasis on intentionality was a recurrent theme among these church leaders.

- "We have a continual emphasis from the pulpit on the need of salvation and soul winning."
- "The key to our evangelistic success is consistency. Everything we do has some evangelistic emphasis."

- "We tell our Sunday School teachers in every weekly Sunday School meeting to share their faith and to encourage others to share their faith."
- "The pastor must be a consistent soul winner, and he must model evangelism for the church."
- "We have an attitude of intentionality; we plan to reach people for Christ each week."
- "We use our youth ministry as a deliberate evangelistic outreach."
- "Our church spends one hour on Wednesday evenings praying for lost people by name."
- "We ask for witnessing testimonies every Wednesday night at our prayer service. Prayer for the lost is emphasized."
- "More than one-third of my sermons are evangelistic."
- "We have three special events per year designed to reach people for Christ."
- "At least one-half of our visits on Monday night outreach are evangelistic."

Repeatedly these church leaders emphasize that evangelism must be an ongoing theme in methodologies, particularly in the basic methodologies of preaching, prayer, and Sunday School. Evangelism rarely takes place unless it is intentional.

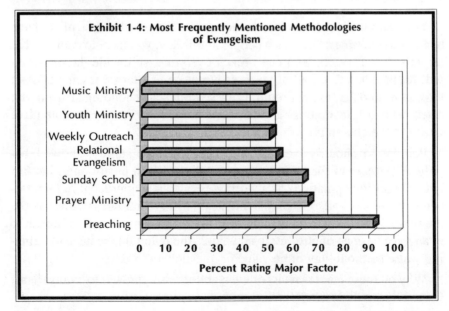

Exhibit 1-4: Most Frequently Mentioned Methodologies of Evangelism

Assessing Other Methodologies

Obviously, several evangelistic methodologies have not been mentioned. The seven discussed thus far included those that were primary evangelistic tools in at least one-half of the churches (although music ministry was slightly under 50 percent). The remainder of this chapter will examine other methodologies that were evangelistically effective plus some that were of questionable value to the responding churches.

Weekday Ministry

The 576 churches we studied were asked this question: "How important are weekday ministries, day care, mom's day out, Christian schools, etc. to your church's evangelistic effectiveness?" Much to our surprise, *only 11 percent* of the churches responded that weekday ministries were a contributing factor or a significant factor in their evangelistic success. Even the megachurches, with an abundance of weekday ministries, saw little evangelistic value in the ministries (17 to 18 percent responded positively). We will examine this issue in the next chapter, which discusses the surprises of this study.

Targeting

The church growth seminar leader spoke the words most of us have heard a dozen times: "To reach people in this day, you have to decide what target you will reach. You can't reach everyone, so decide the ones you will reach. Then focus all of your resources on that target segment." As I looked around the seminar room, I saw several heads nodding affirmingly. The "m" word (marketing) and "t" word (targets) were now accepted language of the church growth vernacular.

Perhaps we should have been surprised when our surveys showed that only *19 percent* of the churches viewed "intentional positioning that targets a specific population" as a worthy evangelistic approach. In fact, target evangelism had one of the highest negative ratings of any of the methodologies. Nearly 44 percent of the respondents saw this approach to evangelism as one of absolutely no value. And over 60 percent said targeting was a methodology of no value or questionable value.

Why do these leaders resist or even abhor this approach to evangelism? Generally we discovered three responses to this question.

One group of leaders had a theological objection to targeting. They view the gospel as the good news for all people. Any attempt to limit evangelistic efforts to a segment of the population thus is contrary to the spirit of New Testament evangelism.

A second group saw no pragmatic value in targeting. While they admit that church members may display a great deal of racial and socioeconomic homogeneity, they claim that such lack of diversity is not sought by the church. Targeting, they say, is not necessary. God will send whom He sends. Most of the homogeneity is the choice of the unsaved rather than the church.

Still a third group expressed discomfort with targeting because the gospel is open to all. Evangelistic resources may focus on the youth or a new subdivision, but such focus is limited. Eventually the church must communicate that the gospel is for everyone.

Event Evangelism

Only *7 percent* of the churches use event evangelism as a significant tool for reaching people. In these churches a special media presentation or a well-known speaker or singer is used to attract the unchurched. Typically the gospel is presented in a low-key fashion; sometimes decision cards are used. But most evangelistic churches gave negative responses about event evangelism. Why? We will see in the next chapter.

Busing Evangelism

The era of busing for church growth has long ended. Still almost one of every ten of these evangelistic churches continues to use some form of busing to reach people for Christ. Surprisingly busing was used more frequently than event evangelism.

Revival Evangelism

Another surprise was the continued emphasis on revivals as an effective evangelistic methodology. More than four out of every ten of these churches use regularly scheduled revival meetings as an evangelistic tool. We have been told that revivals are no longer effective in reaching people for Christ. But just slightly less than half of the most evangelistic churches in America continue to hold regularly scheduled revival meetings. In the next chapter we will see the difference between effective and ineffective revival churches.

Increased Staff

Obviously the larger a church becomes, the more it is financially able to add full-time ministerial staff. Exhibit 1-5 shows that multiple staff increases evangelistic effectiveness for the larger churches.

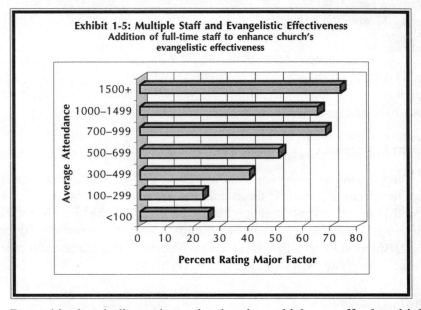

Exhibit 1-5: Multiple Staff and Evangelistic Effectiveness
Addition of full-time staff to enhance church's evangelistic effectiveness

Does this data indicate that only churches which can afford multiple staff can be evangelistically effective? To the contrary, smaller churches that have lay leadership for evangelism indicated better baptismal ratios than the larger churches. (Remember, the information shown in exhibit 1-5 represents church leaders' subjective responses.) In the next chapter we will look at the greatest surprises of this study. For now, we will just share with you that larger is not always better for evangelistic effectiveness.

Conclusion

There is much more to examine, but thus far you have been introduced to some important methodologies in growing evangelistic churches. The chapters ahead will look at some surprises that our study found. We will examine in greater detail the "big three" methodologies: preaching, prayer ministries, and Sunday School. The much-debated issue of worship style will be discussed, and we will delve into such areas as theological beliefs, leadership attitudes, social and family ministries, mission mindsets and the relationship between evangelism and discipleship. For now, let us draw some conclusions about the methodological issues we have examined.

Evangelistic Effectiveness Calls for Renewal of the Basics

Bobb Biehl distinguishes between two broad categories of leaders: goal setters and problem solvers.[3] Goal setters like to attempt new things. They get bored with solving problems of existing products, services, or ministries. They are, as the name indicates, goal conscious. For these goal setters, newer is often better, and quick results are better than slow, long-term results.

Problem solvers, however, cringe at the thought of setting goals. Yet their work (or ministry) becomes a joy when they are challenged to fix or improve something. Making the existing better is often preferred to creating the new.

Biehl, a Christian businessman, argues that any organization, including the church, needs both goal setters and problem solvers. An effective organization must find a balance between the two. However, most church growth literature has been written by goal setters, and many church leaders are convinced that newer is better and the old is for the past only.

Consequently, we are urged to focus on innovation and newness, which is good. But this focus often comes at the expense of improving that which is already proven and established. Thus we hear little about preaching and church growth. We are told that Sunday School, traditional outreach, and revivals are antiquated.

But if we have learned anything from this study, it is that the most effective evangelistic churches seek to be on the cutting edge without abandoning the best methodologies of the past. These church leaders show us that something which is "broken" may need to be fixed instead of discarded.

Assumptions Are Not Always Reality

I had assumed that traditional visitation is ineffective, because I heard such statements from leaders of some great churches. Yet I failed to see the bigger picture of other churches. Almost half of the most effective evangelistic churches in America use traditional outreach. This methodology may also be used of God in your church today. We must depend more on God's wisdom to understand our context rather than the declarations of others.

Intentionality and Repetition Are Critical

A methodology in itself does not engender evangelistic results. But the leaders of these churches make certain that the methodologies *are* evangelistic. And they keep that message before the people of the church repeatedly.

Leadership Attitude Is a Key

In chapter 7 we will see the vital role of leadership attitudes in evangelistic churches. In the methodologies we examined, a clear pattern of positive, encouraging leadership proved to be vital in using the tools effectively to reach people for the kingdom. Perhaps the comment of a pastor from Missouri will convey this attitude more clearly: "I ask God each day to give me the wisdom and attitude to get the people to love one another in spite of their failures, to share Christ, and to worship God from their heart in all that they do."

Balance Is Important

One of the more impressive elements of the leadership style of the pastors of these churches was their approach to methodologies. They believe God uses people in varied ways to reach others for Christ. They were never apologetic in learning and using the "how-tos" of effective methods of evangelism in their churches. But these leaders did not see methodologies as the ultimate solution to their church's needs. They realized that, in all evangelistic methodologies, the true source of their effectiveness was our Lord Himself. The pastors were thus able to keep that healthy tension of using human-devised methodologies in the power of and dependence on a sovereign God.

CHAPTER TWO

Ten Surprises

In every committee of twelve, one will love you and one will betray you.

Lyle Schaller

As I began to assimilate the data in this study, many colleagues and friends asked, "What are the major surprises this study revealed?" Although the study provided more affirmations and insights than surprises, I had to admit several unexpected responses did develop.

Of course, surprise is a relative term. It is the result of expectations not met, or responses not anticipated. When I speak of surprises in this study, I refer to results that are contrary to the conventional wisdom in most recent church growth literature. The surprises noted in this chapter may be totally unexpected by some, yet well anticipated by others. They are presented in no particular order.

Surprise #1

Few Effective Evangelistic Churches Use Event Evangelism

In chapter 1, I mentioned briefly the surprise that most evangelistic churches in the study did not use a major event as a tool to reach people. We described an "event" as a highly-visible or high-profile speaker or musician or performance used to attract the lost to the church and thus to the gospel. (We did not include revivals within our definition of event evangelism; revivals were seen separately as an evangelistic tool.) The surprise was twofold. First, most of the churches did not consider a "big event" to be evangelistically effective. Second, many church leaders expressed rather negative emotions about event evangelism.

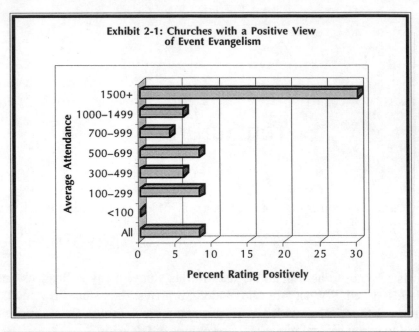

Exhibit 2-1: Churches with a Positive View of Event Evangelism

Exhibit 2-2: Churches with a Negative View of Event Evangelism

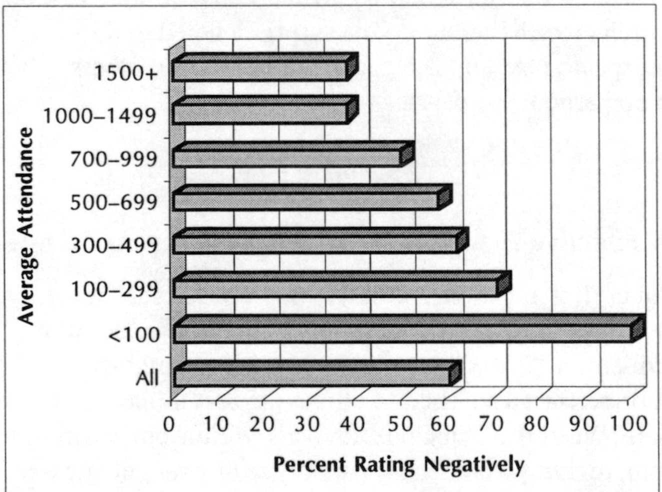

Only 7 percent of these churches use event evangelism to reach people for Christ. That number is fairly consistent in all size churches except for the smallest and largest churches in the study. Many respondents indicated that their churches had used event evangelism in the past but with disappointing results. "We spent tons of money for a well-known speaker. He did a great job and we had a great crowd," one pastor said. "But the decisions for Christ were few. We could have used those same funds for much better results."

Another pastor shared that his church's annual musical was a major event designed to reach the lost. The decision cards indicated that many did accept Christ. But the pastor became disillusioned when he discovered that few, if any, of those people had been baptized and assimilated into the church during the past five years. Were these genuine conversions? If so, why had they not become true disciples in the church? After seven years, the church discontinued the musical.

No single methodology engendered the high level of negative responses as did event evangelism (see exhibit 2-2). Sixty percent of the respondents said, rather adamantly, that event evangelism was of no value in their church's evangelistic ministry. Larger churches were the least negative. Seventy-one percent of churches with an attendance of 100 to 299 viewed event evangelism negatively, while only 38 percent responded negatively in churches with an attendance of 1,000 or more.

Why this difference? In our interviews we gleaned some insight about these attitudes. Church leaders had, for various reasons, high expectations about potential evangelistic success of a major event. Church growth books and periodicals led many to believe that one special event would bring the unchurched into a relationship with believers and, possibly, into a relationship with the Savior. Furthermore, some church leaders heard similar promises of great expectations from their peers.

Disappointment with the event rarely occurred in the first year. A pastor in Missouri commented, "We were extremely excited when nearly two hundred unchurched persons showed up for one of our three days of Christmas celebrations." He continued, "And we were even more positive when twenty-three persons indicated on a response card that they had accepted Jesus. We continued to have those type of responses for three years. But as we were planning for our fourth year, I asked our minister of music to find out how many of the nearly eighty decisions in three years resulted in baptisms and integration into the church. Much to my disappointment and surprise, he could not name one."

Like many other leaders surveyed in this study, the Missouri pastor began to question the real evangelistic effectiveness of his church's major annual event. Were these people who never returned to the church truly saved? Furthermore, the pastor saw the large amount of resources expended on the event. "That's when I became angry," the pastor said. "All of that time, effort, and money, and no results. Now I suppose if any of those people were really saved, then it was worth it. But I'm just not sure that their decisions were genuine."

Most responses to event evangelism were negative, regardless of church size. The smaller churches were especially negative. Perhaps the larger churches who reacted less negatively could more easily afford to expend money, time, and personnel than the smaller churches.

With few exceptions, church leaders tell us that event evangelism is not a good evangelistic tool for the level of resources required. When we presented this information during a conference in late 1995, some of the participants had difficulty accepting these statistics. But our role was primarily to report the sentiments of the 576 churches, not our own. We too were unprepared for this response.

Surprise #2

Revival Evangelism Is Alive and Well

Previously we reported the surprising result that revival evangelism continues to be utilized as an effective evangelistic tool. Slightly less than one-half of the churches in the study continue to hold regularly-scheduled meetings as an evangelistic method. Revivals were eighth in the ranking of the most effective evangelistic methodologies. The following comments are from leaders whose churches are reaching people for Christ through revivals:

- "We normally conduct three revivals each year. The most effective is a summer revival the first week in August."
- "We consistently have two revivals per year."
- "Revivals can be used to reap a harvest if they are done well."
- "I have heard for many years that revivals are 'on their way out!' During these years, our church has continued to reach people for Christ through revivals. We consistently are among the ten leading

churches in our state in baptisms. I hope we never 'learn' that revivals are dead."

- "I have a rather blunt theory about the lack of interest in revivals in some churches. A successful revival requires an enormous amount of preparation and prayer. Many churches want to shortcut that process, or avoid revivals altogether. Frankly, some Christians are just plain lazy."

The pastor's less-than-diplomatic response was a theme we heard in many of our interviews. We asked the pastors of these churches utilizing effective revivals how their churches reach people for Christ when other churches are less successful. Generally they believe the success of their revivals is explained by three major factors.

First, the churches that reach many for Christ plan each revival extensively. Hundreds of hours are involved in locating and inviting the lost, preparing publicity, preparing for prayer, and organizing various events and functions. A pastor in Oklahoma stated rather bluntly, "Yeah, I've heard that revivals don't work today. That's humbug! The problem is that we are plagued with laziness. If church leaders and members would do their work, God would honor their labors."

A second reason given for successful revivals is prayer. While the leaders of these churches work extremely hard to plan the revival, they also recognize that the results are in the hands of a sovereign God. One church devotes an entire week to prayer and fasting prior to their revival. The church is open twenty-four hours a day with people streaming in and out of the sanctuary.

Finally, we were told by many leaders that effective evangelistic revivals usually have a vocational evangelist lead the services. Al Jackson, pastor of Lakeview Baptist Church in Auburn, Alabama, said, "We usually use a full-time vocational evangelist to lead our revival services. Though we have experienced some good revivals with other men, we have found that a full-time evangelist is gifted by God to draw the net."

Average church attendance levels have little to do with the likelihood of having a revival or with the likelihood of having a successful revival. Between 40 and 50 percent of churches in each size category have effective regular revivals.

Of the 576 churches in this study, only ninety-two (16 percent) responded that revival activities did not contribute at all to the church's evangelistic effectiveness. Again, no one methodology is "right" for all churches. This negative response to revivals, however, may seem surprisingly low to some since the methodology has received little or no attention (or even negative attention) in some church growth literature.

Why do only 7 percent of the most effective evangelistic churches avoid event evangelism but almost half embrace revival evangelism? Those asked this question responded with two noteworthy insights.

First, the revival tends to involve the total church whereas the other special event involves a select group within the church. The greater involvement means that more church members will invite people with whom they have a relationship. And these previously established relationships increase the likelihood that a "decision" will result in a "disciple." Though our study does not have conclusive data, anecdotally it seems that the assimilation rate of those who make decisions in revivals is much higher than that of event evangelism.

Second, many church leaders shared with us the importance of a "public" decision typical in revivals. A Missouri pastor explains, "When someone makes a public decision in a revival, he or she has already taken a major step toward identifying not only with Christ, but with the local church. We found that assimilation of new Christians to be extremely difficult unless they first made their decision known to the body."

We must acknowledge a potential bias in the positive responses we received about revivals. Since all of the churches surveyed are Southern Baptist, the likelihood of a pro-revival response may be greater than would be the case with a more diverse denominational group. But even among Southern Baptist churches the strong positive response is surprising.

Surprise #3:

The Best Baptismal Ratios Were in Medium-Sized Churches

Those of us on the research team had no preconceived notion that any particular size category would statistically demonstrate better baptismal ratios. I would not have been surprised if no correlation existed between the size of attendance and evangelistic effectiveness. We were therefore surprised to discover that medium-sized churches were consistently the most effective evangelistic churches as measured by baptismal ratios. For purposes of this study, we define a medium-sized church as one with an average attendance between 100 and 499, encompassing two of the seven categories in this study.

Remember, when we use the phrase "evangelistic effectiveness," we make a statistical evaluation rather than a qualitative evaluation. We considered medium-sized churches to be more evangelistically effective for two reasons. First, more medium-sized churches had baptismal ratios of less than 20:1 than other churches did. In our study, over two-thirds of the effective evangelistic churches had an attendance of 100 to 499.

Second, and perhaps more significantly, the churches of this size had a better baptismal ratio (resident members/baptisms). Whereas the average ratio for the entire study group was 17:1, the ratio for the medium-sized churches was 12:1.

How do we explain this? What factors contribute to greater evangelistic effectiveness in the medium-sized church relative to other-size churches? Our respondents offered their insights.

The difficulty with smaller churches, we were told, was lack of resources and programs. Many of these churches, whose attendance is less than one hundred, do not even have full-time pastors. They tend to have difficulty sustaining an ongoing evangelistic emphasis. One Alabama pastor reported that his church averaged less than 60 in attendance when he first arrived in 1985. By 1995 the average attendance was 170. "I could really tell a difference when our church began to average about 120 to 140," he said. "We were able to offer more programs which attracted more people. As a result, we had more real prospects, people who were really open to becoming Christians."

Why then do churches demonstrate less evangelistic effectiveness when their attendance exceeds five hundred? Many of the leaders of these churches indicated that anonymity becomes easier as churches reach a certain size. One potential negative consequence of anonymity is the lack of accountability. As a minister of education in Georgia shared with us, "In larger churches it becomes easier for people to fall through the cracks. We have trouble keeping up with most of the less-than-regular members, much less holding them accountable for witnessing and evangelism."

What are some implications regarding the size of a church? For one, church planting seems to be an exciting option. Larger churches can sacrificially send one hundred or more of their members to start a new work. It is possible for both churches to become more evangelistically effective.

Yet churches in other size categories need not be discouraged. We found numerous examples of smaller and larger churches that were equally as effective in evangelism as their medium-sized counterparts. The biggest barrier in the smaller churches was power groups that, consciously or not, desired to keep their churches small to retain power. The best opportunity to overcome barriers takes place if just one person becomes evangelistically enthusiastic. For example, consider a church with a resident membership of ninety. If one person led ten people to Christ and those ten were baptized in the church, the baptismal ratio of the church would be 9:1, one of the best in the nation. The advantage of the small church is that one person can have a major impact on the total ministry of that church.

Among the larger churches with better-than-average baptismal ratios we found a recurring theme: small groups are the key to evangelistic accountability. The leaders in these churches recognize that they cannot be responsible for every member. Therefore they organize the church into numerous small groups where a teacher or leader is expected to know the status of group members and develop expectations for them.

With few exceptions in this study, the small group organization utilized was the Sunday School. Of course, one would expect Sunday School to have a dominant role in Southern Baptist churches. But simply having a Sunday School organization does not guarantee evangelistic effectiveness or church health. In a previous study[1] I found three essential characteristics of dynamic Sunday Schools in growing churches. First, organization is evident at all levels of the Sunday School. Responsibilities are clear. Tasks are carried out. Leadership is in place.

Second, quality teaching takes place in the Bible study. Only the most capable and most willing teachers are called to lead the classes.

Third, expectations are high and accountability takes place. It is primarily this aspect of a quality Sunday School that moves the larger church toward more effective evangelistic efforts. All adult classes and their members are expected to be outreach arms of the church. We will take a closer look at the Sunday School and evangelism in chapter 5.

We may conclude that the medium-sized church has a good blend of factors that foster evangelistic effectiveness. The church is large enough to have programs and ministries that draw the lost but is not so large that members remain anonymous indefinitely.

Surprise #4:

Effective Evangelistic Churches Advocate Evangelistic Training More Than They Practice It

Among the 576 churches in this study, 242 churches (42 percent) indicated that some type of evangelistic training program significantly contributed to their evangelistic effectiveness (exhibit 2-4). Though this is a significant percentage, it is less than I anticipated. Yet what is even more surprising is that 444 of the 576 churches, a full 76 percent, disagreed strongly with the following statement: "Effective evangelism requires little training." It would seem, therefore, that more churches advocate evangelistic training than practice it.

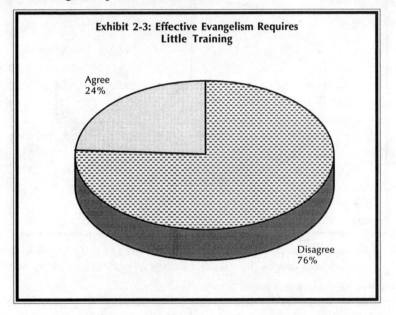

Exhibit 2-3: Effective Evangelism Requires Little Training

Agree 24%

Disagree 76%

If we had any doubt about the perceived value of evangelism training, our respondents quickly dispelled them. The following list includes some of their comments:

- "We are currently involved in sixty days of witnessing. No pressure is placed on people, but we continually ask them to be responsible for the lost people who are in their circles of influence."
- "Soul-winning training comes from an eight-week course taught twice a year, material authored by the pastor."
- "We place each new convert in an Evangelism Explosion or Continuous Witness Training class. We expect our new Christians to share their new relationship with Christ immediately!"
- "We expect, at a minimum, all of our leadership (deacons, teachers, directors, staff, etc.) to take our witness training course."
- "Each of our deacons must take Continuous Witness Training and then share his faith weekly during churchwide visitation."

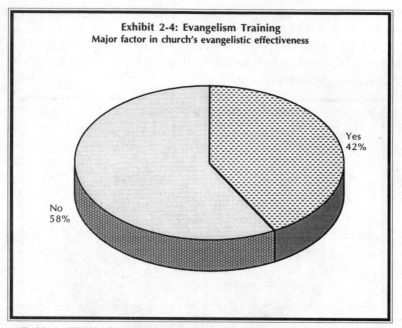

Exhibit 2-4: Evangelism Training
Major factor in church's evangelistic effectiveness

Yes
42%

No
58%

- "I think *CWT [Continuous Witness Training]* in our church in previous years was one of the greatest things to get excited about witness training."
- "We use a marked Bible for evangelism training. The majority of our adult membership has been trained in this method."
- "We hold soul-winning workshops twice a year. All Sunday School teachers must be trained in personal evangelism."

Among the churches stating that evangelism programs were a key factor in their evangelistic effectiveness, the methods of training varied considerably. Pastor Don Phillips leads his Calvary Baptist Church (average attendance 325) in Camden, Arkansas, to once-a-year evangelism training during the Discipleship Training hour. Cana Baptist Church in Burleson, Texas, uses marked Bibles for training. Pastor Thomas Fortune said that laypersons lead Maranatha Baptist Church in Ocala, Florida, to use *CWT [Continuous Witness Training]* tracts for one-on-one witnessing. And at Donahue Baptist Church in Pineville, Louisiana, pastor James Greer and the church's leadership take the entire body through a three-day soul-winning seminar.

Still the discrepancy between attitudes and actions in these churches is large. While only 42 percent affirm the value of evangelism training in their churches' evangelistic effectiveness, 76 percent believe effective evangelism requires training. Why are not 76 percent of the churches actually doing evangelism training if they believe in its value?

In our interviews we discovered that the implementation of evangelism training programs in a church is largely dependent on the expectations of the training. If the leadership of a church expects a single program to produce large numbers of converts and disciples and that result doesn't occur, the likelihood of that church continuing a witness training program decreases. A common response among pastors who no longer advocated evangelism training programs was, "It is not effective." But their understanding of "effectiveness" was conversion, baptism, and assimilation. Nonetheless, more than three-fourths of the respondents believe effective evangelism does require training.

On the other hand, those leaders who see evangelism training programs as a major factor in their churches' evangelistic effectiveness do not expect immediate "results." They see the training programs as methods to equip believers in their daily witnessing relationships.

You will recall from chapter 1 that relationship evangelism was a significant factor in the evangelistic effectiveness of more than one-half of the responding churches. Those who lead their churches in evangelism training typically expect that training to impact the believers' everyday relationships. They are not overly concerned if the church does not baptize and assimilate a large number of people as a direct result of the training.

A second significant reason for using evangelism training is the evangelistic attitude it engenders throughout the church. A minister of education in California comments: "Our primary reason for offering *Continuous Witness Training* every year is the evangelistic environment it creates. Our people know that the leadership of this church holds evangelism as a high priority. *CWT* is one way we keep that priority before the people."

Surprise #5

Weekday Ministries Are Not Effective for Evangelistic Outreach

In chapter 2 we mentioned briefly that only 11 percent of the responding churches indicated that weekday ministries were a contributing factor in their evangelistic effectiveness. As shown in exhibit 2-5, the low response was consistent in churches of all sizes.

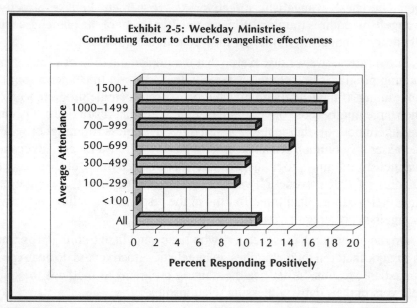

Exhibit 2-5: Weekday Ministries
Contributing factor to church's evangelistic effectiveness

Though the larger churches responded more positively, only 18 percent of the largest churches affirmed weekday ministries' evangelistic value. As we spoke with church leaders, we found that we, the researchers, were among the few surprised. Those church leaders whose churches were involved in weekday ministries registered little surprise at the results of this study.

In his book, *The Seven-Day-a-Week Church*,[2] Lyle Schaller heralds the dramatic growth of many churches that offer ministries and activities throughout the week. He at least implicitly states that a strong correlation exists between growth and weekday ministries such as day care, mom's day out, Christian schools, and other ministries. Yet our respondents indicated that evangelistic growth rarely occurred as a result of these ministries. What are the reasons for the disparity?

Further questioning revealed some fascinating attitudes about weekday ministries. First, the church leaders indicated that such ministries can be effective for church growth but rarely for conversion growth. The programs tend to attract other Christians, but their evangelistic value is questionable.

Some pastors, a sizable minority, told us that their churches' weekday ministries actually detracted from evangelistic emphases. One pastor lamented, "We spend so much time putting out fires in two of these ministries that we take away valuable resources that could be used to reach the lost. They really drain our resources."

Another staff member, whose responsibility includes the coordination of the weekday ministries, commented, "I don't doubt the value of what we do. Many Christians truly benefit from our ministries. But it is really time consuming. We struggle to know the right balance between ministering to Christians and evangelizing the lost."

Other church leaders, however, do believe that weekday ministries can be evangelistic. The problem they see is a lack of evangelistic intentionality. "Our day care became one of our richest sources of baptisms," a church staff member said. "But evangelism had to be planned, encouraged, and emphasized continuously. You should have seen the celebration when one of our day care teachers led a young mother to Jesus!"

Still most church leaders question the long-term viability of weekday ministry as evangelistic tools. They conclude that churches should acknowledge the ministries to be primarily for Christians and use evangelistic resources in other directions.

Surprise #6

Traditional Outreach Is Alive and Well

We covered the topic of traditional outreach in some detail in the previous chapter. Yet if we read much of the literature on church growth, we must register some surprise at the number of churches that told us this methodology was one of their most effective evangelistic tools. In-home visitation, we have been told by many authorities, is waning or ineffective.

The churches that rated this methodology highly (the fourth highest positive rating of any methodologies mentioned) did not believe that resistance to home visits was any greater than in years past. The issue, they told us, was not the receptivity of those visited; the issue was the obedience of the church to "go." Many church leaders lamented that the decline of traditional outreach in some churches is the result of accommodation to culture rather than obedience to the Great Commission.

About half of the churches responding in each size category rated traditional outreach as an effective evangelistic methodology. Somewhat surprising were the responses of the smallest churches (less than 100 in average attendance) and the largest churches (more than 1,499 in average attendance): both gave this methodology a positive rating of at least 60 percent.

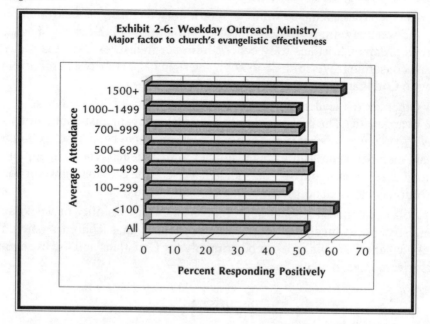

Exhibit 2-6: Weekday Outreach Ministry
Major factor to church's evangelistic effectiveness

Surprise #7

The Age of the Church Is Not Related to Evangelistic Effectiveness

Virtually all church growth and church planting advocates are quick to tell you that newer churches grow faster than older churches, or that newer units grow faster than older units. Indeed, if one were to group statistically all evangelical churches in America, it is likely that the newly-started churches would demonstrate a faster growth rate than those in any other size category. This present study neither examined nor disputed that phenomenon.

Our study differed in two ways. First, the criteria were an absolute number of baptisms (twenty-five) and a baptismal ratio of less than 20:1. In other words, this study was interested in conversion growth rather than total growth.

Second, our study group, using the above parameters, included only evangelistic churches, not all churches. Thus we concluded that among evangelistic churches, the age of the church is not related to evangelistic effectiveness. In fact, we were somewhat surprised that over half the churches were fifty years old or older. Exhibit 2-7 shows the average age of the churches by church size.

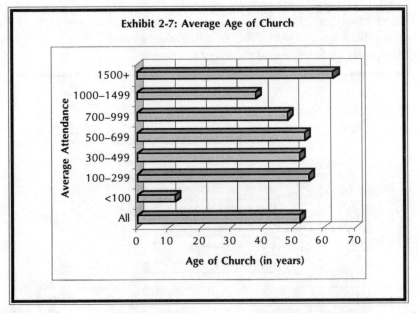

Exhibit 2-7: Average Age of Church

Though the study did not include data of historical attendance trends, we did find anecdotal information in our interviews relevant to this issue. Some church leaders shared their experiences in leading an older congregation to reach people for Christ. Two major themes emerged.

First, the leaders told us pastoral leadership is critical to a church's evangelistic effectiveness. A layman from a small town in central Florida shared with us, "Our church was the classic, small-town First Baptist Church. We had more unwritten traditions than the Bible has verses." The layman, the church's deacon chairman, explained that church attendance had declined for twenty consecutive years. The pattern was reversed in 1986, six years after the present pastor arrived.

"Our pastor," the deacon shared, "did not just tell us to be evangelistic. He lived it! It took his example and leadership over five years before the church caught on. But we eventually got excited about sharing Jesus." The church has grown consistently now for a decade. And a significant portion of that growth has been conversion growth.

A second but related factor is pastoral tenure. Many of the pastors in these older churches experienced opposition and heartaches the first few years of their ministry. Yet they determined that, with God's help and power, they would persevere. The church's evangelistic fervor often became a reality four to six years after the pastor began his ministry at that church.

Exhibit 2-8 depicts the pastoral tenure by church size. Average pastoral tenure of a Southern Baptist pastor is less than three years. Keep in mind that these numbers are averages. We found that older evangelistic churches tend to have pastors whose ministry is ten or more years.

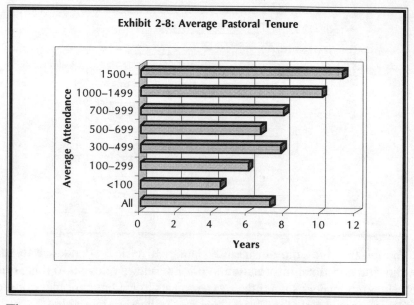

Exhibit 2-8: Average Pastoral Tenure

The average pastoral tenure of 7.3 years in the churches studied is almost three times the average pastoral tenure in the Southern Baptist Convention as a whole. We conclude, therefore, that leading a long-standing traditional church to evangelistic effectiveness requires leadership by example, tenacity, and longevity. These older churches, with an amazingly high average age of fifty-three years, are led by pastors who realize that change does not happen in a day. They approach their calls to ministry with a long-term perspective.

Surprise #8

Location Is Not a Factor in the Churches' Evangelistic Growth

When I took real estate courses in college, we students were told repeatedly that the three most important factors in the sale of property were location, location, and location. Many churches take that same philosophy. Population growth, demographic shifts, accessibility, and traffic patterns often become deciding factors in a church's decision to relocate or to start a new work.

Sufficient evidence abounds in church growth literature to affirm that a good location can enhance a church's opportunity for growth. What has been overlooked, however, is that *conversion* growth does not increase with a better location. The evangelistic churches in our study agreed with this observation. Nearly nine out of ten churches responded that the location of the church, even if it were a factor in total growth, had no impact on conversion growth. Only one percent called the church's location a contributing factor to evangelistic effectiveness.

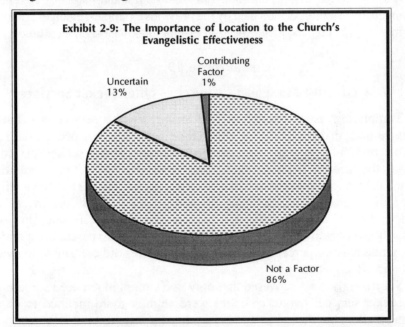

Exhibit 2-9: The Importance of Location to the Church's Evangelistic Effectiveness

Contributing Factor 1%

Uncertain 13%

Not a Factor 86%

Mickey Dalrymple is pastor of Fairview Baptist Church in Columbus, Mississippi, a church whose worship attendance approaches one thousand. Despite its growth and size, Fairview has maintained evangelistic effectiveness. The church's baptismal ratio is below 20:1. According to Pastor Dalrymple, the church is not in an ideal location. It is a neighborhood church located three blocks off a main thoroughfare. The location, he says, has not enhanced the church's evangelistic effectiveness.

Wally Portmann is minister of pastoral care at East Side Baptist Church in Fort Smith, Arkansas. Portmann called East Side's location ideal but emphasized that it is beneficial to transfer growth rather than conversion growth. He said that "the key is to have people who develop personal relationships with others and then share their faith."

David Dills, pastor of Center Hill Baptist Church in Loganville, Georgia, called their current location an "obstacle." Nonetheless the church of 250 in attendance continues to reach people for Christ. "Location isn't everything," Dills said. "Just let the people know where you are and that you care about them. Lift up Christ and He will draw the people in."

Church leaders contemplating leading their church to relocate should therefore consider the words of the great majority of the leaders whose churches were in this study. Moving from one location to another may be God's will for the church, but such a move does not automatically engender evangelistic growth. As indicated by the previous examples, evangelism must be intentional and persistent. Location cannot guarantee such an attitude.

Surprise #9

Few Effective Evangelistic Churches Offer Seeker Services

Terminology is important here. We defined a seeker service as a church service designed explicitly for unsaved persons. Every aspect of the service is mindful of a largely unredeemed audience. Thus a seeker service is distinctly different from a seeker-sensitive service. The latter is sensitive to the presence of lost persons in a worship service, but the service itself is for believers who are worshiping the one true God. Therefore, we asked the leaders of the 576 churches, "Is a seeker service a factor in your church's evangelistic effectiveness"? A resounding 60 percent responded no, while only 10 percent said that seeker services did contribute to evangelistic effectiveness.

Surprisingly we discovered that only one church in ten used some kind of seeker service. Larger churches were slightly more inclined to do so than smaller churches.

Surprise #10

Offering Choices Does Not Necessarily Help the Church's Evangelistic Effectiveness

The effective growing church has been characterized by some church growth pundits as a "cafeteria" church. A wide array of choices is available in these churches: worship services at different times; small group meeting times; support groups; youth ministries; children's ministries; singles ministries; and so on. But many of the leaders of these 576 churches have a dif-

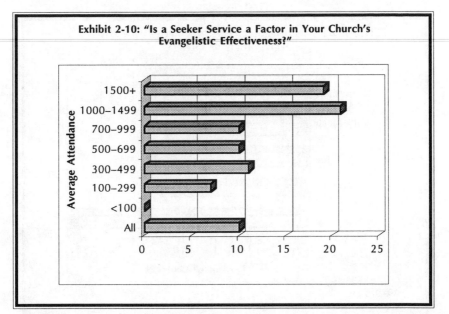

Exhibit 2-10: "Is a Seeker Service a Factor in Your Church's Evangelistic Effectiveness?"

ferent perspective. Their responses to the statement "Evangelism occurs when people are given a wide variety of choices," were anything but consistent.

Our in-depth interviews with some of these church leaders helped us understand the ambiguous responses. On the one hand, many of these leaders believe that a diversity of ministries and times can reach people, resulting in both total growth and conversion growth. On the other hand, these leaders spoke with conviction of a tension between contextualization and accommodation. *Contextualization* means that the church understands its community or context. This awareness indicates that the church knows certain ways to reach the lost and unchurched at their point of need. *Accommodation* means that the church has let the world dictate its standards and values. The gospel no longer is authoritative; all authority resides in culture.

These responses told us that the question would have received an overwhelmingly positive response if it had been worded differently. For example, we suspect that responses would have been strongly affirmative to the following revised question: "Evangelism occurs when people are given a wide variety of choices without compromising the integrity of the gospel." Throughout the interviews, we found these leaders wary of any fad or trend that detracts from the cost of following Christ. Choices are not inherently

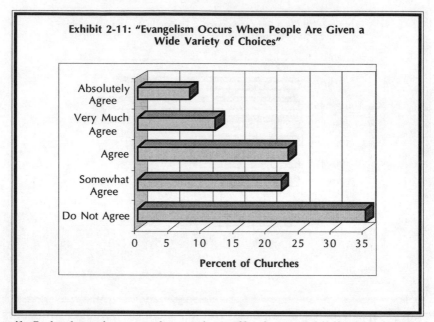

Exhibit 2-11: "Evangelism Occurs When People Are Given a Wide Variety of Choices"

evil. Indeed, options can be used as effective and biblical evangelistic tools. Yet we must never compromise the full truth of the gospel message. Following Christ is never the easiest or most convenient way. If our array of choices in any manner conveys such easy believism, then perhaps the choices or options should no longer be made available.

Back to Basics

Perhaps more than any single theme, we discovered that the churches successfully reaching the lost focus on the basics: biblical preaching, prayer, intentional witnessing, missions, and comprehensive biblical training in small groups (usually called Sunday School). That theme recurs throughout this book.

If a methodology or approach to evangelism appears to stray from these basics, the churches rejected it. If a methodology or approach to evangelism enhanced the basics, the churches embraced it. These church leaders showed little interest in the latest church growth methodology. They simply desired to know how to be more effective in the basics. And one of those basic elements of effective evangelism was biblical, expository preaching. To that topic we turn in the next chapter.

CHAPTER THREE

The Pulpit Is Still Primary

The supreme work of the Christian minister is the work of preaching. This is a day in which one of our great perils is that of doing a thousand little things to the neglect of one thing, which is preaching.

G. Campbell Morgan

Imagine a sermon that concludes with three thousand people accepting Christ. Such a response would be miraculous by almost any standard. When the Holy Spirit came at Pentecost, the result was "about three thousand were added to their number that day" (Acts 2:41). A common explanation for the significant number of conversions is the power of the Holy Spirit, which filled the believers, and the accompanying miraculous signs from God.

Although Pentecost would not be Pentecost without the coming of the Spirit and the miraculous events, these supernatural signs alone did not engender conversions. To the contrary, some nonbelievers mocked the believers, exclaiming that the phenomenon was the result of drunkenness (Acts 2:13, 15).

Without debating or minimizing the extraordinary events of that day, we must acknowledge that the plentiful harvest of souls on Pentecost followed the *preaching* of the first sermon of the New Testament church. The preacher was Peter and the "congregation" was a large number of Jews in Jerusalem. His texts were Joel 2:28–32, and Psalm 16:8–11 and 110:1. The words of Peter's sermon are found in Acts 2:14–36, and the "invitation" is in Acts 2:38–40. The response is in Acts 2:41.

Though signs and wonders were already plentiful that day, the growth of the church did not begin until one man preached a powerful message about the fulfillment of Old Testament prophecy in the person of Jesus Christ. Preaching was primary at Pentecost.

In the plethora of church growth literature, rarely is the role of preaching analyzed or discussed. In some of his previous books, C. Peter Wagner asks for more research and discussion on the topic of preaching and church growth.[1] The response to his plea has been minimal.

Few on our research team were surprised that preaching and church growth are related, particularly preaching and conversion growth. The surprise was in the intensity and quantity of the responses. *Among all the possible factors that led a church to evangelistic growth, preaching was clearly the most important element. Over 90 percent of the respondents indicated preaching was a major factor in their churches' evangelistic effectiveness.*

Of course most churches have pastors who preach sermons. However, few of these churches, less than 4 percent by the criteria of this study, are evangelistic churches. What are the characteristics of sermons in evangelistic churches? Are they different in content, context, style, or delivery from the sermons in other churches? Do pastors in evangelistic churches utilize the pulpit for emphases beyond the sermon?

Of all the evangelistic methodologies described by these 576 churches, the topic of the pulpit and preaching required more follow-up than any other issue. We interviewed dozens of pastors, staff persons, and laypersons to determine why preaching was deemed the single most important factor for evangelistic effectiveness.

Listening to the Churches

James Greer is pastor of Donahue Baptist Church in Pineville, Louisiana, a church with an attendance of approximately two hundred. Pastor Greer believes the preaching ministry is central to the church's evangelistic effectiveness. Most of his messages are expository, though he also preaches topic sermons. But beyond the actual sermons, the pastor believes the ministries of the church, particularly evangelism, "rise and fall on leadership." His leadership is seen especially in the pulpit, whether for a particular emphasis, announcements, or the sermon itself.

Likewise, Houston Roberson, pastor of Bethel Baptist Church in Chesapeake, Virginia, says that preaching is central to that church's evangelistic efforts. "If there is no power in the pulpit, there is no power in ministry," he commented. "Power comes from prayer. A praying preacher is mandated by God. If the preacher doesn't pray . . . then the people will not catch the fire."

Pastor Roberson's preaching is expository with an evangelistic thrust. In fact, he stated that every message, whether an explicitly evangelistic message or not, "always contains an evangelistic thrust."

Pastor Roberson's comments are representative of hundreds of pastors to whom we spoke, as well as laypersons in their churches. He mentioned three key elements of preaching that were repeated several times over. In these three areas we thus began to see the power of the pulpit in evangelistic churches, compared to the possible lack of power in other churches.

One key facet of preaching in evangelistic churches is that the sermon is guided by the Bible rather than the nebulous insights of a preacher or other authority. Scripture is the source of authority and power for the messages. The Word of God, they told us, is powerful. Therefore any message should be anchored to the Bible.

When we examine theological issues in chapter 7, you will see that the leaders of these churches are, for the most part, conservative evangelicals who hold a high view of Scripture. Exhibit 3-1, for example, demonstrates that 90 percent of the respondents hold a view of Scripture best described as inerrancy.

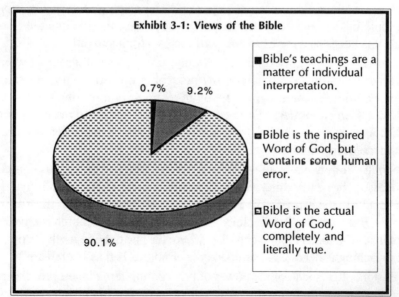

Exhibit 3-1: Views of the Bible

- Bible's teachings are a matter of individual interpretation.
- Bible is the inspired Word of God, but contains some human error.
- Bible is the actual Word of God, completely and literally true.

0.7% 9.2%

90.1%

Such is one characteristic of the preaching in these evangelistic churches. The messages are guided by Scriptures in which the preacher has complete trust. In some ways this perspective of preaching affirms a book written over twenty-five years earlier by Dean Kelley, *Why Conservative Churches Are Growing.*[2] Kelley, an executive with the National Council of Churches, created a stir with his book. Yet his thesis still holds today. Those churches that maintain a higher view of Scripture are more likely to grow than other churches.

But conservative theology alone cannot explain the power of the pulpit in these evangelistic churches. In fact, the word *power* was used frequently to describe an aspect of preaching dependant upon a high view of Scripture, but extending beyond inerrancy. Listen to some of the comments about "power" in preaching:

- "Our pastor preaches not only with authority, but also with power. His messages are truly anointed by God."
- "The deacon leadership prays before each service with our pastor. They lay hands on him, with sincere prayers for power in his message."
- "I [the pastor] can see the impact of God-powered preaching. When I depend upon Him, the response is amazing. When I depend upon my own scholarship and eloquence, the service falls flat."

If the second characteristic of preaching in evangelistic churches is "power," how do these pastors acquire it? The response to this question is the topic of the next chapter: the power of prayer. At this juncture, however, it is necessary for us to speak of the two topics together.

A pastor in Georgia explains: "Seven years ago a small group of women began to pray for me, especially my preaching ministry. Three or four of them would alternate praying for me in a small room during the worship services." He continues, "Their commitment so impressed me that I began to become a prayer warrior myself. It is unbelievable the difference prayer has made in my ministry, particularly my preaching."

Similar comments were made by a deacon who has served his church in Tennessee for nearly thirty years: "I would not attend any church that does not believe in the inerrancy of Scripture. I am as conservative as most anyone I know. But conservative theology alone does not mean a church is alive." He explains, "I've been around churches where the pastor believes the Word, but his preaching is dead. Cold orthodoxy is almost as bad as liberalism."

Pastors often speak of the power of prayer "anointing" their preaching. In fact, prayer was mentioned over five hundred times in our interviews! Lay persons confirmed that they could discern a certain quality of preaching that went beyond style, oratory skills, or even preparation. Descriptive words were used such as *anointing*, *power*, *Spirit-filled*, and *blessed*. Pastors, whose preaching style was described with these words, explained that their pulpit ministry had been transformed at some point through the power of prayer.

A third frequently mentioned characteristic of preaching in effective evangelistic churches is evangelistic intentionality. J. T. Reed is pastor of First Southern Baptist Church in Lompoc, California, a church with an average attendance of 350. He tells us that preaching is primary and that every sermon has some type of evangelistic thrust. Most leaders of these churches affirm that most of their messages have an intentional evangelistic thrust even though most are not purely evangelistic sermons.

As best our research team could discern then, preaching is primary if three key elements are present. The pastors hold a high view of Scripture. Evangelistic intentionality is evident in most of the sermons preached. And something less tangible but no less real, the preaching of these pastors is anointed by the power of God, power that comes from prayer.

To Whom Did We Listen?

A potential problem in our study related to the individual respondents. Over 80 percent of the survey respondents were pastors; fewer than ten of the 576 surveys were answered by laypersons. If preaching was the most-frequently mentioned factor in the evangelistic growth of these churches, was it not likely that the numbers were skewed since *preachers* answered the survey? Recognizing a possible conflict of interest, we did extensive follow-up by interviewing laypersons in these churches.

The results of these follow-up interviews were fascinating. Almost without exception, the laypersons indicated that perhaps the pastors *understated* the role of preaching in the church's evangelistic growth. In on-site interviews with several laypersons at East Heights Baptist Church in Tupelo, Mississippi, the significance of Pastor Steve Bain's preaching was unambiguous. One deacon shared with me: "We could probably point to several factors that have helped our church grow and reach people for Christ, but all of those factors pale in comparison to what Brother Steve's preaching means to our church." Or listen to one woman's comments about Pastor Bain's preaching. (Note the three elements we have highlighted.) "Our pastor's preaching is the main reason people are accepting Christ. You never have any doubt about his stand for the Word or how to become a Christian. I've heard many preachers, but his sermons just seem to be anointed by God."

David Butler is pastor of Springdale Church in Louisville. Interestingly, Springdale is an eight-year-old church with a vision to reach the unchurched in Louisville's east end. Part of that vision meant that church-as-usual would not be the order of business. The worship services are contemporary. No hymnals or choirs can be seen in the worship services. The pastor is committed to maintaining a church on the cutting edge of reaching the community for Christ. Many people refer to Springdale as "innovative," "contemporary," or "nontraditional."

But in our discussions with some members of the church, we found that the pastor's preaching was perhaps the dominant factor in the growth of the church. "You have no doubt about David's commitment to the Bible. His preaching is powerful. While we try to get the unchurched into our worship services, it is David's preaching that communicates the gospel so effectively."

Dennis Williams recently joined the Southern Baptist Theological Seminary in Louisville as dean of the School of Christian Education. He and his wife Cornelia visited many churches in the Louisville area while searching for a church home. They chose not to join Springdale because of their preference for a more traditional worship service. However, Dr. Williams' comments about Springdale were insightful. "We visited many churches in the area, and the first thing that stands out about Springdale is its contemporary format." He continued, "But that is the initial impression only. The real difference at Springdale is the powerful preaching of David Butler. That church would be growing regardless of its worship style."

These examples were typical of the hundreds of comments we received from laypersons. We concluded that the pastors' comments about preaching being primary were accurate and, perhaps, even understated.

The Overwhelming Response

Let us review the overwhelming response preaching received as the most important factor in these churches' evangelistic effectiveness. We identified seven methodologies as the most frequently mentioned by these churches. The second highest response was prayer ministries with nearly 70 percent responding, followed by Sunday School at slightly above 60 percent. Relational evangelism, weekly outreach, and youth ministry received responses of 50 percent or higher. Music ministry was slightly below 50 percent.

But preaching as a methodology for effective evangelism was cited *above 90 percent* by the respondents! No other methodology came close (see exhibit 3-2).

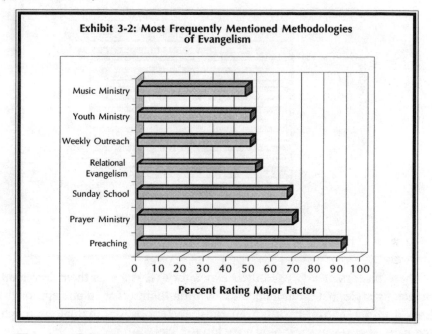

Exhibit 3-2: Most Frequently Mentioned Methodologies of Evangelism

Percent Rating Major Factor

The size of the church, measured in average attendance, did not change the overwhelmingly positive response to preaching. In churches with an attendance above 1,500 or below 100, the two extremes in our study, *100 percent* of the respondents called preaching the most important factor in their churches' growth. That response never fell below 85 percent for any size church (see exhibit 3-3).

What Type of Preaching?

Exhibit 3-4 describes the various sermon models that were presented to the respondents. We asked them to identify their dominant approach to preaching.

The respondents did not believe that the differences between expository and textual, and topical and thematic were sufficient to call them different preaching models. Consequently we combined the four categories into two.

Exhibit 3-5 shows the overwhelming preference for the expository/textual preaching model by the pastors of these evangelistic churches. Many

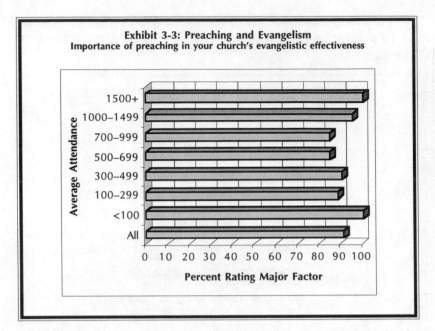

Exhibit 3-3: Preaching and Evangelism
Importance of preaching in your church's evangelistic effectiveness

of these pastors clearly used their expository message as their dominant preaching style, but did not necessarily limit themselves to one approach. Less than one-half of pastors who chose the expository/textual approach indicated that it was their *only* preaching model.

Expository/Textual

The dominance of the expository/textual preaching style (73.6 percent) is somewhat related to the conservative theology of the respondents. Our discussion with a pastor in North Carolina is representative of this attitude. "If one truly believes that the Bible is the Word of God without error, then the Bible must be the basis for the sermon." He further explained, "While we who preach the Word must use our God-given abilities to make the text applicable for today, we still first preach the text in its historical context. It is the preached Word that has power, not the opinions of men."

Such responses are common among the leaders of these 576 churches. To them the expository sermon indicates both a belief in and fidelity to Scripture. Though these pastors did not infer lack of fidelity to Scripture when other preaching approaches were used, their consensus was that the expository approach to Scripture was the *most* faithful.

Exhibit 3-4: Preaching Models

Expository	An expository sermon contains a clear statement of the biblical idea that is legitimately derived from a passage or passages of Scripture.
Textual	Textual sermons tend to be shorter text than expository sermons and lean toward topical styles, but they are focused on a biblical text and the message of that text.
Topical	The best understanding seems to be that this approach is driven by a subject and the subject matched to Scripture. Usually used when it does not appear that there is text that speaks directly to the subject.
Thematic	The purpose of this sermon is to identify the principles that help Christians understand God and their faith. The better use of this model will carefully show how the listeners can apply the message of the text in their own walk of faith.
Narrative	The narrative sermon is a story that, from the outset to conclusion, binds the entire message to a single plot as theme. This is a sermon-as-story understanding of the text.
Other	Anything that does not fit into the above models.

The strong preference for expository/textual preaching among these evangelistic churches seems to go against trends today, even in evangelical churches. A recent analysis of sermons from two major preaching journals over a ten-year period revealed some fascinating insights into modern-day preaching. The study classified the published sermons into four categories.[3]

The first category would best be called expository because the content of the sermons and their organization were determined by the biblical passage. Sermons in the second category included biblical content, but the preacher imposed his own organization topically. The biblical passage did not determine the organization.

The third group of sermons had no biblical passages to determine the content or the organization, yet the messages were identifiably Christian. And finally, the fourth category of sermons were neither biblical in their organization or content, nor did the messages have any discernible Christian truths.

Less than one-fourth of these sermons prepared and preached by "evangelicals" could be classified as expository. And, surprisingly, over

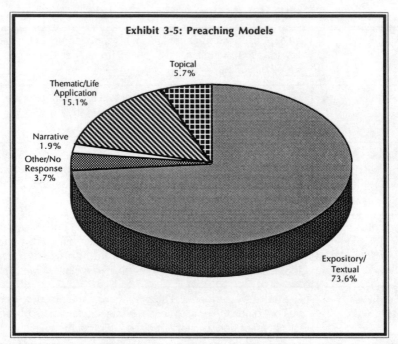

Exhibit 3-5: Preaching Models

Topical
5.7%

Thematic/Life
Application
15.1%

Narrative
1.9%

Other/No
Response
3.7%

Expository/
Textual
73.6%

one-half of the sermons had *no* biblical passage as the basis for truth. This contrasts sharply with the group of evangelistic churches in this study where the expository approach to preaching was dominant.

Topical/Thematic/Life Application

Our respondents once again had difficulty distinguishing between the two preaching approaches of topical and thematic/life application. In follow-up interviews we were told that our initial survey would have been less confusing if we had merged the two approaches. Three major themes emerged in our discussions about the topical/thematic preaching style.

First, this approach to preaching is clearly the second choice among our respondents. Its second-tier status does not mean that it is avoided by advocates of expository preaching. To the contrary, the majority of expository preaching proponents indicated that they preach thematically or topically on occasion. In fact, nearly 60 percent of the respondents indicated that they approach sermons thematically on a regular basis. This percentage is revealing when compared to only one-fourth of the respondents who advocate topical and thematic preaching as the *primary* preaching approach.

Second, pastors who are positive about thematic and topical preaching believe it is no less faithful to Scripture than the expository advocates. The pastor of a church in Alabama whose attendance exceeded seven hundred said, "The majority of my sermons are topical, but that does not mean they are unbiblical. When I preach on a topic, I always ask what the Bible says first. I may not go verse-by-verse in one book of the Bible, but the Word is the basis for the truths I proclaim."

Third, the preaching style is only slightly related to the worship style. Some of us on the research team anticipated a higher correlation between contemporary worship and topical preaching. Our findings indicated a greater *likelihood* of topical preaching in contemporary worship, but the degree of correlation was lower than we anticipated. Expository *and* topical preaching were found in all worship styles.

Narrative/Other Preaching Approaches

Less than 2 percent of the respondents indicated that the narrative approach to preaching was their style of preaching. And less than 4 percent either did not respond or answered "other" for their preaching style. Because of this low response, we did not conduct follow-up interviews for these approaches to preaching. We concluded that first expository/textual preaching and then topical/thematic/life application preaching dominated the preaching style of the pastors who responded.

Other Roles of the Pulpit

I could have entitled this chapter "Preaching Is Still Primary," rather than "The Pulpit Is Still Primary." Our main concern in the study was the role of preaching. A secondary issue arose, however, regarding the primacy of the pulpit. Perhaps some of the comments from the pastors, other staff, and laypersons will provide a glimpse of some of our discoveries.

Comments by Pastors:

- "The opportunity to stand before the congregation in a worship opportunity is tremendous. Even when I am not preaching, I take the opportunity to exhort our people when we are all gathered together."
- "My leadership role has its greatest momentum when I speak to the entire congregation. When we are facing critical issues, I typically speak to the entire body after I preach."

- "I have discovered that, even in the announcements I make and the prayers I pray in the worship service, the emphases of our church through me are discerned."
- "One of my chief joys is taking time to welcome people, members and guests, in our worship services. I have been told that my enthusiasm (or lack of enthusiasm) during this time affects the whole church."
- "One of the most important opportunities I have as a pastor is the opportunity to speak before the entire gathered congregation. I can do so through the sermon, but it is not limited to the sermon."

Comments from Church Staff Other Than Pastors:

- "Every week in our staff meetings, we discuss the needed emphases from the pastor when he speaks to the congregation. The church knows that our direction for leadership comes from the pulpit in both preaching and other contexts."
- "[Our pastor] does a wonderful job of keeping our church focused through a part of the worship services called 'Focus.' He reminds us prior to the message who we are and whose we are."
- "As a staff, we had no idea how important the announcement time was until we made a deliberate decision for the pastor to speak on key areas each Sunday. We don't announce every minute event in the church, but [the pastor] does remind us of the important happenings in our church."

Comments from Laypersons:

- "I remember one Sunday morning worship where the pastor said he just wanted to share some thoughts from the bottom of his heart before he preached. The church was in a financial crisis at the time and morale was low. [He] reminded us that God was in control and that God would provide. I have forgotten hundreds of sermons, but I will never forget that talk!"
- "The pastor asks the deacons to lead the way to pray in front of the pulpit. Anyone else is welcome to join them. He then leads in prayer. The entire direction of the worship service is set by that moment of pastor-led prayer."
- "Preaching is the most important. But the pastor has other leadership roles during Sunday services that make a big difference."

We were reminded by dozens of such comments that the pastor's leadership during worship services can come from several opportunities other than the sermon. I speak of these opportunities as "pulpit" opportunities rather than "preaching" opportunities. The comments in our survey indicated that such leadership roles can be classified into three broad categories.

The first category, mentioned more frequently than others, was the role of leadership and modeling. The leaders in these evangelistic churches indicated that most of their church members view their pastors through their words, actions, and demeanor on Sunday mornings. "It's a tremendous challenge," shared the pastor of a California church. "I know that my leadership is often measured by what I do or say on Sunday morning." Yet the pastor sees possible advantages as well. "The 'captive' audience of Sunday morning means that I can share the dreams and visions with a large number in the church. It is a true opportunity for leadership."

"I can be a model of Christlikeness on Sunday morning or I can be the epitome of carnality," another pastor explained. "My members know that I am not perfect, but they look to me to set an example, especially when the greatest number see me on Sunday morning."

A second leadership role that many pastors assume on Sunday mornings is the role of encourager. "Whether I'm preaching or just making announcements," a Tennessee pastor shared, "I try to be a 'Barnabas' to my people. They need encouragement and exhortation."

A Texas pastor encourages from the pulpit by recognizing one or more persons each Sunday for their work and ministry. The people in his church expressed sincere appreciation for the pastor's desire to give credit and encouragement to them.

Perhaps the most significant role of the pulpit beyond preaching and leadership was the opportunity to emphasize major thrusts in the church's ministry. "Whenever our church needs a push in a certain direction, I go to the pulpit to speak forthrightly to the people. We recently concluded a major missions emphasis, and we broke all giving records!"

One final observation about the power of the pulpit is noteworthy. The longer the tenure of a pastor, the greater the likelihood that the pastor uses the pulpit for leadership opportunities. We already noted that the average pastoral tenure of these evangelistic pastors is three times the denomination's average (see exhibit 3-6). Those pastors with ten or more years tenure in one church mentioned the use of the pulpit for leadership persuasion quite often.

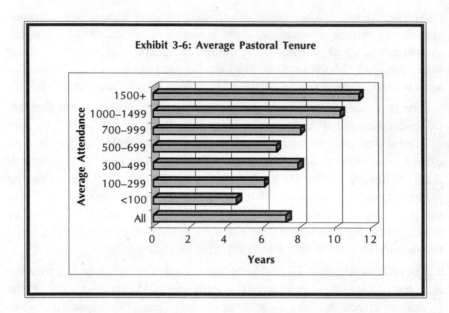

Exhibit 3-6: Average Pastoral Tenure

Evangelistic Preaching or Preaching for Evangelism?

Do the pastors of these evangelistic churches preach evangelistic sermons? We asked 10 percent of the respondents this question and were somewhat surprised to discover that "pure" evangelistic sermons were the exception rather than the rule. We described an evangelistic sermon as one prepared specifically for the lost, with a clear gospel message present. The sinfulness of humanity, the atoning sacrifice of Christ on the cross, repentance, faith, and forgiveness were among the elements of the kerygma present in these messages.

While almost all of the pastors preached straightforward evangelistic messages on occasion, very few gave the members a steady stream of such sermons. Bruce Watford, pastor of Lugoff Friendship Baptist Church in Lugoff, South Carolina (worship attendance 307), does not necessarily preach an evangelistic message per se in every sermon. He does believe, however, that "the sermon . . . must always present the plan of salvation." Similarly, Houston Roberson, pastor of Bethel Baptist Church in Chesapeake, Virginia (attendance 250), says that his sermons "always contain an evangelistic thrust."

Such comments were repeated throughout out interviews. Evangelistic preaching takes place on occasion. But even more frequently, sermons are preached with an evangelistic intentionality. As one pastor in Michigan said, "Even if I am preaching from Ecclesiastes, I will somehow communicate the gospel in every sermon."

The Power of the Word Proclaimed

Because preaching was seen as the most important element in these evangelistic churches, we must be certain of the implications of these findings. The key elements are grouped below into four major observations.

Observation #1: Preaching Is Highly Important for Evangelistic Growth

Church growth methodologies offer a certain fascination and temptation. With the right tools, programs, and ministries, the argument goes, growth is certain to come. But our research shows that absolutely nothing is of greater importance to evangelistic growth than the preaching of the Word. Such preaching presumes trust in the Scriptures, intentionality in evangelism, and power that comes from God through the pastor's prayer life and the intercessory prayer of others.

Why then has the role of preaching for evangelistic growth been sorely neglected? Volumes of preaching books have been written, but few broached the issue of preaching for growth. Likewise, church growth books rarely mention the role of preaching. Perhaps a possible answer is that preaching is a long-discussed topic that offers no "newness" in its methodology. It is as tried and true as Peter's sermon at Pentecost.

A church growth-informed pastor from California offered these insights: "Much of the church growth literature has a bias toward the new and the trendy. I believe that the relationship between the two disciplines is an untapped reservoir for study."

Indeed, I pray that someone will expand this major facet of our study. No methodology (if preaching can truly be labeled as a methodology) was mentioned nearly as often as preaching for the evangelistic effectiveness of the church. The primacy of the pulpit for evangelistic growth is a topic worthy of pursuit for years to come.

Observation #2: The Primacy of Preaching Means a Reevaluation of Pastoral Priorities

In my earlier book, *Giant Awakenings*,[4] I commented on a growing trend among pastors, a trend I called "the Acts 6 revolution." Church growth methodologies, counseling leadership training, and other areas will be important, but the growing trend is for the pastor's time to be spent like the apostles of Acts 6—in prayer and ministry of the Word.

The results of this study confirmed those earlier observations. Pastors can easily fill an eighty-hour week battling the tyranny of the urgent. But many pastors of these evangelistic churches have shifted their priorities to make certain they spend adequate time in study of the Word and in sermon preparation. These pastors realize that they are not omnicompetent; they can "feed the flock" only after hours are spent in the Word each week. Other urgent matters become less urgent; pastoral priorities are reevaluated.

"What it meant for me," said an Oklahoma pastor, "is whether I will do good things or whether I will do well that which God called me to do: preach the Word." A perceptible shift, particularly noticeable in these evangelistic churches, is underway. The Bible is returning as the key church growth manual. Pastors are waking up to the fact that long-term, evangelistic growth can only take place when the people are nurtured, taught, and educated in God's Word.

Observation #3: Evangelistic Intentionality in Sermons Is as Important as Evangelistic Preaching

One easily discernible observation about this study has been the attitude of evangelistic intentionality in the churches and their leaders. In every methodological and ministry-related area, church leaders are searching for ways of reaching people for Christ. This observation is certainly true about preaching. The pastors may not preach a point-by-point evangelistic sermon, but they are aware of the potential evangelistic impact each message has. Lost persons may be listening with receptive ears and hearts, and Christians may be moved to become evangelistic themselves.

Observation #4: Preaching and Prayer Are Closely Related

Many of these pastors stated explicitly that the power in their preaching directly relates to both their prayer lives and the intercessory prayer of others. It is difficult to speak of dynamic sermons without speaking of the role of prayer in evangelistic churches. Therefore it is no surprise that prayer was the second leading "methodology" of growth in these churches. To that subject we turn in the next chapter.

CHAPTER FOUR

Churches That Pray

The only sure foundation for a church is intercessory prayer. Only then will the outpouring of the Holy Spirit come, and people in the world will be drawn to Christ. More than half of the people who ever lived are alive today. We must believe fervently that they are really lost before we can intercede effectively for them.

R. A. Pegram

Throughout this book you have heard or will hear the testimonies of hundreds of leaders in evangelistic churches. My primary role in this project was one of listening. Though my interpretations are offered at points, my primary desire is to let others speak to you, the readers.

I must, however, share with you my own heart and testimony for prayer, especially for prayer in churches. In a previous book,[1] I shared the story of the miraculous healing of my son Sam in 1982. Many people in churches across our nation prayed specifically for Sam on one specific night. His healing was dramatic and immediate.

Two years later my father, also named Sam, was diagnosed with a rapidly spreading cancer. I once again called on prayer intercessors across the United States. This time God chose not to heal Dad physically but to take him home. And though the prayers were not answered as I had asked and hoped, I was nevertheless overwhelmed with the power of prayer.

God led me in 1986 to write my doctoral dissertation on C. Peter Wagner, a key leader of the church growth movement. Though my initial interest in Wagner was on the methodological insights he provided to growing churches, his influence on me was greatest in the area of prayer. Peter Wagner has had his share of critics. They have accused him of everything from racism to Pelagianism. Yet I suspect that most of his critics have no idea about the enormous influence he has been on church leaders whose lives were changed by the power of prayer.

In 1992, primarily because of Peter Wagner's influence, I began to pray that God would raise up intercessors for my ministry and my family. I was the pastor of a large church in Birmingham, Alabama. As I reflect upon those days, I now see that they were the most difficult times I had known in pastoral ministry.

But God did call several people to intercede daily for me. I began to know the power of prayer for ministry as I had never known before. God was once again showing me the priority and power of prayer.

Another significant influence upon me has been the prayer lives of my three sons: Sam, Art, and Jess. For years now, each of my boys has been praying daily for one person. They have sensed the call of God to be intercessors for three special leaders. Sam prays daily for Timothy George, the dean of Beeson Divinity School. Art never misses a day praying for Lewis Drummond, my mentor and former president of Southeastern Baptist Theological Seminary. And Jess, now eleven, has been praying for C. Peter Wagner almost since he learned to talk!

The Leaders Speak on Prayer

Before we turn to the statistical results of prayer and evangelism, let me share with you some of the stories we heard from the churches. The power of prayer truly is being unleashed for evangelism across our land.

Riverland Baptist Church, Fort Lauderdale, Florida (200 attendance), Ron Mensinger, pastor: "We have a prayer room where members volunteer one hour per week to pray specifically for lost people. We also have a Saturday night prayer session for evangelistic prospects."

Peniel Baptist Church, Palatka, Florida (160 attendance), Dannie Williams, pastor. We interviewed Greg Bearden, minister of music: "Billy Graham was baptized in our church, so we have a great legacy of evangelism. We have prayer leaders in every Sunday School class. The deacons pray before worship services, then a ladies' group prays during the services. An ongoing prayer ministry is maintained in the church's prayer chapel. Prayer for the lost is incorporated into the church's Watchman prayer ministry."

Post Falls Baptist Church, Post Falls, Idaho (200 attendance), Bill Hohenstreet, pastor: "We keep a prayer list for salvation. The interesting thing is that a member cannot place a person's name on that list without first personally witnessing to that person. The church now has four thousand names on this list [remember, this church has two hundred in attendance], which means there have been at least that many personal soul winning confrontations. After a person is converted, the name stays on the list as the church continues to pray for real spiritual growth."

Crown Point Baptist Church, Jacksonville, Florida (230 attendance), Steve Thompson, pastor: "Prayer is considered to be of primary importance in our evangelistic efforts. Every week one person from each Sunday School class is selected to go to the prayer room and pray specifically for the lost to be converted. Every morning I pray over a specific list of names of known lost people."

First Southern Baptist Church, Lompoc, California (350 attendance), J. T. Reed, pastor: "Each Sunday people are encouraged to fill out a card that lists some known lost person. On Sunday evenings, the staff prays for the people who have been named on these cards. Saturday night is set aside for groups to gather to pray specifically for non-believers."

The testimonies of these leaders could continue for pages. What the printed word cannot communicate adequately, however, is the sense of enthusiasm and excitement these leaders conveyed as they spoke to us. Prayer is truly a priority in most of these evangelistic churches.

The Survey Results

Exhibit 4-1 highlights the importance of prayer in these churches' evangelistic effectiveness. Nearly 70 percent of the churches rated prayer as a *major* factor in their evangelistic success. Except for those with attendance of 700 to 999, at least 60 percent of churches in every size category identified prayer as a major factor.

Interestingly, the strongest responses came from the extremes of the smallest and the largest churches. Since our survey size was too few in the smallest churches, we could not offer a categorical explanation for their responses. However, many of the largest churches had a staff person, either full-time or part-time, responsible for prayer ministries. This focus tended to make the churches more aware of their need for greater emphasis on prayer.

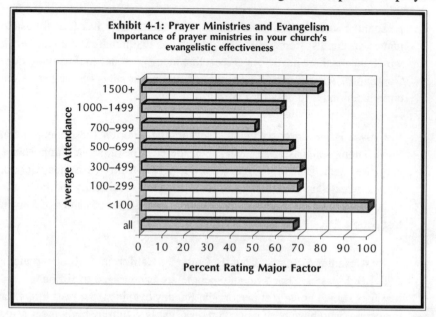

Church leaders were asked to respond to the statement, "Prayer is foundational to effective evangelism." As shown in exhibit 4-2, over 80 percent responded that they absolutely agree prayer is most important. The number who responded "agree," "very much agree," or "absolutely agree" accounted for over 98 percent of the churches. Only 1 percent did not agree with the statement.

Earlier surveys by C. Peter Wagner, George Barna, Kirk Hadaway, and others discovered a direct correlation between prayer and church growth. Our study confirms their work, but specifically in the area of evangelistic or conversion growth. Whereas the 1960s and 1970s was a time of intense interest in methodological approaches to growth, we now see a greater balance which recognizes spiritual realities such as prayer to the sovereign God.

Our research team also asked questions about the implementation of prayer ministries for evangelistic effectiveness. We wanted to know if their attitudes resulted in actions. Church leaders were asked to respond to the statement; "We are committed to prayer as an essential element of any successful outreach venture." Two obvious conclusions are drawn from the results.

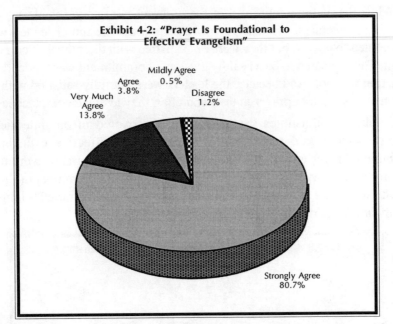

Exhibit 4-2: "Prayer Is Foundational to Effective Evangelism"

Mildly Agree 0.5%
Agree 3.8%
Very Much Agree 13.8%
Disagree 1.2%
Strongly Agree 80.7%

First, these evangelistic churches *are* committed to prayer. Nearly 90 percent responded "very much agree" or "absolutely agree, most important" to the above-mentioned statement. Only 1 percent did not agree that their churches were committed to prayer for evangelistic outreach (see exhibit 4-3). Some of the quotes received in our interviews demonstrate this level of prayer commitment.

- "An attitude of fervency of prayer has taken hold in our church since we began praying for the lost specifically by name."
- "Prayer, corporate prayer, explains the evangelistic turnaround in our church."
- "We are now a church of prayer and fasting, something we have never done before."
- "I believe the primary reason that God has His hand on our church is our commitment to the foundation of prayer."
- "Our growth through conversions? It's the result of our prayer ministry that takes place seven days a week."
- "Prayer, prayer . . . and more prayer."
- "Our evangelistic growth can best be explained by our ongoing prayer ministry."

While the commitment level of these churches to prayer is clearly discernible, a second pattern emerged in the responses. The church leaders *were* committed to prayer, but they *were not* satisfied with their level of commitment. This appeared to be a healthy tension—commitment was evident; satisfaction was not. And because the leaders were not fully satisfied with the depth and breadth of prayer in their churches, they avoided complacency.

Exhibit 4-3 illustrates the tension we discovered in our interviews. Eighty percent said prayer was foundational to effective evangelism (exhibit 4-2), yet less than 65 percent believed their churches were truly committed to prayer for outreach. While the level of commitment (almost two-thirds of the churches) is very high, we nevertheless noted a longing for even greater depth of commitment.

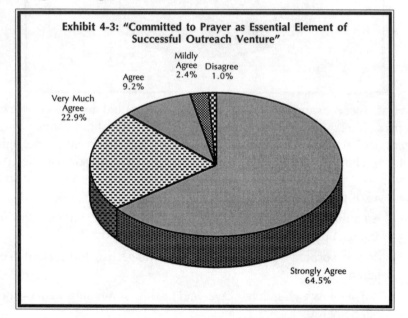

Exhibit 4-3: "Committed to Prayer as Essential Element of Successful Outreach Venture"

Mildly Agree 2.4% Disagree 1.0% Agree 9.2% Very Much Agree 22.9% Strongly Agree 64.5%

One pastor in South Carolina shared his frank assessment of his church's prayer ministry. "With each passing day," he said, "I recognize God's plan for prayer in my life personally and in my church." After a brief pause he continued, "But neither I nor my church are where we should be in our level of commitment to prayer. We have made great strides, but we have so far to go. I just don't think we will ever be fully satisfied." Many other church leaders made similar comments. Because of this attitude, we anticipate even greater levels of commitment to prayer in the years ahead.

C. Peter Wagner estimates that 5 percent of churches in America have a dynamic prayer ministry.[2] Among the 576 evangelistic churches in this study, over three-fourths had a churchwide prayer ministry. Though not all could be called "dynamic," our impressions were that most were truly vibrant and made a difference in the life of the church. If Wagner's assessment is correct, and if our numbers are valid, the contrast between praying and non-praying churches is stark. Wagner's estimate of only 5 percent is dramatically below our measure of approximately 75 percent. Therefore, we conclude, with conviction, that most evangelistically growing churches are also praying churches.

How They Are Praying

Ed Young, pastor of Second Baptist Church in Houston, Texas, leads one of the largest and fastest-growing Southern Baptist churches in the nation. Numerous articles have been written on the church, particularly on its methodologies to reach baby boomers.

Wagner notes, however, that the explosive growth of the church is associated with the beginning of a churchwide prayer ministry in 1982.[3] This vibrant twenty-four-hour ministry consists of two prayer intercessors in a prayer room at separate work stations. One intercessor receives prayer needs over a telephone prayer line while a second intercessor prays for the telephone requests as well as many other requests. The church needs 336 persons (168 hours times two) to serve in the prayer room each week. With on-call substitutes, the ministry, known as the "First Watch" ministry of Second Baptist involves nearly 400 church members. A few years ago, a "Second Watch" was formed to provide intercessory prayer in all geographic regions of Houston.

Second Baptist has a full-time prayer ministry director and a full-time prayer secretary. Most of the churches in our study were unable to have either part-time or full-time staff devoted specifically to prayer ministries. This void, however, did not deter the church leaders from moving forward with several approaches to corporate praying.

A Lay Leader for Prayer

In many of the churches, we discovered that God had raised up one particular person with a passion for prayer. In most cases this was a woman. This person had a distinct call to develop prayer ministries in the church.

The success of the prayer ministry she (or he) attempted to develop and lead was largely dependent upon four factors.

1. A passion for prayer. The prayer leader's entire life is directed by and focused upon prayer. His or her burning passion for prayer influences others to become prayer intercessors. The following comments of a prayer ministry coordinator reflect this attitude: "I simply cannot understand why *all* of our church members are not giving our prayer ministry one or more hours a week. Prayer is such a precious privilege. You would think the people would be in line to sign up!"

2. The support of the pastor. One vital role of the pastor is that of supporting the prayer ministry and the prayer leader. "I knew God was calling me to lead this ministry," a California woman shared with us. "But I simply could get nothing more than token support from our pastor. Rather than making an issue of him, I gave the matter to God in prayer. Would you believe that within one year, the pastor was called to another church? Our new pastor is a man of prayer and enthusiastically supports the ministry!" Perhaps there is a lesson for pastors in her comments!

3. Leadership and organization. We noticed that leaders of prayer ministries truly are called leaders because they have willing and excited followers. A church's prayer ministry often has more people involved than any other church ministry, with perhaps the exception of Sunday School. For that reason, good organizational skills are a requisite for these leaders.

4. A church that is ready. Not all churches are ready for corporate prayer ministries. The level of readiness is not as much dependent on financial and personnel resources as it is spiritual factors. As one rather blunt prayer leader told us: "Some churches make Laodicea look like a paradigm of passion. These churches must have business meetings and a majority vote just to decide if they are going to pray."

Upper Room Ministries

Special prayer rooms are not new, but I first heard Don Miller of Fort Worth, Texas, call this place the "upper room." In simplest terms, an upper room is a place in the church's building that is specifically set aside for prayer. Basically, two kinds of upper rooms can be seen in churches.

The first type is a room where people can come and go at random. It really is more like a small chapel than an organized intercessory prayer room. Unfortunately, with rare exceptions, these rooms are vacant much of the day and night, and little intercessory prayer takes place.

A second type is a room that is specifically organized and designed for intercessors to pray at designated hours of the day. Though we did not ask about prayer rooms on our initial survey, we discovered in follow-up interviews that about one-third of the evangelistically effective churches had dynamic intercessory prayer rooms.

A pastor in Kentucky led his church to begin an upper room prayer ministry in 1993. He initially was reluctant because he had heard that this kind of ministry needed someone in the prayer room twenty-four hours a day, seven days a week. The 168 required persons was more than the church's average attendance!

Instead, he began with ten persons who were willing to come to the church one hour per week for intercessory prayer. Cards containing prayer requests were placed in a room with a Bible, a comfortable chair, and a pen and paper for additional prayer requests. Now, three years later, the number who come to the upper room has grown to twenty, and the church has witnessed remarkable changes, not the least among them greater evangelistic harvests.

A pastor in Alabama described the organization of his church's prayer room. Six Rolodex files are placed on one long table. The files include cards in one of six categories.

1. Lost persons—by name or relationship to someone ("a friend of John Smith").

2. Physical needs, sickness, etc.

3. Other intercessory needs: financial, job, relational, grief, etc.

4. Church, staff, and denominational needs, including missionaries.

5. All church members' names and their families.

6. The praise file—answered prayers!

Each person is instructed to spend ten minutes at each Rolodex "station." A colored clip marks the point where the previous intercessor ended. The person in the room moves the clip to his ending point as well. The pastor commented that many of the people had never before prayed for one hour without interruption. They testified of their own spiritual growth as an intercessor.

Worship and Preaching Intercessor

Nearly half of those questioned in follow-up interviews indicated that their prayer ministries included a group of intercessors who prayed during worship services. Although they prayed during the entire service, many focused upon the time of preaching as the time of most intense intercession. These intercessors sometimes prayed in a designated upper room, or simply used any vacant room during the worship services.

Prayer Chains

Few of these churches use prayer chains. A minister of education in Texas commented, "Our prayer chain became a gossip chain. We had more problems than prayers, so we simply stopped emphasizing it. The chain died a natural death."

Wagner notes that prayer chains are often used only for emergencies.[4] But he advocates the use of prayer chains for concentrated prayer effort for any specific concern or issue. Perhaps it is the crisis-only mentality that causes some prayer chains to degenerate into a gossip chain.

Wagner also asserts that the vitality of a prayer chain depends upon sharing answered prayers. "One other principle for maintaining the vitality of prayer chains is to design and implement an efficient way to share answered prayer with prayer chain members. Without answers to prayer, the ministry can become tedious."[5] None of the interviewed pastors or staff indicated that their prayer chains, whether in place or discontinued, included the element of answered prayer.

Wednesday Night Praying

Some churches responded that their prayer life became vital when they began focusing Wednesday evening services on prayer. Others indicated that their churches had drifted away from devoting Wednesday services to prayer because of low attendance and sheer boredom. As a Florida pastor said, "Wednesday nights had become 'who's who in the hospital.' Our young people avoided the service like the plague."

One church built a worship service around corporate prayer. Praise teams sang. The congregation participated in hymns and choruses. Someone gave a testimony on answered prayer. Then, for about twenty minutes, the church would intercede in prayer as the pastor announced the prayer needs. The conclusion of the service included some element of expectancy for answered prayers in the days ahead.

The Prayers of the Pastor

Most of the pastors we studied have a singular devotion to prayer. They believe their prayer lives are critical for two reasons: (1) their own spiritual growth and relationship to God; and (2) their example to their congregations. Listen to how some of these pastors articulated their self-expectations of prayer.

- "I believe that I [the pastor] must model a heart for prayer."
- "I [the pastor] should never ask our people to do anything I am not willing to do. And the absolutely most important thing we should be doing is praying."
- "We have a weekly time set aside where the pastor invites anyone to join him in intercessory prayer."
- "The pastor and staff meet regularly to pray specifically for the lost. Any church member can join them in this time of prayer."
- "I [the pastor] pray and fast one day a week. Though I do not advertise it, the church has become aware of it and many have followed my example."

Pastoral leadership is vital in all areas of the church, and prayer is no exception. Wagner, who has probably done more research on prayer in the local church than anyone else, is adamant about the example that pastors must set for prayer in the church: "The churches I have found with dynamic congregational prayer ministries have pastors who have given prayer a high enough visible priority in their lives and ministries to assume the leadership of the prayer ministry."[6] But Wagner is not advocating a solo prayer ministry by the pastor. "This does not mean they themselves do all the prayer ministry. Far from it. But they do hold themselves responsible and accountable for the quantity and quality of prayer in their church. The buck stops with them."[7]

Prayers for the Pastor

Many pastors shared with us that they knew of church members who prayed for them daily. Some of these pastors send letters to inform known intercessors of their prayer needs and the prayer needs of their families.

A pastor in California told us that the intercessory prayer of others was the key factor in his remaining in ministry. "As I see how God is blessing our church today, I remind myself how close I came to leaving the ministry altogether. God convicted me that I had become too self-dependent. Because of pride, I would not let anyone help me."

During that difficult time the pastor sank into despair and desperation. "I finally confided in a spiritually mature man in the church. When he saw my hurt and desperation, he simply said, 'Pastor, we need to get some people standing in the gap for you.'" Within a few days, fifteen men were praying for the pastor daily. Not only did he stay in the ministry, but the church went from virtually no conversion growth to become one of the selected churches for this study.

Prayers for Evangelism and Conversions

A word we kept hearing in this study was "intentional." Sermons were intentional about evangelism. Outreach was evangelistically intentional. Ministries intentionally were designed to reach people for Christ. Sunday School was organized intentionally to be evangelistic. Many church leaders reported that same attitude about prayer. "I think it's unbelievable," said a pastor, "that we do not ask God for souls to be saved. We have the great power of prayer, yet we do not ask Him to give us the souls of men and women. Most of our churches are not evangelistic because we fail to ask God."

While the intensity and frequency of prayer in these evangelistic churches in commendable, equally noteworthy is the *type* of prayers offered corporately by the churches. Repeatedly pastors, staff, and laypersons told us that their churches prayed for lost people by name. Matthew Leilich, minister of education at Cana Baptist Church in Burleson, Texas, said, "Every week we distribute a list of known lost people to our intercessory prayer groups." As I noted earlier in this chapter, the members of Riverland Baptist Church in Fort Lauderdale, Florida, volunteer one hour per week to pray specifically for lost people. Consequently, most of Riverland's growth has been conversion growth.

Wayside Baptist Church in Miami, Florida, has grown to seven hundred in worship attendance. Leslie Williams, minister of education, told us that their church's small groups pray specifically for the lost. Additionally, "the pastor and staff meet regularly to pray for the lost." And Bobby Harrell, pastor of First Baptist Church of Leesburg, Georgia, spoke excitedly about their strong prayer ministry which has specific concern for the unsaved. "Our two strongest prayer groups are our deacons and senior adult ladies. They regularly pray for the lost."

I recently reviewed my consultation notes of dozens of churches I visited over the past few years. Most of them were in a slow decline that we sometimes mislabel "plateau." Perhaps more than any single factor, the absence of dynamic corporate prayer ministries was the contrasting element compared to these 576 evangelistic churches. More specifically, I could not find one declining church that had an ongoing prayer ministry specifically for the lost. Perhaps these dying churches have not because they ask not.

Observations and Lessons

The results of this study reminded or perhaps awakened us to the unbelievable power of prayer through the insights of church leaders in evangelistic churches. Since my heartfelt desire is for this book to be more than a presentation of data, I have attempted to offer observations and lessons as we deal with many of these issues. Of course, in doing so I leave the objective for the subjective. Nevertheless, it would be a travesty if we simply heard facts about praying churches without asking how our own churches might utilize the data.

Therefore I again assume the role of consultant to share some of the lessons from this study. Armed with the data, I offer the following conclusions and lessons to any church that is interested.

Lesson #1: Corporate Prayer Is Vital to the Health of a Church

Though this lesson may seem too obvious, we need to be reminded of the clear correlations evident from this and other studies. Few declining churches have good corporate prayer ministries; most growing evangelistic churches do. Churches that are asking for souls are receiving evangelistic harvests. Prayer should be the priority for evangelistic growth.

Lesson #2: Prayer and Fasting Can Prepare a Church for Ongoing Prayer Ministries

I recently concluded an interim pastorate at Highview Baptist Church in Louisville, Kentucky. Highview has a far-reaching prayer ministry and a multi-room upper room ministry. Each November the church members recommit themselves to prayer. A day is set aside for prayer and fasting. For twenty-four consecutive hours members come to the church and seek God's face for another year of prayer commitment. The following Sunday is a time of massive commitment to prayer by the church body.

Many of the churches in this study indicated that they spent months preparing their people for a greater emphasis on prayer. In other words, they told us that they prepared for prayer by praying!

Some churches simply are not ready for a new and intense emphasis on prayer. Leaders in the church may pray and fast themselves before proposing corporate prayer ministries to the church. Then again, other churches, like Highview, prepare the people on a regular basis for a renewed emphasis on prayer.

Lesson #3: An Upper Room Ministry Is Common in Many Evangelistic Churches

The upper room ministry mentioned earlier in this chapter was the common methodological link in a great number of the evangelistic churches in this study. What the upper room ministry offered was a level of organization and accountability not offered in some other prayer ministries. The upper room is also a visible indicator to the congregation of the church's commitment to prayer. Typically the ministry also provides an easily accessible vehicle for members and others to communicate prayer concerns.

Lesson #4: Not All Prayer Is Evangelistic Prayer

Any sincere prayer is important. But not all prayers are specifically for evangelism. Many churches, perhaps most churches in America, focus their corporate prayers on physical needs—sickness, bereavement, and hospitalizations. While these prayer needs are valid and need fervent intercession, the eternal needs of those without a relationship to Jesus Christ are critical. Several church leaders interviewed in this study indicated that both the attitude of the members and the atmosphere of the church improved significantly when prayer included prayers for the lost.

As an Arkansas pastor told our research team, "Praying for the lost did more to refocus our church than any single factor. We became a church with an outward focus after being an inwardly focused church for years."

Lesson #5: Acknowledging Answered Prayers Is Important

A significant number of churches in this study have established a process to inform church members about answered prayers. On a small scale, some churches keep a written record of answered prayers. Anyone can go to an upper room or designated area to see the answers to prayers.

On a larger scale other churches take part of the time in selected worship services to celebrate answered prayers. A layperson in a church in Mississippi told us, "I always look forward to our worship services on the final Sunday of each month. Several of the answered prayers from our upper room are shared with us through a variety of ways. But we close that part of the service with a thunderous hymn which gives thanks to God. It's an awesome service!"

Evangelistic Churches Are Praying Churches

Prayer was mentioned as the second most important methodology for reaching people for Christ in these evangelistic churches. But even that statistic may be understated. In every methodology—preaching, Sunday School, ministries, etc.—prayer was the underlying strength to the methodology. If, as Wagner believes, a great prayer movement began in churches in the early 1970s, the twenty-first century may see the fruit of that prayer as millions accept Christ through the ministry of local churches.

CHAPTER FIVE

The Sunday School Factor

If the Sunday School is to become more evangelistic, then the importance of the Sunday School must be communicated all the way to the grass roots, where every Sunday School member accepts responsibility for reaching out to others with the good news.

R. Wayne Jones

Those who predict the demise of the Sunday School are betting against history. The Sunday School is almost as old as our nation and, with only a few exceptions, has mirrored the growth of the United States. The movement had its beginnings in England in the late 1700s when Robert Raikes, editor of the *Gloucester Journal*, hired teachers for impoverished children.

Sunday School quickly moved to the United States and was aided by other forces pushing for social reform. Just before 1800, Sunday School had spread to Massachusetts, New York, Pennsylvania, Rhode Island, and New Jersey.

After 1800, the purpose of Sunday School expanded to both education and evangelism. The first national Sunday School effort began in 1824. The American Sunday School Union's stated purpose was to organize, evangelize, and civilize. The Union trained leadership, published literature, and formed thousands of Sunday Schools by 1880.

Though the Sunday School movement began by educating children in England, it eventually became the teaching, nurturing, and evangelizing arm of the church. Sunday School outreach was especially effective. By 1900 about 80 percent of all new church members in America first came to the church through the Sunday School.

Sunday School has weathered two centuries of theological and ecclesiological storms because it has remained true to its purpose: to be the vehicle through which the truths of Scripture are taught to all generations. Contrary to some critics, effective Sunday Schools do not use archaic methods. No long-standing organization can survive two hundred years without methodological adaptation. The Sunday Schools in many of these evangelistic churches today are vibrant organizations used effectively to teach and reach thousands.

Those who think something is inherently wrong with Sunday School should consider two things. First, many Sunday Schools are quite effective—the leaders in these evangelistic churches will attest to that. Second, churches with ineffective Sunday Schools violate the very principles that make Sunday School a viable organization: they dilute biblical teachings, fail to train effective teachers, replace systematic Bible teaching with other types of group activity, and relegate Sunday School to the status of one more church activity.

What Is a Sunday School?

Perhaps part of the critics' problem with Sunday School is perceptual. For some, Sunday School means listening to a long and boring lecture on the Bible in an uncomfortable metal folding chair in a room with peeling paint. We asked the leaders of these evangelistic churches specifically how they defined Sunday School. Their responses focused on four general characteristics:

- Sunday School includes systematic teaching of Scripture. They have some level of accountability and organization in place to insure that such teaching is offered to everyone.
- Sunday School gives regular Bible teaching for all ages. This is the "cradle to grave" concept advocated by many leaders.
- Sunday School provides small group ministry and fellowship within each class. Multiple small groups may be necessary in larger classes.
- Sunday School ensures regular outreach beyond the people in the class.

Note that they did not define Sunday School as an organization meeting at a certain time, day, or place. Though most of the church leaders preferred on-campus classes for accountability, they did not limit the Sunday School to a room in the church building. To the contrary, many churches were quite innovative with their times and locations.

What about Small Groups?

Only 2 of the 576 churches indicated that they had replaced Sunday School with in-home or off-campus small groups. There was some confusion, however, concerning the definition of small groups. Several mentioned that the location (home or off-campus) was the deciding factor, though they were willing to call their off-campus groups Sunday Schools. Others spoke of the "intimacy factor" afforded by small groups, but then quickly responded that care groups in Sunday Schools were just as effective. A minister of education in Georgia said, "Sunday Schools have had small groups meeting in the homes for decades. We have called them fellowship groups, care groups, and other names, but they essentially served the same purpose as small groups do today."

Many church leaders indicated that they had struggled with the debate of Sunday Schools versus small groups. Should they lead their churches to begin small groups to replace Sunday School? Or should small groups supplement Sunday School? The leaders did not think they could expect their people to be fully committed to two open-ended groups. Consequently, most of them chose to keep the Sunday School. Nearly one-fourth, however, indicated that short-term small groups had done well in their churches. The key, they told us, was for the small groups to have a clear termination date and a specific purpose.

What about the Southern Baptist Bias?

Since we studied Southern Baptist churches, we might expect a better response to Sunday School methodology than we would have received had we studied another group. In fact, everyone on our research team was prepared for what we called "the Southern Baptist bias." But we were surprised at the intense loyalty these evangelistic churches have to Sunday School. Many Southern Baptists have perceived that Sunday School's effectiveness is waning. But the most evangelistic churches in the denomination responded with a resounding affirmation of Sunday School. Sixty-three percent ranked Sunday School as a major factor in their evangelistic effectiveness. *Nearly 90 percent of the churches in the follow-up interviews identified Sunday School as their most effective assimilation tool.*

The Statistical Results

Our initial survey asked only one question about the Sunday School: "Rank your Sunday School in terms of its contribution to the evangelistic effectiveness of your church." Because our survey was only concerned with matters related to evangelism, no other questions were asked about the Sunday School. Although more information came through in our follow-up interviews, we will address those issues later. For now, let us review again the relationship of evangelism to Sunday School.

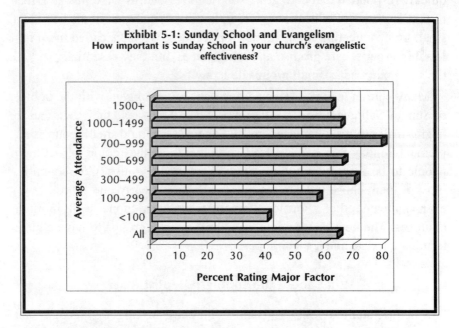

Exhibit 5-1: Sunday School and Evangelism
How important is Sunday School in your church's evangelistic effectiveness?

Sunday School as a methodology for evangelistic effectiveness ranked only third, below preaching and prayer. We were somewhat surprised to find that larger churches (more than 300 in attendance) use Sunday School as an evangelistic tool more than smaller churches. Even in the largest churches (one thousand and above), over 60 percent ranked Sunday School highly as an evangelistic methodology.

Smaller Churches

Since so few churches with an attendance of less than one hundred were included in our study, we looked at the two categories of churches with attendance of less than three hundred. The number of churches this size in the study numbered 227.

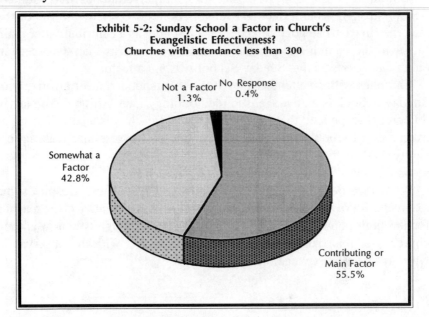

Exhibit 5-2: Sunday School a Factor in Church's Evangelistic Effectiveness?
Churches with attendance less than 300

Not a Factor 1.3%

No Response 0.4%

Somewhat a Factor 42.8%

Contributing or Main Factor 55.5%

Few churches in any size category said Sunday School is *not* a factor in their evangelistic effectiveness. Those with fewer than three hundred in attendance had the fewest number (55.5 percent, exhibit 5-2) that rated the methodology as a contributing or main factor. Why did the smaller churches respond in this manner? Our follow-up interviews identified two interesting patterns.

First, leaders of these churches were more intentional about other facets of Sunday School ministry—assimilation, teaching, or ministry—than about outreach. Evangelism seemed to be *more* intentional in larger churches. Why? Perhaps our second observation explains.

Smaller churches were more pastor- or staff-dependent for evangelism than the larger churches. For example, a pastor of a smaller church with fifty annual baptisms may have been personally responsible for half of the witnessing encounters that resulted in conversions. Yet once attendance grew beyond a certain threshold, the pastor or staff could no longer be responsible for most of the evangelistic activities. Thus, the Sunday School became the intentional evangelistic arm of the church.

Larger Churches

Exhibits 5-3 and 5-4 show that these larger churches rank Sunday School strongly as an effective evangelistic tool. Over two-thirds of the churches in each category ranked Sunday School as a contributing or main factor in the church's evangelistic effectiveness. Less than 3 percent in either category said that Sunday School was *not* a factor.

Churches with an attendance of 700–999 responded most positively to Sunday School as an evangelistic methodology (see exhibit 5-5). Nearly 80 percent responded that Sunday School outreach was a contributing or main factor to their evangelistic effectiveness. The response was significantly higher than churches in any other category. The next highest response was a full eighteen percentage points lower.

What factors could explain these different responses? Despite some extensive follow-up interviews, we were unable to identify clear reasons for the high popularity of Sunday School as an evangelistic arm among churches of this size category. We are simply left with the observation without a certain explanation.

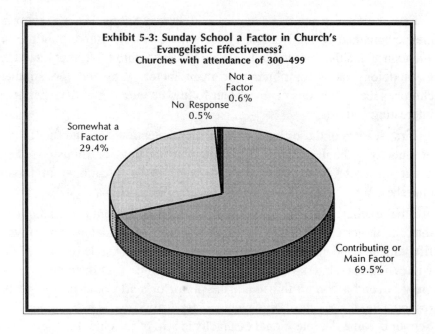

Exhibit 5-3: Sunday School a Factor in Church's Evangelistic Effectiveness? Churches with attendance of 300–499

Not a Factor 0.6%
No Response 0.5%
Somewhat a Factor 29.4%
Contributing or Main Factor 69.5%

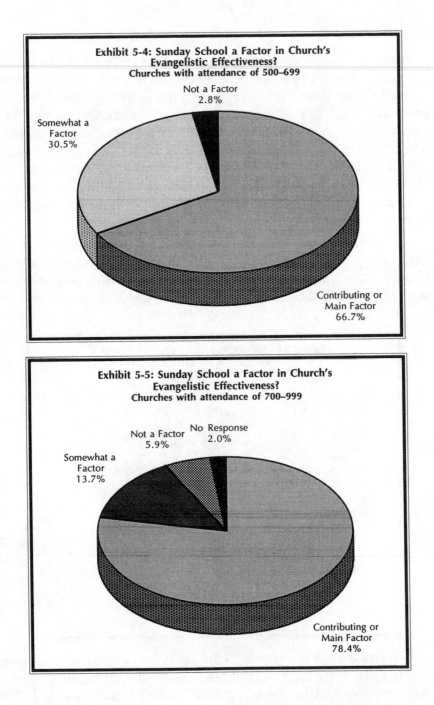

Exhibit 5-4: Sunday School a Factor in Church's
Evangelistic Effectiveness?
Churches with attendance of 500–699

Not a Factor
2.8%

Somewhat a
Factor
30.5%

Contributing or
Main Factor
66.7%

Exhibit 5-5: Sunday School a Factor in Church's
Evangelistic Effectiveness?
Churches with attendance of 700–999

Not a Factor   No Response
5.9%   2.0%

Somewhat a
Factor
13.7%

Contributing or
Main Factor
78.4%

Largest Churches

During my interim pastorate at Highview Baptist Church, I asked assistant pastor Norman Coe how many people were involved in leadership positions in the Sunday School. Highview has an average Sunday School attendance of 1,500. Two Sunday School organizations meet at two different times, 9:30 A.M. and 10:50 A.M. Each of these Sunday Schools has multiple classes available for every age group. In addition, "early bird Sunday School" meets at 8:30 A.M. Norman Coe's records indicated that 450 people were involved in Highview's Sunday School leadership! An incredible amount of energy and resources was needed just to maintain the organization.

Yet maintenance was not the main goal of the megachurches in our study. The leaders of these churches believe Sunday School must always be focused outward. Nearly two-thirds see their Sunday Schools as an important factor in their churches' evangelistic effectiveness (see exhibits 5-6 and 5-7).

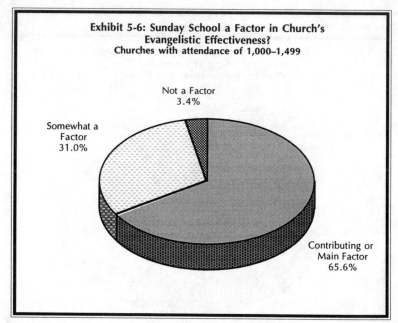

Exhibit 5-6: Sunday School a Factor in Church's Evangelistic Effectiveness?
Churches with attendance of 1,000–1,499

Not a Factor 3.4%

Somewhat a Factor 31.0%

Contributing or Main Factor 65.6%

Although the task of organizing a Sunday School for evangelism is massive in these megachurches, the leaders believed such organization was necessary and vital for the evangelistic health of their churches. "The

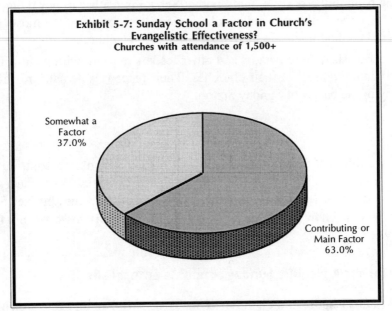

Exhibit 5-7: Sunday School a Factor in Church's
Evangelistic Effectiveness?
Churches with attendance of 1,500+

Somewhat a
Factor
37.0%

Contributing or
Main Factor
63.0%

larger our church became," said one megachurch pastor, "the more I believed that we also had to become smaller. As a result, we began to become more intentional about our small groups in our Sunday School classes. Those groups accounted for at least one-half of our conversion growth last year."

Statistical Reality: Sunday School for Evangelism Regardless of Church Size

The survey results indicate that Sunday School is an effective evangelistic tool in most of these churches, regardless of size. With the exception of one size category (0 to 299 attendance), over two-thirds of the churches responded enthusiastically about Sunday School's evangelistic effectiveness.

Our follow-up interviews revealed more about the level of enthusiasm for Sunday School. Leaders have not been oblivious to comments about the prospective demise of the Sunday School. They expressed bewilderment that a methodology so effective in their churches was declared terminally ill by pundits. Indeed, several pastors shared that they had listened carefully to the critics, trying to determine if they and their churches were about to be left behind in a future methodological wave. But ultimately all came back to the position that Sunday School is neither ill nor dying nor dead. On the contrary, Sunday School, done well, is one of the most God-blessed methodologies in the recent history of the church.

So we asked these pastors and other leaders to share with us how they use Sunday School in their churches. Their responses actually reviewed many of the basics of Sunday School.

Sunday School Lessons

Two-thirds of the churches identified Sunday School as a contributing or main factor to the churches' evangelistic effectiveness. We made a special study of these churches to learn in greater detail how they utilized Sunday School. Their responses are categorized into four "lessons" and four "keys to success."

Lesson #1: A Healthy Sunday School Is Evangelistic

At Cana Baptist Church in Burleson, Texas, Minister of Education Matthew Leilich told us that their Sunday School evangelistic outreach is alive and well. Class members are taught to mark their Bibles and "go out with the Paul and Timothy model to do one-on-one soul winning." Each Sunday School department meets for dinner on Monday nights; they then go to the homes of prospective members and unchurched persons. Accountability takes place through the minister of education.

Johnny Williams, minister of music at Morningside Baptist Church in Valdosta, Georgia, told us of a similar outreach approach. The church averages above 650 in attendance. Pastor Wayne Robertson has led their growth through a variety of methodologies, but outreach is still done primarily through the Sunday School. A structured outreach program assembles on Sunday afternoon and is directed totally through the Sunday School program.

In Laurinburg, North Carolina, Pastor Lewis McLean told us a similar story about Stewartsville Baptist Church. This evangelistic church, with an attendance of four hundred, conducts its outreach through care groups in each Sunday School class. Each care group has five members, one of whom is the leader. On Tuesday nights, two of the five members visit prospects for their classes. In the actual Sunday School classes, the plan of salvation is presented on a regular basis.

Such stories could lengthen this book by several hundred pages. I confess that I was surprised at the level of intensity by which evangelism is carried forth through the Sunday School in many of these churches. In 1987, R. Wayne Jones offered a prophetic voice on the future of Sunday School: "The most important task that keeps the Sunday School as a viable organization in the world today is the task of reaching people for Christ. . . . No matter what else the Sunday School does, no matter how appropriate or good it may be, if churches fail to reach people for Christ, they have failed."[1]

Church growth literature of the past twenty-five years has offered churches many methodologies to grow and to reach people for Christ. While these methodologies captured the attention and excitement of many Christians, Sunday School methodologies continued to be used effectively without much fanfare.

Leaders of the churches we studied were keenly aware of the latest developments in church growth methodology. Many regularly attended conferences and read the latest church growth books. They had tried many of the innovative methodologies and approaches to outreach, some with great success, others with less success. Yet most of the pastors and staff members kept returning to the basics of Sunday School outreach as one of their key evangelistic tools.

Why has the traditional Sunday School maintained its usefulness in these evangelistic churches? A pastor in California explained, "We simply have found no other way to train all age groups in Scripture; to have small groups in place without creating a new organization; to have outreach accountability; and to have groups which naturally provide ministry to one another within their fellowship."

Lesson #2: A Healthy Sunday School Provides Biblical Education to All Age Groups

In *Giant Awakenings*, I cited a study about mainline churches by mainline authors Dean Hoge, Benton Johnson, and Donald Luidens.[2] The surprising conclusion of the study was that mainline churches were declining because they had failed to provide or emphasize regular biblical training for all age groups. Thus an entire generation grew up in the church without comprehending biblical truths, the uniqueness of the Christian faith, and the demands of discipleship. Without an anchor to hold them, millions left mainline churches.

Evangelical churches affirm the total truthfulness of Scripture. But mere affirmation of the trustworthiness of Scripture is of little value if these churches fail to train their members in the complete revelation of the Bible. One reason these evangelistic churches continue a strong emphasis on evangelism is their equipping of members in God's Word. "As we study different books of the Bible," a Mississippi layperson told us, "we are regularly reminded of the good news of Jesus Christ which must be shared with others." Here are other comments from church leaders:

- "We believe our people cannot become equipped to carry out the Great Commission until members are attending Sunday School on a regular basis."

- "Any new member is immediately enrolled in a Sunday School class where he or she learns Scripture to understand fully the responsibilities of being a Christian, including sharing one's faith."

- "Our church trains everyone, from children to senior adults, in God's Word from Genesis to Revelation. I believe a large part of the explanation for our increase in baptisms can be explained by our faithfulness to biblical training."

- "Enrollment in Bible study classes is critical to the ongoing spiritual maturity of our members."

- "We notice a major failure to get people involved in evangelism when they weren't first involved in Bible study. We had tried a lot of methodologies for outreach, but found that the tried-and-true Sunday School was most effective."

After listening to hundreds of comments about the vital importance of ongoing biblical training, I see clearly now the significance of the Hoge study mentioned earlier. The church that fails to educate all generations in the totality of Scripture is headed for decline and possible death.

Lesson #3: A Healthy Sunday School Provides Means and Opportunities for Ministry

In chapter 8 we will examine more fully the role of ministries and evangelism. For now we will simply mention that, in over half of our follow-up interviews, the pastor or other interviewee indicated that the Sunday School was a primary instrument of ministry. While the emphasis of this study was the outward focus of the Sunday School, we were told repeatedly that a healthy Sunday School has ongoing ministry to its own as well.

Lesson #4: A Healthy Sunday School Assimilates Church Members

No other aspect of Sunday School received more comments than its role in assimilation and discipleship of new members and new Christians. Part of the reason for the overwhelming response we received came from a simple question we asked in our survey (see appendix 2): "What specific measures do you take to ensure that the people baptized remain involved in the church?" Hundreds of churches told us that their specific measure for assimilation was the Sunday School.

We will discuss this further in chapter 10. For now, we simply say that over 90 percent of the assimilation and discipleship methodologies were directly or indirectly related to Sunday School. An Ohio pastor told us, "We have tried closing the back door a dozen different ways, but it seems like we always come back to Sunday School."

The Keys to an Effective Sunday School

The mere existence of a Sunday School organization does not guarantee effective evangelism, effective assimilation, effective ministry, or effective teaching. Indeed, the leaders of these churches expressed concern about the *ineffectiveness* of many Sunday Schools they had observed. "Poor Sunday Schools," shared an Alabama pastor, "are certain obstacles to growth. But quality Sunday Schools are the key to effective churches."

What are the keys to an effective Sunday School? We received over seven hundred responses to this question (more than the total survey group), both solicited and unsolicited. The responses are classified into four basic keys.

Key #1: Quality Leadership

The churches in this study took seriously the role of leadership for effective Sunday Schools. Many indicated that they used spiritual gift inventories and assessments to place people in various positions. One pastor stated that their Sunday School organization "began to be transformed when they placed real leaders in leadership positions and quality teachers in teaching positions."

Some church leaders reported that the quantity of available persons was reduced initially when they began to focus on quality. "We had so many of our best leaders in the wrong positions that we had to wait about two years before we could utilize them in Sunday School leadership," a Mississippi minister of education said. "But we actually let some positions go unfilled until the right person came along."

The Sunday School teacher became a critical position when churches focused on quality. "We realized that what they were teaching had eternal impact on children, youth, and adults," a Virginia pastor observed. "We could no longer be satisfied with just filling all the openings. We had too many square pegs in round holes."

Training was a major factor for Sunday School leadership in these churches. A combination of one to three different elements of training was apparent in many of the churches.

One method was teacher training, where a "master teacher" communicated key essentials to others. Some churches used a short-term cycle of teacher-training classes during the Sunday School time.

A second method provided means for teachers and leaders to attend conferences and seminars, watch videos, and read books. Many times these resources were not specifically focused on direct Bible learning but on concepts such as leadership, pastoral care, and witness training.

A third method of training was the apprentice method. A prospective teacher or leader would spend time observing and questioning a quality teacher or leader within the organization. After this prospective teacher was ready and qualified to lead his or her own class, new apprentices were assigned to each of the two teachers.

Maintaining quality teachers and leaders in Sunday School is a struggle. Quality teachers are difficult to recruit and train, and poor teachers are often difficult to "retire." A few of the church leaders to whom we spoke would actually ask a teacher to step down if he or she was deemed unqualified by the pastor, staff, or Sunday School leadership. But "firings" were the exception.

Church leaders usually tried to work around a less-than-competent teacher. For example, one situation involved a teacher who taught older baby boomers, but his class was dry and dull. Only six persons remained in the class, but those six were intensely loyal to their incompetent teacher. When it became apparent that "firing" the teacher would be divisive in the church, the leaders opted to create new classes led by new teachers, without disturbing the class in question. Within two years the class still had six persons while the two newer classes averaged twelve persons each in attendance.

One cannot be around these pastors and other church leaders long without hearing the high priority they place on quality for all the people who are in positions of responsibility in the Sunday School. This focus on quality requires commitment of time and other resources well beyond the norm in other churches I have observed. Yet these leaders told us that the hours of work and the tremendous energy expended is well worth the effort.

Key #2: Accountability

Another recurring theme in the responses was accountability. At GraceWay Baptist Church in Augusta, Georgia, Pastor Gene Swinson leads an accountability group in which every person in the church receives a call from someone else. Many churches are extensively organized. The Sunday School class members are accountable to their small group leaders. The small group leaders are then accountable to the Sunday School teachers. The teachers report the developments of their classes to a division or department director, who in turn is accountable to the director of the Sunday School program. This director gives account for all the Sunday School ministry to a staff member or committee.

Although many churches have organizational charts that reflect the above scenario, few see the process to fruition. "Accountability is the major reason for our Sunday School's success," said a Louisiana minister of education. "But we have to work constantly to keep the lines of communication open, and we have to motivate constantly to keep the people accountable to one another."

Accountability is engendered by high expectations. A church in West Virginia asks all of its Sunday School workers to sign a covenant each year. This covenant involves all aspects of the Sunday School: witnessing and outreach to others; ministry through small groups; regular attendance; preparation of lessons; and a lengthy list of other expectations.

We found a significant correlation between the level of expectations placed upon Sunday School workers and the ability of the church to keep ongoing accountability among its volunteer workers. "When we first started asking Sunday School workers to sign a covenant," the West Virginia pastor told us, "we met a pretty high level of resistance. Some told us that we had no right to tell volunteers what to do." But the leaders persisted, though a few of the workers quit in protest. "Today," he said, "we see our accountability system as one of the best things that happened to our church. It was painful but it was worth it."

Key #3: Organization Quality

Without exception the church leaders who told us their Sunday Schools were instrumental in their evangelistic growth also had one or more key individuals involved in the program who had organizational or administrative gifts. In larger churches this person was often a staff person, but laypersons were also utilized in churches of all sizes.

In order to have a regular source of good leadership and to keep an accountability system in place, a well-designed and well-maintained organization is a must. Our research team spoke to many church leaders whose organizational skills were obvious. Rarely did we hear of an evangelistic Sunday School which was not well organized.

Key #4: Evangelistic Intentionality

Mountain View Baptist Church in Tucson, Arizona, is less than ten years old. Its second pastor, Barry Jude, is leading the church to exciting levels of evangelistic growth. Though its attendance is in the five hundred to six hundred range, the church has reached a level where it is baptizing around two hundred persons per year.

One does not have to be around Barry Jude long to understand a major reason behind Mountain View's growth. In virtually every program and ministry of the church, the pastor asks how that aspect of the church is evangelistic. This evangelistic intentionality permeates everything the church does, including the Sunday School. The Sunday School program at Mountain View is evangelistic by design, not by accident.

It is amazing what this intentionality can do for the conversion growth of a church. Many of the Sunday Schools in these 576 churches are evangelistic because they try to be evangelistic. Intentionality is the key, and intentionality leads to accountability.

Many leaders of these churches indicated that the Sunday School had been written off as an evangelistic tool by others because more and more seekers and visitors come to worship as their initial entry point into the church. They agree that Sunday School is not the entry point it once was. But they believe it can still be evangelistic.

The pastors and other interviewees said that the small group accountability function of the Sunday School engendered evangelistic responsibility as effectively as other approaches. "We realize that, as our members develop relationships with the unchurched, they are most likely to get them to visit a worship service first," a minister of education told us. "But the Sunday School is where accountability for inviting and evangelism takes place. And if that unchurched person does come to a few worship services, he or she will probably visit a Sunday School class. That is where the relationships have developed in our church, and that is where many people have been saved."

Furthermore, the evangelistic efforts that take place in the Sunday School are more likely to have a lasting impact. Several church leaders told us that new members or new converts who did not become involved in the Sunday School were likely to drop out of the church within a year.

The Sunday School: Methodology of the Twenty-First Century?

The quantity of comments about the importance of Sunday School surprised us. But our team was not prepared for over 90 percent of the respondents to comment about the role of Sunday School in their churches' evangelistic and discipleship efforts. Indeed, the fact that Sunday School was the third most often mentioned evangelistic methodology, ranking only below preaching and prayer, was a surprise itself.

Our surveys and interviews revealed that these leaders believe a Sunday School becomes ineffective only because it does not receive the attention it must have. "I have been a pastor in California, Florida, and now in Texas," one respondent commented. "In each of these churches, because of different contexts, we had to make some adjustments in our Sunday School organization. But the bottom line is that basic Sunday School principles worked in a blue-collar Florida church, a California yuppie church, and a Bible-belt middle class Texas church. Sunday School works if it is worked right!"

This statement and others we received from church leaders tell us that Sunday School may be experiencing a renewed level of interest. As more churches discover that some of the most evangelistic churches in America use Sunday School effectively, they may examine their own Sunday School organization to see if it is on the right path to evangelistic, ministry, and discipleship effectiveness.

If the responses we received are indicative of evangelistic churches across America, we may anticipate that Sunday School, a methodology from the eighteenth century, will be a methodology of the twenty-first century. Churches will continue to make changes in Sunday School, as they have for two hundred years. But the essential functions of reaching, teaching, discipling, and ministry will probably take on a new priority in the renewed Sunday School of the twenty-first century.

CHAPTER SIX

Worship Styles in Evangelistic Churches

Ever since you moved the offering to the end of our worship service, the Holy Spirit has not been present.

Note to the author, then serving as a pastor, from a disgruntled church member

Most church leaders know the pains of change. And most church leaders know the pains associated with making changes in worship services. Few factors can engender the divisiveness that even a minor modification in worship services produces. For example, in a previous pastorate, I had to deal six months with the issue of moving the offering to the end of the service. And I never heard the end of complaints about our printing words to *some* of the hymns and choruses in the church bulletin. These complaints continued despite the fact that hymnals were available for any church member or visitor who chose to use them!

When consulting with churches across the country, the issue of worship style and changes in worship services inevitably becomes a topic of discussion. It is not unusual for church leaders to receive more protests about those seemingly peripheral issues than a major doctrinal deviation. Why do church members hold tenaciously to worship paradigms? Why are they willing to fight rather than reason?

For many, the worship service is, in a very deep and emotional way, the church. They use the terminology "going to church" when they mean they are going to a worship service. Therefore, what happens on Sunday morning from 11:00 A.M. to noon is what happens in the church. To tamper with the slightest detail, especially introducing a new and unknown music style, is nothing less than heretical. While we who are church leaders lament this deficient ecclesiology, we must nevertheless acknowledge the reality of the pain.

Another factor is equally significant in the worship service debate. Many church members in America have a background that is largely monocultural. They have not been exposed to diversity in cultures, particularly diversity in religious cultures. Therefore they cannot view other worship styles as equally orthodox or equally worshipful. For many in fact, deviations in their worship style are truly deviant. In a recent book I addressed the turbulent history of changes in worship styles.[1] The controversy and debate are as old as Christianity itself, and have been particularly divisive for the past three hundred years.

A new and significant trend has developed, however, in recent years. Monocultural eyes are opening to the different cultures around the world and around the nation. The simple act of turning on a television set places us in a different area of the world. Slowly old attitudes of "different is inferior" are breaking down. One consequence has been a growing acceptance of multiple worship styles. While most people continue to prefer a familiar and comfortable style of music and liturgy, we notice increasing acceptance of other worship styles as equally orthodox and worshipful.

Nevertheless, the debate is not over. And certainly the interest in worship styles is as intense as ever. Church Growth Institute reports that their highest attended seminars in 1995 were those related to worship styles.[2] This chapter will look specifically at the issue of worship in the 576 evangelistic churches we studied. Perhaps one of the more significant points of discussion is the lack of contentiousness about worship styles. Indeed, the leaders of these churches indicated that their choice of worship style was more a factor of context and outreach possibilities than an attitude that one particular style was inherently superior to another.

Definitions of Worship Styles

Exhibit 6-1 lists the definitions we gave to the respondents. They may not have been in complete agreement with our definitions, but at least they understood what we meant when we referred to a particular style.

The respondents surprised us with the manner in which many of them dealt with worship styles. For example, we had many respondents express confusion over the specific differences between "contemporary" and "seeker," and also between "traditional" and "revivalist" styles. Conse-

Exhibit 6-1: Definitions of Worship Styles

Liturgical	Mood: formal, solemn, majestic. Music: pipe organ, traditional hymns, classical anthems. Purpose: "To lead the church to give corporate recognition to the transcendent glory of God." Favors reverence over relevance. It runs counter to the cultural obsession with contemporary entertainment. Biblical model: Isaiah 6.
Traditional	Mood: orderly, majestic, contemplative. Music: organ and piano, traditional and gospel hymns, traditional and contemporary anthems. Purpose: "To lead the congregation to praise and thank God for His goodness and to hear Him speak through His word." Geared for people from a religious culture and background. The most frequent Southern Baptist format. Biblical model: Col. 3:16–17.
Revivalist	Mood: exuberant, celebrative, informal. Music: organ, piano, and taped music, gospel hymns, contemporary Christian songs and anthems. Purpose: "To save the lost and encourage believers to witness." More evangelistic than contemplative worship. Biblical model: Acts 2–3.
Contemporary	Mood: expressive, celebrative, contemporary, informal. Music: keyboard, piano and taped music, praise choruses and contemporary Christian songs. Purpose: "To offer a sacrifice of praise to the Lord in a spirit of joyful adoration." This is contemporary worship for believers, but does attract some non-Christan and unchurched. Biblical model: Psalm 150.
Seeker	Mood: celebrative, contemporary, informal. Music: piano, taped music, synthesizer and band, scriptural music and contemporary Christian music, little congregational singing in the traditional sense. Purpose: "Present the gospel in clear non-God talk terms and modern forms." An upbeat, non-threatening evangelistic service for non-Christians seeking God. Biblical model: Acts 17:16–34.
Blended	Combination of elements in both tradtional and contemporary.
Other styles	[Respondent indicates other style]

quently those four categories were combined into two categories. When all the data was finally gathered, we came to the following conclusions:

- Worship styles are not monolithic in Southern Baptist churches.
- Though less than previous years, the traditional worship service style is still the most common.
- Liturgical worship is rare in Southern Baptist evangelistic churches.
- The fastest-growing worship style is the blended approach.
- Contemporary/seeker worship styles are more common in larger churches. Three out of ten churches with an attendance greater than one thousand have contemporary worship styles.
- Four out of ten churches with an attendance greater than one thousand have traditional worship styles.
- Blended worship styles appear consistently in three out of ten evangelistic churches in all size categories.
- Most evangelistic churches in this study do not "target" their "audiences" with their worship services.
- Seeker services are rare in these evangelistic churches.
- Intercessory prayer in the worship services is vital to the evangelistic effectiveness of these churches.
- These churches expressed a wide variety of responses and attitudes toward evening worship services.
- Pastors consistently reported a hunger for authentic, biblical worship.

We will examine some of these findings in detail. Others we will mention briefly.

What Are the Dominant Worship Styles?

Though we did not have empirical data to determine worship patterns in past years, our interviews indicated several trends beyond the statistical information. The empirical data of exhibit 6-2 shows that the traditional/revivalist style is the dominant worship approach among the churches in this study. Slightly over 44 percent of the churches indicated that this style described their primary worship service. The blended style (traditional/revivalist blended with contemporary/seeker) is second with just over 31 percent. The contemporary/seeker approach is the style in over 21 percent of the churches. The liturgical approach to worship has never been present in a significant number of Southern Baptist churches, and our survey did not find it to be a significant factor among effective evangelistic churches.

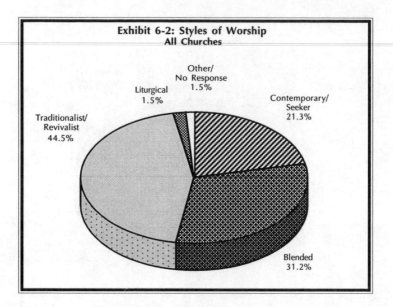

Exhibit 6-2: Styles of Worship
All Churches

Other/No Response 1.5%

Liturgical 1.5%

Contemporary/Seeker 21.3%

Traditionalist/Revivalist 44.5%

Blended 31.2%

Worship Styles among Smaller to Mid-Sized Churches

Since our data on churches with less than 100 in attendance was limited, we could assess only those churches with an attendance greater than 100 (see exhibit 6-3). When we examined churches, therefore, with an attendance between 100 and 299, we were really looking at churches that could be classified as both smaller and mid-sized.

Perhaps the surprising aspect of comparing this data with similar data for all churches in the study is the *lack* of significant differences in worship styles between the two groups. For example, the traditional worship style is the dominant approach in almost half the smaller to mid-sized churches. But that number is not significantly higher than the 44.5 percent for traditional worship in all of the churches in the study. Close comparisons hold as well for other types of worship styles.

Worship Styles among Larger Mid-sized Churches

As the circle graph indicates in exhibit 6-4, the larger mid-sized churches in this study do not have significantly different worship styles than either the smaller churches or all of the churches collectively. What we discerned in our follow-up interviews, however, was a potential future trend not noticed in smaller churches. Many of the worship leaders and

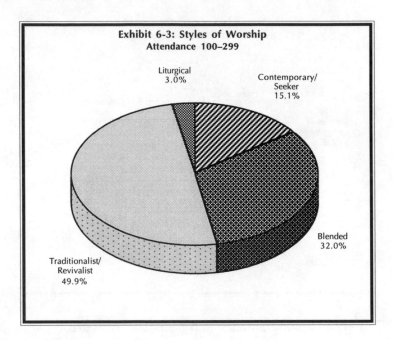

Exhibit 6-3: Styles of Worship
Attendance 100–299

Liturgical
3.0%

Contemporary/
Seeker
15.1%

Blended
32.0%

Traditionalist/
Revivalist
49.9%

pastors in both the traditional/revivalist churches and, to a lesser extent, in the contemporary/seeker churches, indicated that their worship style was transitioning to a blended approach of the two styles. If this trend does come to fruition, we could expect the blended approach to be the dominant style in the twenty-first century.

A pastor in Georgia told us his church could still be classified as traditional in its worship style but that it was making incremental changes. He anticipates that, within two years, the worship approach will be legitimately called blended. "Our members don't respond well to sudden or massive changes," he said. "We have to be very careful as we introduce new or different elements to worship."

Several leaders of churches with contemporary worship styles indicated that they planned to introduce a few more traditional elements in the months or years ahead. "We never thought we would be a church with hymns," a Kentucky pastor shared with us. "But in a few 'test' cases, our people responded with enthusiasm. We may very well be a 'blended' church in the next couple of years."

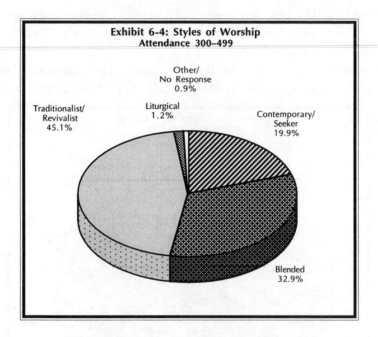

Exhibit 6-4: Styles of Worship
Attendance 300–499

Other/
No Response
0.9%

Traditionalist/
Revivalist
45.1%

Liturgical
1.2%

Contemporary/
Seeker
19.9%

Blended
32.9%

Worship Styles among Large Churches

The most noticeable difference in churches with an attendance from 500 to 999 was in the contemporary/seeker worship style. Only in churches with more than 500 in attendance did this approach exceed 20 percent of the total group. In fact, in every category more than 500 in attendance, the contemporary/seeker style exceeded one-fourth of the total group.

The growth of the contemporary style in churches with an attendance from 500 to 699 came primarily at the expense of the traditional approach (see exhibit 6-5). But in the attendance category 700 to 999 the contemporary style grew at the expense of the blended approach (exhibit 6-6). In the churches with an attendance of 700 to 999, the traditional worship style remained surprisingly strong.

What reasons explain the significant increase of the contemporary/ seeker approach in churches with an attendance more than 500? The leaders indicated that the pain of change was still evident, but their larger numbers in membership and attendance allowed the pastors or worship leaders to withstand the charges of the critics. "When I pastored a smaller church," an Ohio pastor said, "I could have never moved a church at the pace of this larger church. A few disgruntled families in a church of closely-tied families can kill a pastor in a small church. At most, in my present situation the few disgruntled families are in a significant minority. We may lose them, but the church will be okay."

Many leaders in churches of all sizes want to make changes in worship styles, but many cannot handle the loud cries of protest that will erupt.

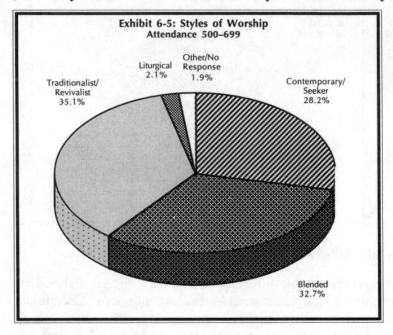

Exhibit 6-5: Styles of Worship
Attendance 500–699

Liturgical 2.1%

Other/No Response 1.9%

Traditionalist/ Revivalist 35.1%

Contemporary/ Seeker 28.2%

Blended 32.7%

Worship Styles among the Largest Churches

Churches with an attendance between 1,000 and 1,499 have worship-style patterns similar to churches in the smaller category of 700 to 999. Approximately the same percentage, 27 percent, have contemporary/ seeker services (see exhibit 6-7). The larger churches have a higher percentage in blended and a lower percentage in traditional/revivalist. Significantly, still 40 percent or more of these churches have a traditional worship style until their attendance exceeds 1,500. In other words, the traditional worship style is clearly the dominant approach in all but one of the size categories.

That one category which is the exception to the pattern is the largest group in our study, 1,500 and more in attendance. A significant shift in worship patterns is noticeable at this megachurch level (see exhibit 6-8).

While the traditional worship style is still in the greatest number of churches, the edge over the contemporary approach is statistically insignificant. In rough terms the worship styles of churches with an attendance greater than 1,500 are almost spread equally between traditional, contemporary, and blended.

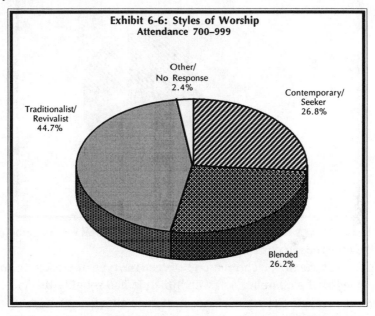

Exhibit 6-6: Styles of Worship
Attendance 700–999

Other/
No Response
2.4%

Contemporary/
Seeker
26.8%

Traditionalist/
Revivalist
44.7%

Blended
26.2%

The contemporary worship style grows significantly in this largest attendance category. As exhibit 6-8 depicts, over 35 percent of the churches with an attendance greater than 1,500 described their worship services as contemporary or seeker.

Preaching and Worship Styles

In chapter 3 we analyzed the critical importance of preaching to evangelistic growth. No single methodological factor was deemed more important to the evangelistic growth of these 576 churches than preaching. We further saw that expository preaching was the dominant approach to preaching with topical preaching a distant second.

Anecdotally, our research team had heard from numerous sources that topical preaching was more common in churches with contemporary or seeker services than other worship styles. We decided to review the

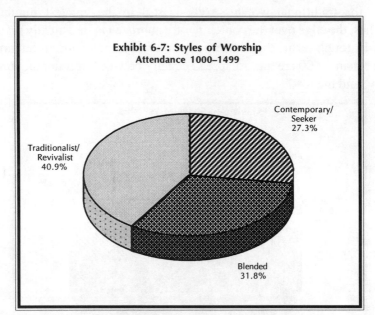

Exhibit 6-7: Styles of Worship
Attendance 1000–1499

Contemporary/
Seeker
27.3%

Traditionalist/
Revivalist
40.9%

Blended
31.8%

churches by their worship styles to see if such anecdotal evidence held true with the churches in our study.

We found virtually no correlation between the type of preaching and the worship style of a church. Each worship style had roughly the same proportion of preaching approaches. And in each category of worship style, expository preaching was the dominant approach.

What we *cannot* determine from this study is a relationship between worship styles and preaching approaches for all churches in America. Among these 576 evangelistic churches, however, the only conclusion we can make regarding a relationship between preaching and worship style is that the expository approach to preaching was consistently preferred regardless of worship style.

What Are the Major Worship Issues?

What factors determine a church's worship style? Most of the responses to this question in our interviews are placed in one of three categories.

Know Your Context

Decisions for a particular approach to worship were typically contextual decisions. The context was both inside the church and outside the church.

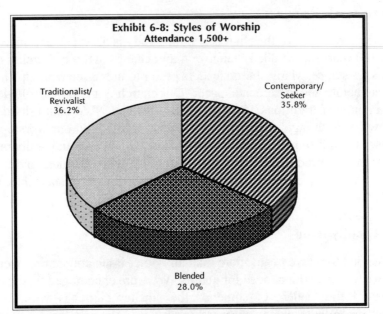

Exhibit 6-8: Styles of Worship
Attendance 1,500+

Traditionalist/
Revivalist
36.2%

Contemporary/
Seeker
35.8%

Blended
28.0%

A concern for the context inside the church often meant finding the most meaningful worship style for a changing church population. Each generation usually has its own music preferences. The church leadership often responds by making changes that reflect the new composite membership.

Several church leaders have warned us about the presumptuousness of assuming that a certain generation prefers one particular music style. "I attended a baby boomer seminar in 1991," a worship leader shared with us. "We were led to believe that only a certain flavor of 'Christian rock-n-roll' would meet the boomers' worship needs. That general statement was the furthest thing from the truth for the boomers in our church."

Most churches in this study were concerned about the context of the community they were trying to reach. Though many avoided the use of the word *target*, church leaders were aware that certain worship styles were more palatable than others. Indeed, the single most-often-given reasons for transitioning from a traditional worship to a blended or contemporary worship service was "to reach the unchurched." But the leaders said repeatedly that too many pastors or worship leaders *assume* that a contemporary worship will attract the unchurched. "It's a lot more complex than one single issue," an Indiana music leader observed. "Churches are headed for problems if they haven't done their homework well."

Incremental Change

The average age of the churches in this study is 53 years, and many are over 100 years old. Sudden change or major change in these churches often meets resistance. Many church leaders prefer to introduce worship change at a deliberate and incremental pace. "Our church is a 150-year-old downtown house of traditions," one pastor commented. "We could divide the fellowship with rapid and unwise changes, especially in our worship services. Our staff thinks through every change with prayer and deliberation, and then we introduce the change to the church with openness and a willingness to reverse our decision if we discern that a mistake has been made."

The Quality Issue

The one topic we heard more than any other issue concerning worship service was the critical need for quality. We were encouraged by the comments of the leaders of some of the smaller churches with limited resources. "What we do in our worship services," the pastor of a 120-attendance church said, "is to try to do a few things well. We don't have a lot of outstanding musicians with a variety of experiences. So we concentrate on a few things that we can do well."

Some comments indicated that the quality of the worship services was more important than utilizing a particular worship style. In a day where most homes have access to quality music through radio, cassettes, and CDs, worshipers quickly detect poor-quality music. The potential evangelistic growth of a church may be hindered by poorly planned services and low-quality music. It is no surprise that the churches in this study felt that quality was of paramount importance.

Multiple-Style Worship Services?

First Southern Baptist in Lompoc, California, has a worship attendance of 350, and a baptismal ratio of 7:1, among the best in the entire study group. Pastor J. T. Reed shared that his church utilizes two different worship approaches. "We have two distinct worship styles. The early service is contemporary and informal. There is no public invitation. Instead, people respond by completing a card." The second service offers a distinct contrast and alternative. "The second service is very traditional with a more traditional, open invitation."

First Southern is the exception. Less than 4 percent of the churches in the study indicated that they had multiple services with different worship styles. We discovered three reasons that few churches offered multiple-style worship services.

1. A slight majority of the churches had only one morning worship service.

2. Some church leaders did not believe that their congregation or their community had enough diversity to warrant two different worship services. A North Carolina pastor commented that the two contemporary worship services at his church met both the internal and outreach needs of the church. He saw little value in offering a different worship style.

3. Many leaders indicated that their churches lacked resources to offer multiple-style worship services. Although some would like to have that option, they do not see such a possibility considering the present level of resources of time, talent, money, and persons.

Churches like First Southern Baptist, though a distinct minority among these evangelistic churches, offer an interesting approach for churches with the necessary resources available. However, our study gives no indication that multiple-style worship services will be a growing trend.

Seeker Services?

Our survey simply asked if seeker services contributed to the evangelistic effectiveness of the churches. As we indicated in a previous chapter, only 10 percent of the responding churches responded positively. Even among the megachurches, only 20 percent used seeker services (see exhibit 6-9).

We first made certain that our respondents understood that we were referring to services designed explicitly and totally for lost persons. Many people still confuse seeker services with seeker-sensitive services, which are not services specifically for the lost but services with an awareness of, or sensitivity to, the presence of lost persons in the service. Our concern was unfounded and, as usual, we found the respondents well informed. They understood our terminology well.

Can we therefore conclude that seeker services are ineffective because only 10 percent of the churches surveyed use them for evangelistic effectiveness? Not necessarily. Most churches in the study have never

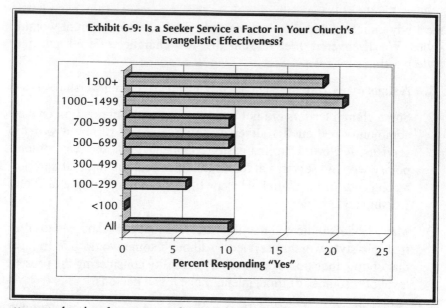

Exhibit 6-9: Is a Seeker Service a Factor in Your Church's Evangelistic Effectiveness?

attempted to implement a seeker service and therefore responded no when asked if a seeker service enhanced their churches' evangelistic effectiveness. Furthermore, some churches that desire to offer seeker services do not have the resources to do so. The best-known advocate of the seeker service, Bill Hybels of Willow Creek Community Church, insists that only a minority of churches have the right mix of pastor and other resources to implement a seeker service.

We state with caution, therefore, that true seeker services are not playing a major role in the evangelistic effectiveness of the great majority of these churches. Yet we acknowledge that some life-changing churches may be enjoying major success through seeker services.

Prayer in and for the Worship Services?

Since an entire chapter has already been devoted to prayer in evangelistic churches, only brief mention is made of the topic at this point. Its importance is noteworthy.

We simply cannot ignore the overwhelming response we received to the role of intercessory prayer in the worship services. As shown in exhibit 6-10, *over 90 percent* identified intercessory prayer as most important or very important to the worship services. Only 1 percent did not agree that prayer was important in their worship services.

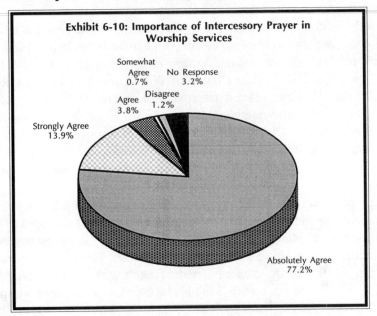

Exhibit 6-10: Importance of Intercessory Prayer in Worship Services

Somewhat Agree 0.7%
No Response 3.2%
Agree 3.8%
Disagree 1.2%
Strongly Agree 13.9%
Absolutely Agree 77.2%

The most common expression of intercessory prayer during the worship services was where one or more people prayed in an upper room or any other room as the service progressed. Several of the pastors attested to a change, a greater power, in their own pulpit ministry when people began to pray during the service. "If you desire to see the 'engine' that provides power for our church, visit our upper room during a worship service," a pastor told us. "You will see ten or more people pleading to God for a service of power and conviction. We never cease to be amazed at the miraculous answers to prayers each Sunday."

Worship: Still the Front Door?

In recent years church growth literature has discussed at great length the role of worship in the growth of the church. Indications are that the growing unchurched population is more likely to "test" a church through its worship services, than through a small group such as the Sunday School. How did our study group respond to this thesis?

In our follow-up interviews, the church leaders overwhelmingly agreed. "We know that almost all of our unchurched visitors will first come to our worship services," an Arizona pastor said. "Christians who move to our town from other locations may visit a Sunday School class first, but not the unchurched."

Yet the pastors and worship leaders warned us not to view the worship service as a panacea to reach a growing unchurched population. First, they told us, conversions are rare during the worship service time itself. Larry Craig, pastor of First Baptist Church of West Columbia, Texas, said that "most conversions take place during the week as a result of traditional outreach and neighbor-to-neighbor relationships." John Moody, pastor of Sewell Mill Baptist Church in Marietta, Georgia, concurred: "Most converts who 'walk the aisle' have made their decision for Christ during the week. They are making a previous decision public during the worship services."

In chapter 5 we saw that many of these evangelistic churches viewed the Sunday School as the place where relationships are built that lead to decisions for Christ. Many evangelistic leaders consider the presence of the unchurched at worship services a first step at best. "If we don't eventually get them into the Sunday School to make friends with other Christians, we know that they will not remain long in the anonymity of our worship services," a megachurch pastor told us.

Our study verified the thesis that worship is the front door, that quality and meaningful worship is critical as churches strive to reach a lost generation. But the worship service alone is no panacea. Unless active Christians build relationships with the unchurched, conversions are unlikely and assimilation is nearly impossible.

The Sunday Evening Service

One final worship issue we addressed was the status of Sunday evening worship services. Anecdotally we had heard for years that the Sunday evening worship was a dying tradition. Responses in our follow-up interviews gave us no clear indication about the future of these services.

Exhibit 6-11 shows a mixed response. As you look at the categories in the aggregate of the exhibit, you see indication that the Sunday evening worship is in trouble. In 51 percent of the churches, evening services are plateaued, declining, or significantly declined. Another 8 percent of the churches do not offer or have discontinued the service altogether. Nearly 60 percent of the churches, therefore, have plateaued or declining evening services, or they do not offer them at all; and we are speaking of growing, evangelistic churches only. A study more representative of all churches may show an even bleaker outlook for the Sunday evening worship.

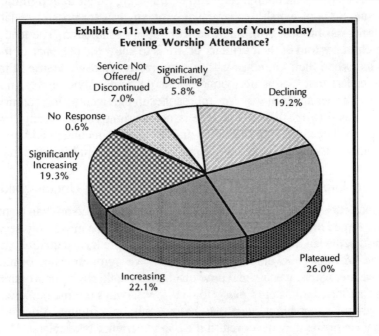

Exhibit 6-11: What Is the Status of Your Sunday Evening Worship Attendance?

Service Not Offered/ Discontinued 7.0%

Significantly Declining 5.8%

Declining 19.2%

No Response 0.6%

Significantly Increasing 19.3%

Plateaued 26.0%

Increasing 22.1%

Yet the status of Sunday evening worship in many of these churches is positive. Over 22 percent indicated that attendance was increasing, and another 19 percent said that attendance was increasing significantly. Over 40 percent of the churches, therefore, conveyed a positive outlook for their Sunday evening worship services.

We looked for patterns to explain why some churches had increases in evening attendance while others showed declines. Unfortunately we found none related to geographical location, socioeconomic composition of the membership, church age, or age of the congregation. The future of the Sunday evening worship service is an area we must leave for future study.

Three Final Observations

Worship and church growth has been a topic of fascination for years. Our study attempted to make some observations about worship and *evangelistic* growth. We conclude this topic with three major observations.

The Debate Is Slowly Ending

The debate over the "right" type of worship service is slowly coming to a close. The American church seems to be maturing rather than fighting over the issue. Style of worship is largely a contextual factor possibly related to outreach possibilities. Still, multiple worship styles abound. The leaders of these churches told us their primary desire is to know the presence of the living God when their churches gather corporately. And we learned through these leaders that God is not bound to one particular style of worship. We may see further shifts in worship approaches in the twenty-first century, but the reasons for the shifts will not be issues of right versus wrong. Rather, changes will occur as church leaders discern their own context and outreach possibilities, then seek God's wisdom to worship Him in truth and in love.

The Worship Service Experience Is Critical for the Unchurched

Repeatedly we were told that seekers or unchurched persons can be immediately turned off to the church by a negative experience in worship services. Therefore, the leaders of these churches determined to have a quality worship service for both believers and unbelievers. "We communicate so much of who we are, whose we are, and how much we care through our worship services," a Florida minister of music told us. "We always remind ourselves that one particular worship service may be our only opportunity to reach a lost person. He or she may never return if a bad experience takes place."

Attitude of Leadership Is Vital

Leaders describe their worship services with words such as *warm, exciting, loving, vibrant, hopeful,* and *worshipful.* Though humans cannot manufacture an environment without the power of a sovereign God, we found that God uses the hearts and minds and attitudes of church leaders to impact the atmosphere of worship services. An upbeat and exciting worship service usually has leaders who are upbeat and exciting. A loving and accepting worship service often reflects a pastor's loving and accepting attitude.

Throughout our interviews regarding worship two words were repeated hundreds of times: *intentionality* and *attitude.* These church leaders seek to create worship services that intentionally demonstrate the love and hope that can only be found in the person of Jesus Christ. Consequently the leaders' expectancy and hope spills over into the excitement of the worship services. Thus attitude is vital in the worship services. But attitude is important in *all* areas of these evangelistic churches. We will thus examine this issue in the next chapter.

CHAPTER SEVEN

Attitudes, Beliefs, and Evangelism

You just need to wake up each morning and ask God to set your-self and your church on fire for Jesus. You just have to tell the world about Jesus. You must have a . . . passion—that's it—a passion for Jesus . . . you know what I mean?

Pastor of one of the churches in this study

Pastors are one of the hardest-working, lowest-paid, least-respected groups in America. I visit dozens of churches each year, and I am still amazed at the dedication of these men. I was recently in a church in Mississippi. Five minutes before the pastor was to lead the service and preach, an irate woman rebuked him because "the toilet in the women's restroom [was] clogged again!"

Being a pastor is not an easy job. In fact it is an impossible job unless God has called him. I have seen pastors emotionally beat up and verbally torn down, yet only one hour later found praying and ministering to someone filled with fear over upcoming surgery.

My pastor is David Butler of Springdale Church in Louisville, Kentucky. Springdale is one of the 576 churches in this study. I watch in amazement as my pastor, one of the most respected leaders in our denomination, leads our eight-year-old church through its growing pains and victories. David and his wife Gayle pour out their lives daily for the Lord they serve through Springdale. As I was writing this chapter, my pastor called to check on me, just to see how things were going. David apologized for being intrusive. I responded, "It's just like you, isn't it? You're taking time out of your busy day to call me, and you apologize for being intrusive!" It is no wonder I love him and his family so much.

Part of my sense of call to the position I hold is to be a pastor to pastors. I also have a deep burden to share with congregations across America to pray, love, support, and encourage their pastors. I do not advocate placing pastors on pedestals, but we must respect them and their divine calling.

The pastors of the 576 churches in this study blessed me throughout my conversations with many of them. As I listened to their insights, passions, and agitations, I was once again reminded of the high calling to be a pastor. These pastors and others like them across our nation deserve our prayers, respect, and love.

A Profile of the Pastor

No singular description characterizes the pastors in this study. The churches they serve range in attendance from sixty to megachurch size and are as young as two years or older than two hundred years. The pastors are young, middle-aged, and . . . well, some are as old as Moses when he received his burning bush call to ministry. Their places of ministry include inner cities, rural America, old suburbia, new suburbia, and small communities.

Though three-fourths of the pastors are seminary graduates, the other one-fourth enjoy successful and blessed ministries without the benefit of graduate theological studies. The pastors in this study have served their churches from one to over thirty years. The average pastoral tenure among these churches is 7.3 years, three times their denomination's average.

But these pastors cannot be known by years, demographics, or size of church. You have to listen to them, feel the excitement they feel, understand the passion that drives them in ministry. George Barna interviewed thirty-three pastors of evangelistic churches. His description of them conveys some of the emotions I felt during this study's interviews: "Interviewing the pastors of the most successful evangelistic churches is nothing short of fascinating. You can fire questions at them about budgets, organization structures, staff development, and program expansion, and they can answer with precision and insight."[1]

Barna's comments especially reflect my sentiments when he states, "Ask the pastors about the evangelistic heart and agenda of the church and you are suddenly speaking to new people. Their enthusiasm and commitment regarding evangelism is obvious and contagious. It would be virtually impossible to work for such a pastor, or to last long in a church led by him, without sharing the same enthusiasm for reaching the unreached."[2]

The Vitally Important Role of Leadership's Attitude

The above quote from Barna communicates something that statistics and written surveys cannot convey. They communicate the passion for evangelism and ministry that is both far-reaching and contagious. The leaders of these churches are not necessarily the most gifted orators in the world, nor do they all possess the shrewdest leadership skills and acumen. What they do have is a deep conviction of their call and unwavering belief that Christians go to heaven and lost persons go to hell.

In his classic work *Evangelism in the Early Church*, Michael Green notes that the drive and passion for evangelism of the first-century believers was fueled by a deep concern for lost people. This deep concern motivated the early church to share the good news of Jesus Christ with urgency and enthusiasm. Green notes that "concern for the state of the unevangelized was one of the great driving forces behind Christian preaching of the gospel in the early Church."[3] That motivation continued for a full century. "This lively awareness of the peril of those without Christ persisted as a major evangelistic motive in the second century. The stress on judgment in the subapostolic writers is so great that it was the subject of ridicule among some pagans."[4]

I recently listened to Bill Hybels speak on the gift of leadership. He stated that church leaders must possess those certain qualities that engender fellowship in a church. At least he indicated implicitly that pastors should be gifted for leadership. Though I cannot deny the God-given leadership abilities of Bill Hybels, what I see in his tremendous ministry at Willow Creek has been more *passion* than leadership. You cannot listen to him long without catching the fire for evangelism and for the church.

What impressed me most about the pastors in our study is that intangible factor called "enthusiasm" or "passion." People in their churches catch their enthusiasm for the church and for reaching lost people. An atmosphere of expectancy and love saturates the congregation due, in an earthly sense, to the passion of the leadership.

Can this enthusiasm or passion be learned? Or must some pastors simply accept that they can never be *that* kind of leader? Though better persons than I disagree, I believe that pastors *can* catch this enthusiastic attitude, which in turn can be caught by the church membership. This study convinced me more than ever of that truth! To illustrate these sentiments, I share some lengthy portions of an interview with a pastor in Alabama whom I will call John (although he gave me permission to be quoted, he has asked to remain anonymous). Other pastors made similar comments.

John graduated from seminary with some nagging doubts. "I really bought into the higher critical approach to the Scripture. As a result, I questioned the validity of any obvious biblical truths. In fact, my most persistent doubts related to the reality of hell. I should have listened to some good friends who had recommended that I go to an evangelical seminary."

John took those doubts into his first pastorate, and his burden for evangelism was virtually nonexistent. "How can we have a burden for evangelism when we are uncertain ourselves about someone's eternal destiny?" he asked. "But, you know," he pondered, "I have friends today who say they are conservative theologically. Yet they act as if lost people don't really matter. How can you sleep in peace if you really believe lost people are going to hell, and you're doing nothing about it?"

John reached what he called a "theological crisis." After weeks of prayer and study he returned to the view of the complete authority of Scripture. "Inerrancy was not a political fighting word for me," he said. "It was a view that had eternal implications."

Yet returning to an evangelical view of Scripture did not immediately cause John to be evangelistic. "I thought once the authority issue was settled, I would be knocking on doors giving an EE [*Evangelism Explosion*] presentation to everyone I met. Much to my surprise, evangelism did not come naturally."

How did John become a contagious evangelistic Christian? His pilgrimage was twofold. "First, I sought a deeper prayer life. And as I prayed, I asked God to give me His eyes for lost people, and His heart for lost people. My attitude began to change and my enthusiasm began to grow."

"The next step," he said, "was critical. I made an intentional decision to place myself under the teachings of great leaders who have a passion for evangelism. Some of these leaders are peers with whom I meet on a regular basis. We share stories and excitement about evangelism."

But John's learning did not end with peers. "I now listen to some of the evangelistic leaders in our world today through tapes and conferences," he shared. "And I also read biographies of some of the heroes of the faith and in the Word. That's where the fires of evangelism are lit for me!"

After listening to dozens of pastors, I am convinced that leadership can catch evangelistic passion. The pastors in these churches are amazingly diverse in personality, gifts, and leadership abilities; but excitement and enthusiasm is common to all of the leaders with whom I spoke. And that leadership attitude helps create an atmosphere within the church for evangelistic ministries and meaningful worship. The leadership's attitude is vitally important for the evangelistic effectiveness of a church.

The Attitude of "Going"

The leaders of these churches affirm that relationship evangelism is important. When we asked the respondents the importance of the relational witness of their church members, over 60 percent indicated that it was a contributing factor (40.8 percent) or main factor (19.4 percent; see exhibit 7-1). Larger churches particularly had this attitude (exhibit 7-2), but these evangelistic leaders insisted that relational evangelism alone was not sufficient. Their responses came from two directions.

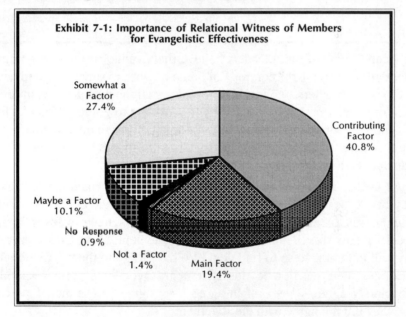

Exhibit 7-1: Importance of Relational Witness of Members for Evangelistic Effectiveness

Somewhat a Factor 27.4%

Contributing Factor 40.8%

Maybe a Factor 10.1%

No Response 0.9%

Not a Factor 1.4%

Main Factor 19.4%

First, leaders told us that relationship evangelism must eventually become confrontational evangelism. Dan Wade, pastor of Town 'n' Country Baptist Church in Tampa, Florida, said that he "teaches and preaches a lifestyle of relationship evangelism." But he says the gospel cannot go unspoken indefinitely. "That is one of the reasons I have developed a soul-winning tract that I and others use when we confront people with the claims of the gospel."

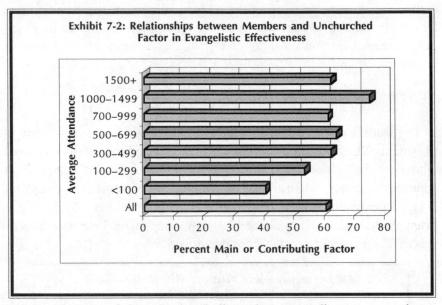

Exhibit 7-2: Relationships between Members and Unchurched Factor in Evangelistic Effectiveness

Second, most of these leaders believe that evangelism means going—intentionally leaving the comforts of home or work to share the good news of Christ with others. A Washington pastor said the evangelistic environment of his church can be gauged by faithfulness to going. "You can feel an apathy in our church when we aren't doing outreach on a regular basis. We therefore concern ourselves more with faithfulness to going out rather than conversion successes."

As further indication of the attitude of going, we asked the leaders if they had a "search theology." Did they believe that the believers in their churches must seek unbelievers to tell them the good news of Jesus Christ? Specifically we asked them to react to this statement: "Non-Christians usually will not come to us to find God. We have to go to them." Exhibit 7-3 illustrates their reaction to this statement. Over 90 percent responded "absolutely agree," "very much agree," or "agree." Less than 1 percent said they did not agree with the statement.

Multiple Encounters with the Gospel

The need for an attitude of going was further evidenced by the leaders' belief that multiple encounters with the gospel were usually required before a person accepted Jesus Christ as Lord and Savior. We used the

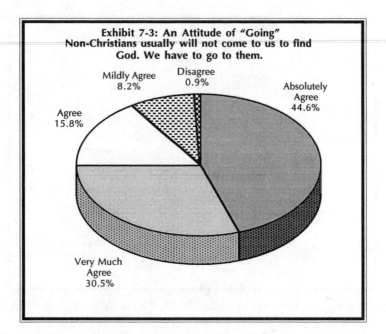

Exhibit 7-3: An Attitude of "Going"
Non-Christians usually will not come to us to find God. We have to go to them.

- Mildly Agree 8.2%
- Disagree 0.9%
- Absolutely Agree 44.6%
- Agree 15.8%
- Very Much Agree 30.5%

number "five or more" in our statement regarding multiple encounters with the gospel. The response was one of overwhelming agreement among all the churches in our study. Three-fourths of the respondents said "absolutely agree," "very much agree," or "agree." In the strongest response categories—"absolutely agree" or "very much agree"—nearly half responded affirmatively. Less than 8 percent did not agree with the five or more multiple-encounter approach (exhibit 7-4).

We found a significantly higher affirmation of the multiple-encounter approach among the larger churches. When we asked leaders whose churches average more than five hundred in attendance, the strongest affirmation categories ("absolutely agree" or "very much agree") were ten percentage points higher than the responses of all the churches in the aggregate (exhibit 7-5). Let us first examine the issue of reaching people for Christ through numerous encounters with the gospel. Then we will attempt to discern the reasons larger churches advocate this approach more than smaller churches.

In our follow-up interviews we discovered an attitude among the leaders best illustrated by the Engel scale.[5] Several years ago, James Engel developed a scale that depicts eight progressive steps an unbeliever makes

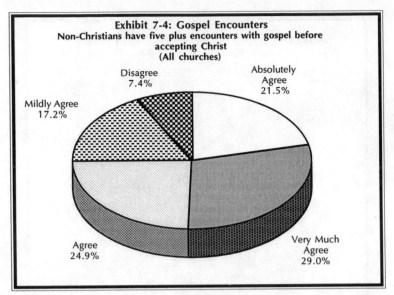

Exhibit 7-4: Gospel Encounters
Non-Christians have five plus encounters with gospel before accepting Christ
(All churches)

Disagree 7.4%

Absolutely Agree 21.5%

Mildly Agree 17.2%

Very Much Agree 29.0%

Agree 24.9%

before becoming a believer in Jesus Christ. The scale then shows three further steps after salvation.

-8 Awareness of a supreme being, but no effective knowledge of the gospel.

-7 Initial awareness of the gospel.

-6 Awareness of the fundamentals of the gospel.

-5 Grasp of the implications of the gospel.

-4 Positive attitude toward the gospel.

-3 Personal problem recognition.

-2 Decision to act.

-1 Repentance and faith in Christ.

The person is regenerated and becomes a new creature.

+1 Post-decision evaluation.

+2 Incorporation into the body.

+3 A lifetime of conceptual and behavioral growth in Christ.

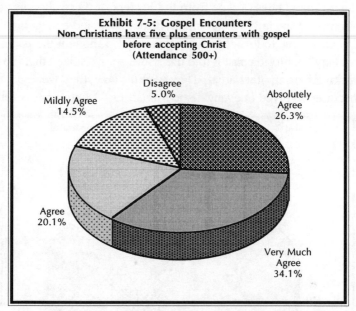

Exhibit 7-5: Gospel Encounters
Non-Christians have five plus encounters with gospel before accepting Christ
(Attendance 500+)

These church leaders in our study believe that one or just a few confrontations of a believer with the gospel may move him or her closer to the cross. But the evangelistic efforts that God uses to draw people to Himself may require multiple exposures to the gospel. One gospel presentation may bring a person from "-7" to "-6" on the Engel scale. Yet God may use numerous exposures to bring a person to the point of regeneration.

Why do leaders in larger churches affirm the importance of multiple encounters with the gospel more than smaller churches? In our interviews we found that the larger churches' ability to offer programmatically more gospel encounters made them more likely to advocate such evangelistic steps. Even so, the smaller churches were in agreement with the larger churches. The *intensity* of the feelings, however, was greater with the larger churches.

Attitudes about the Laity Going

One of the highest negative responses we received in our survey came in answer to this statement: "Evangelism is the easiest and most natural of all the ministries in the church." More than 55 percent of the churches responded with an unequivocal "do not agree" (exhibit 7-6). Only 14 percent answered with a strong affirmation.

We heard many tales of woe from the leaders of these churches as they tried to motivate the laity to participate in outreach and evangelism ministries. "When I came to this church six years ago, I thought the people were just plain lazy," a Florida pastor told us. "But I soon realized that the people were working hard in other areas. They weren't lazy; they were just unwilling to become involved in evangelistic ministries." Many pastors felt that a

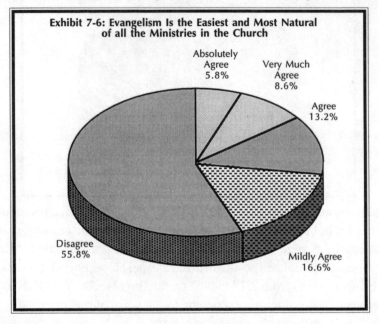

Exhibit 7-6: Evangelism Is the Easiest and Most Natural of all the Ministries in the Church

Absolutely Agree 5.8%

Very Much Agree 8.6%

Agree 13.2%

Mildly Agree 16.6%

Disagree 55.8%

perceptual hurdle had to be overcome before the laity would participate in evangelism ministries. Exhibit 7-7 depicts church leaders' beliefs that laypersons are inhibited because of irrational fears about evangelism. "I found out that my deacon chairman thought evangelism meant he had to get a person to 'accept Christ' every time. He had this idea that he would be arguing with an unbeliever for hours," a Texas minister of education said. Over three-fourths of the respondents agreed that unfounded fears prevent a person from being a part of the church's evangelistic ministry.

What does a church leader do to overcome these perceptual barriers? "Unfortunately, cognitive education usually will not work," the Texas church leader shared. "We found that experience was about the only way to get people involved in evangelistic outreach. But experience means that they must first be willing to get involved. It's a catch-22!"

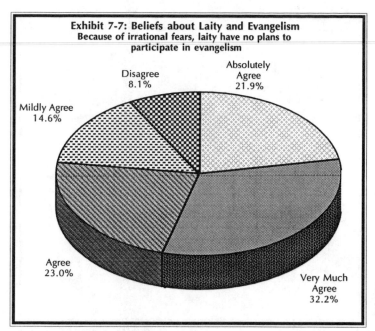

Exhibit 7-7: Beliefs about Laity and Evangelism
Because of irrational fears, laity have no plans to participate in evangelism

- Disagree 8.1%
- Absolutely Agree 21.9%
- Mildly Agree 14.6%
- Agree 23.0%
- Very Much Agree 32.2%

The ultimate answer to getting people involved in evangelistic ministries is patience, persistence, and the leaders' example. Though often a slow and laborious process, it will eventually yield its fruits and rewards.

Other Important Attitudes

We will look briefly at church leaders' attitudes on other issues although they are covered in other chapters. It is fascinating to see some of the issues about which these pastors and other leaders are dedicated.

The Primacy of Prayer

In chapter 4 we discussed prayer as a programmatic issue that is very much on the hearts and minds of pastors and other leaders. (See exhibit 7-8.) Leaders of these churches have an *attitude* of prayer. Over *98 percent* agreed without hesitation that prayer is the foundation to effective evangelism. No other single attitudinal factor measured this strongly.

Social Ministries

In the next chapter we will examine a host of issues dealing with social ministries and evangelism. The holistic view of ministry these pastors

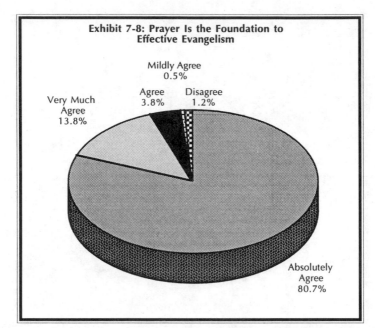

Exhibit 7-8: Prayer Is the Foundation to Effective Evangelism

Mildly Agree
0.5%

Agree
3.8%

Disagree
1.2%

Very Much
Agree
13.8%

Absolutely
Agree
80.7%

possess was impressive. Most of them certainly held to the priority of evangelism, but this priority was no excuse to neglect social ministries.

Cana Baptist Church in Burleson, Texas, has an average worship attendance of 425. Its evangelistic ministries are many, but an attitude of love and concern permeate everything that the church does and represents. Matthew Leilich, minister of education, responded thoughtfully to our question "What can we learn from your church?" He simply responded, "The key to our church is love and a caring concern for people. It takes a concerted effort to care. There is no easy fix." Cana Baptist operates a home for unwed mothers and a large benevolent ministry. Said Leilich, "Social causes are supported by this church in order to help people get back on their feet. This aid is for all people in need regardless of their membership ties. This church tries very hard to encourage our members to be active in ministry in our community."

Discipleship Ministries

Another impressive attitude of these leaders was their commitment to discipleship ministries. As we will see more fully in chapter 10, these churches are serious about Great Commission evangelism including the making of disciples. No other issue received as much unsolicited comment as the issue of discipleship.

Missions beyond the Local Community

One of the most fascinating churches of the twentieth-century is Willow Creek Community Church. I know of no American church that has been evaluated, analyzed, and discussed as much as Willow Creek. Lynne Hybels, pastor Bill Hybels' wife, recently wrote a revealing history of the church.[6] The blessings of God have been obvious in the church for twenty years. But it was not until 1994 that Willow Creek began a ministry beyond its local community. Lynne Hybels shares insights about this issue: "One of the gifts of maturity, it seems, is that it gives a person or an institution the ability to do two things at once. For Willow Creek, relative maturity means we have finally reached a developmental point that allows us to enter a new era of worldwide extension without jeopardizing our God-ordained local ministry."[7]

Nearly twenty years after the founding of Willow Creek, the church began to have a global outreach. "This aggressive expansion of International Ministries was launched in November 1994, when Bill [Hybels] announced to our congregation that the entire amount gathered through our end-of-the-year giving would go to help the poor and the lost worldwide."[8]

Most leaders of evangelistic churches do not see local church outreach and global mission support as an either/or choice. "It is amazing and absurd to me," said a Tennessee pastor, "that some pastors refuse to lead their churches to greater mission giving and support because it will take away from their local ministries. They act like they serve a God of limited resources. God *always* blesses those churches that give resources out of faith and trust!"

Numbers Are Not Everything

Church growth proponents are often accused of being overly numbers conscious. Some perceived this as a numbers-for-numbers-sake attitude. We did not find that attitude in any of the churches we interviewed.

In fact, we were somewhat surprised at the responses to our statement, "Numerical growth is not vitally important but should be monitored." Exhibit 7-9 illustrates that 60 percent of our respondents agreed strongly with that statement.

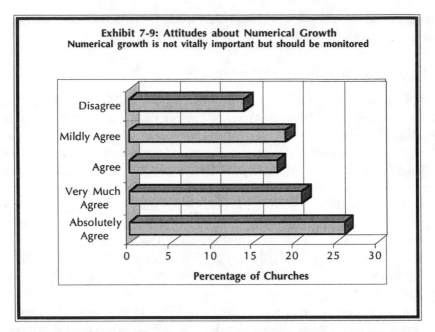

Exhibit 7-9: Attitudes about Numerical Growth
Numerical growth is not vitally important but should be monitored

Regardless of their specific response to the statement in exhibit 7-9, the primary sentiment of these leaders toward numerical measurements was one of *balance*. They rejected the critics who saw evil in any numbers. "Numbers have their place in ministry," an Oregon pastor commented. "They allow us to measure progress and to remain accountable. I cannot imagine not having statistics and numbers to help us to understand many of the dynamics of our ministries."

But most of these pastors were also careful to avoid idolizing numbers. They rejected a numbers-are-everything mentality. They did not live or die according to numerical results. But they also felt that many critics were negative about numbers because the critics themselves did not want to remain accountable to numerical realities. "The most vocal critics about our numerical growth," a Virginia pastor observed, "are pastors whose churches are declining."

Theological Beliefs

Our survey asked few theological questions. And, quite honestly, the way we worded the questions caused some level of confusion. Nevertheless, any doubt about these leaders' theological beliefs was quickly dispelled in our follow-up interviews. These pastors and other staff are clearly conservative evangelicals.

Earlier in this book I mentioned the "Southern Baptist bias" concerning theological issues. As a denomination, Southern Baptists are typically regarded as a conservative evangelical body. Should it be a surprise then that the churches and their leaders reflect this same theological positioning? Probably not. In fact, I would not be surprised to discover that we were looking at some of the more conservative churches within the conservative denomination.

Despite the obvious bias in this study, research of the past twenty years has indicated a strong, positive correlation between conservative theology and church growth. As I shared in chapter 3, one of the earlier books on the issue was written in 1972 by an executive in the National Council of Churches, Dean Kelley. *Why Conservative Churches Are Growing*[9] engendered significant discussion and debate. Even in recent years some writers have tried to counter Kelley's thesis that conservative churches are more likely to grow than liberal churches.

But abundant evidence seems to support Kelley's claims. Although isolated exceptions to the rule may be found, most churches that are growing *are* conservative. While theological conservatism does not guarantee growth, theological liberalism is most often a guarantee for decline.

We asked our respondents three theological questions. These dealt with their view of Scripture, their understanding of God, and their beliefs about sin and salvation. Although we asked only three questions, we certainly received a great deal of unsolicited responses about theological beliefs.

Views of the Bible

A response of over 90 percent to a statement is overwhelming. But I suspect, as a consequence of follow-up interviews, that the number is actually understated. As depicted in exhibit 7-10, 90.1 percent of the respondents described the Bible as the actual Word of God, completely and literally true. But we asked further questions among that 9.2 percent who responded that the Bible is the inspired Word of God but contains some human error. The respondents to whom we spoke understood the statement differently than we intended. They interpreted "human error" in the statement to refer to translators rather than the original writers of Scripture. I suspect that the true number of respondents who affirm the theological

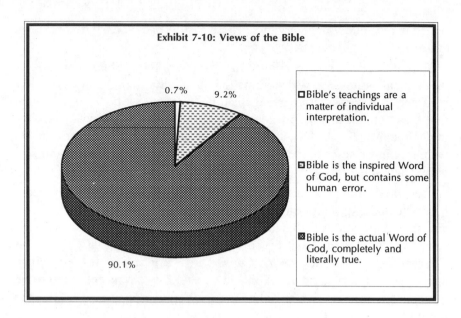

Exhibit 7-10: Views of the Bible

0.7% 9.2%

□ Bible's teachings are a matter of individual interpretation.

□ Bible is the inspired Word of God, but contains some human error.

☒ Bible is the actual Word of God, completely and literally true.

90.1%

position called inerrancy, which we tried to communicate in the earlier statement, is over 95 percent.

Beliefs about God

The respondents clearly had an orthodox understanding of God. Once again, our choice of words in one statement was not altogether clear. Follow-up interviews indicated that almost all the leaders would have affirmed the statement "God is constantly at work in the world."

Beliefs about Sin and Salvation

Exhibit 7-12 shows leaders who are clear on their understanding of the salvific role of Christ. Only 2 of the 576 respondents view the matter differently, well within the statistical margin for error in marking answers.

Other Theological Comments

In the miscellaneous responses to the survey, numerous church leaders indicated the critical importance of theology to evangelistic growth. The following is a sample of their comments.

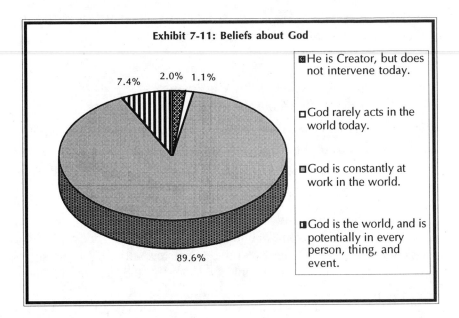

Exhibit 7-11: Beliefs about God

7.4%   2.0% 1.1%

89.6%

☒ He is Creator, but does not intervene today.

☐ God rarely acts in the world today.

☐ God is constantly at work in the world.

☐ God is the world, and is potentially in every person, thing, and event.

Exhibit 7-12: Beliefs about Sin and Salvation

All people are inherently good; they simply must realize their human potential.	0.0%
All people participate in God's salvation, even without faith in Him.	0.0%
All people are sinful and must ask God for His forgiveness to be saved.	99.7%
All people are sinful and must live a good life to earn salvation.	0.3%

- "We believe that all of our church members must understand and affirm the fundamentals of the faith."
- "We believe the Bible literally, and live it instead of 'lipping it.'"
- "Our church believes and loves the Word of God."
- "We are a solidly conservative church."
- "We are conservative and believe that the Bible is the Word of God."
- "We constantly emphasize these principles: the Scriptures are without error; God never contradicts His Word; Scripture is the best interpreter of Scripture; and disobedience to God and His Word will bring discipline."

- "I don't see how a church can be faithful to God's Word unless the people believe with all their heart that the Bible is perfect, without error, and Holy Spirit inspired."

Concluding Comments:
Conservative Churches with Biblical Balance

Almost all of these 576 churches are conservative, evangelical churches that affirm the total truthfulness of Scripture. Most of the pastors of these churches have a passion to reach people for Jesus Christ and that passion becomes contagious in the churches they lead.

But many detractors over the years have concluded that such "on-fire evangelistic types" are narrow in their understanding of God's mission for the world. The leaders of these churches may be stereotyped with other such personalities who are narrow-minded persons with little or no social conscience. That stereotype simply did not fit the pastors of these churches.

These leaders are biblically-balanced. They affirm the priority of evangelism, but they insist that the church must show Christlike compassion through social ministries. They believe in the local church and its mission, but they insist that the mission of the church must be worldwide in its scope. They know that evangelism usually begins relationally, but they urge their members ultimately to confront believers with the claims of Christ. They believe that a sovereign God controls this world, but they also know that prayer moves mountains. They eagerly seek to obey God and see nonbelievers become converts, but they insist that converts become disciples. And they believe that numbers are not everything, yet they realize that numbers are important.

The leaders of these churches are leaders because they are balanced in the truest biblical sense. They know that they are not perfect; many confessed openly their inadequacies. But most of them in some way or another told us that they are "pressing toward the goal to win the prize for which God has called them heavenward in Christ Jesus." It is little surprise that these pastors and leaders are being used by God to reach their communities and world with the saving gospel of Christ.

CHAPTER EIGHT

Community Ministries and Evangelism

I am reasonably sure that evangelical churches which give priority to the evangelistic mandate are in the long run actually doing more for the poor, the dispossessed, the exploited, and the marginal citizens of America's cities than more liberal ones. . . . Study a major metropolitan area and see where the physically and mentally handicapped are attending churches in considerable numbers. Locate the churches that have active and growing programs for the deaf. . . . Most likely such churches will be of an evangelical nature.

C. Peter Wagner

The myth exists and persists: A church must choose to be either a community- or social-ministry church or an evangelistic church—it cannot be both. Or so we have been told. Yet, studies of the past two decades have not only dispelled the myth, they have shown that a direct correlation exists between evangelistic growth and the level of ministries offered by a church.

For example, a recent study by C. Kirk Hadaway found that newly growing churches are more likely to be involved in community ministries than declining churches. Hadaway spoke of these as "breakout churches," churches that reversed a pattern of numerical decline to achieve numerical growth. Hadaway unhesitatingly says, "It is clear that breakout churches (and growing churches generally) tend to have a greater presence in their community."[1]

Hadaway's study found that the outward focus of an evangelistic church engenders an outward concern for ministry as well. Evangelistic churches "are less inward looking and see the role of the church as helping people, whether they are members of their congregation or not. As a result, persons in the community are aware that the church exists and that it is available in time of need."[2]

But Hadaway's research also showed that the growing churches did not provide community ministry as simply a means to add to their membership roles. "The goals of providing ministry to the community were not designed to produce growth in these churches, but it would appear that growth can be seen as an unintended consequence."[3] Indeed, the community's perception of an evangelistic church is often significantly improved as the church reaches out in both evangelism and ministry. "The ministering church is seen as an open, accepting congregation, rather than a restricted social club. Those who have received help or support and those on the outside who have worked on joint ministry projects with the church may establish relationships with the pastor or members, come to know Christ (if they do not already), and eventually join the fellowship."[4]

Our study affirms and concurs with Hadaway's research. The evangelistic churches in this study are very ministry-minded and community-oriented. Why then do misperceptions still abound? Why do many well-intentioned people still see a dichotomy between evangelism and social ministries? The roots of the misperceptions are found in a historical reality.

A Historical Excursion

As the nineteenth century came to a close, the understanding of mission shifted dramatically. The social gospel movement was influencing churches, and mission changed in perception from the simple task of winning converts to the complex task of social justice, betterment, and reconstruction.

Evangelicals began to build defenses against the social gospel. In doing so, evangelicalism was rightly affirming the importance of evangelism but wrongly avoiding any recognition of social ministries as being a part of missions. A dichotomy emerged in which conservative evangelicals raised the flag of evangelism and liberals touted the cause of social ministries. For conservative church leaders, an outspoken position on involvement in social ministries would have been tantamount to theological treason.

After nearly six decades of debating about evangelism and social ministries, evangelicals began to recognize that they were overreacting against social ministries. Scripture favors an evangelistic priority, they argued, but not to the neglect of temporal needs. Signs of the more balanced and biblical change were noticeable at the Berlin Congress of 1966, but the shift was explicitly stated at the International Congress on World Evangelization, held in Lausanne, Switzerland, in 1974. The Lausanne Covenant affirmed "that evangelism and sociopolitical involvement are both part of our Christian duty. For both are necessary expressions of our doctrines of God and man, our love for our neighbor and our obedience to Jesus Christ."[5]

If the evangelical world was returning to a more balanced understanding of missions, the word about the return was not spreading rapidly. Evangelistic churches, most all of which were conservative, evangelical churches, were still stereotyped in the minds of many. They were perceived as single-faceted, "notch-belt" evangelistic machines with little concern for people who are hurting. But as Hadaway, Wagner, and others have shown us, evangelistic churches have taken up the banner for social ministries. Our study only enhanced those observations.

We noted in the previous chapter the ministry of Town 'n' Country Baptist Church in Tampa. In our follow-up interview with pastor Dan Wade, we listened to his story of a church that seeks biblical balance. Look at their ministries in both evangelism and community involvement.

Evangelistic Ministries:

- Continuous evangelism training program designed by pastor. Program focuses on three graduated levels of involvement: visiting, witnessing, and soul winning.
- Teaching and preaching of lifestyle evangelism.
- Deacons, Sunday School leaders, and their spouses expected to spend one and one-half hours per week in soul winning.
- Every morning at 8:00 A.M. the pastor meets with some of the laity to pray specifically for lost people to be saved.
- Wednesday night prayer meetings include a time to pray for lost people specifically by name.
- An ongoing ministry where a trained soul winner takes an apprentice on visitation until that person is ready to train someone else.
- Youth of the church receive soul-winning training.

Social and Community Ministries:

- Prison ministries.
- Backyard Bible clubs.
- Ministry in retirement homes.
- A Spanish mission was recently meeting in this church's facilities, but they have moved into their own facilities.
- Ministry to troubled youth through the local sheriff's department.
- Philosophy to meet people where they are and meet their needs.

Town 'n' Country Baptist has seen consistent growth through its balanced ministries in the community and in evangelism. Today most of its growth is conversion growth.

An Attitude of Caring

We asked some questions about community and social ministries. Two of these related directly to an attitude of caring for those in need. We asked leaders to respond to this statement: "Everyone who loves Jesus will have a heart for the poor, sick, lost, widowed, and homeless." As exhibit 8-1 shows, over 53 percent agree without equivocation that such is the attitude of all Christians.

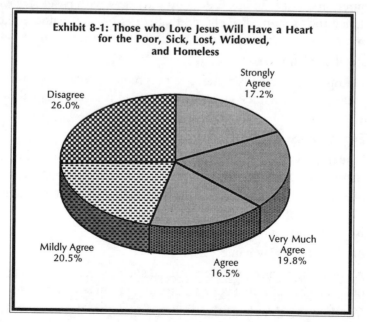

Exhibit 8-1: Those who Love Jesus Will Have a Heart for the Poor, Sick, Lost, Widowed, and Homeless

Strongly Agree 17.2%

Disagree 26.0%

Very Much Agree 19.8%

Mildly Agree 20.5%

Agree 16.5%

In our follow-up interviews we spoke to leaders who responded "do not agree" or "somewhat agree." Their responses in no way indicated an aversion to social ministries. They simply did not believe that all who love Jesus will *naturally* have a heart for the poor, sick, lost, widowed, and homeless. Said a pastor in Oklahoma, "I wish that everyone *did* have that kind of compassion. It certainly is the model of Jesus. Unfortunately, I don't think our love for Christ is always reflected in our love for the down-and-out. It should be, but it's not."

We also asked leaders to react to another statement: "Non-Christians may not remember what they have been told regarding God's love, but they always remember what they have experienced as God's love." Many leaders related this statement to ministries in their churches. A minister of education from California told us, "We began a ministry in 1991 similar to big brother and big sister ministries. The greatest reward that we receive on earth is the look of gratitude of the children and their single parents. It's a tough world for them, and I thank God that we are helping just a little. That's the ministry I recall when you mentioned experiencing God's love in the survey."

As we discovered in our interviews, the responses of exhibit 8-2 are more indicative of the attitudes of these leaders. They truly have a heart for people who are hurting. They are leading their churches to diverse community and social ministries. And they are seeing balance in ministries between temporal and eternal needs.

Diverse Ministries

No one type of community or social ministry is dominant among these evangelistic churches, though we found that almost every church was involved in some kind of intentional social ministry. Since our survey did not ask respondents to name the ministries in which they were involved, we cannot with confidence convey a level of involvement with any particular ministry. We can, however, name some of the ministries that were mentioned in our interviews or in the miscellaneous portion of our survey.

Benevolence Ministries

Many churches mentioned a significant involvement with benevolence ministries. Some were as basic as providing budgetary funds for emergency needs. Others were much more complex and involved. When we

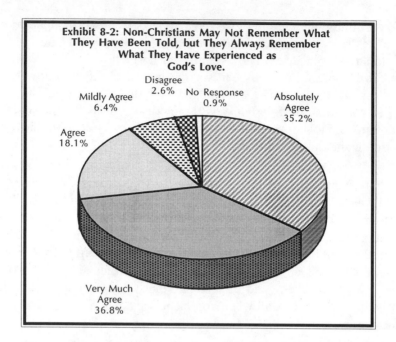

Exhibit 8-2: Non-Christians May Not Remember What They Have Been Told, but They Always Remember What They Have Experienced as God's Love.

- Disagree 2.6%
- No Response 0.9%
- Mildly Agree 6.4%
- Absolutely Agree 35.2%
- Agree 18.1%
- Very Much Agree 36.8%

asked one pastor the key to his church's growth, he responded: "Ministry! A church is effective evangelistically when it is reaching out in compassion to a hurting community. Recovery groups, food assistance, clothing, shelter, and other services are an excellent way to model the love of Jesus. The gospel embodied is essential to the gospel proclaimed if people are going to be reached."

We also heard leaders frankly assess their own churches' involvement or lack of community involvement. "We are committed to providing benevolent ministries," said an Arkansas church layperson. "But our commitment has been greatly tested since some of the recipients of our ministry began attending our church. These people are of a lower socioeconomic status than the membership, and some folks are not sure about 'those kind of people.' Our pastor is leading us to work through some of those issues and to learn to accept all people as God's creation."

Ministries to Military Personnel

Some churches in the study are located near military bases. The turnover of membership is high, but we received several rewarding testimonies from church leaders who are trying to lead their churches to make a difference in the lives of these military personnel.

Ministry to Women

If this study is indicative of future trends in ministry, we should see a continued growth in ministries specifically for women. Numerous churches in this study were in some manner involved in pregnancy ministries. For example, Christopher Road Baptist Church in Shelby, North Carolina, is a relatively new church started in 1987. Among the numerous ministries in which they are already involved is a crisis pregnancy ministry led by the Baptist Women, a missions group in the church.

Though fewer in number than the churches involved in crisis pregnancy ministries, some of the churches are also involved in meeting the needs of abused and battered women. A few of the churches even have their own facilities for these ministries.

Support Groups

As many as one-fourth of the 576 churches had some type of ongoing support group. The most commonly mentioned support group was for divorce recovery. Others were formed for alcoholics, persons with eating disorders, single parents, compulsive spenders, and those with drug addictions, to name a few. Though these groups meet at a variety of times on every night of the week, the most frequently-mentioned meeting time was Sunday evening.

Ethnic Ministries

Several of the churches (130 of the 576) have begun ministries to ethnic groups (see exhibit 8-3). The most common expression of these ministries has been the availability of church facilities to a particular ethnic group. First Southern Baptist Church in Garden City, Kansas, worships each Sunday morning while a Vietnamese mission worships at the same hour in the same facility.

Bus Ministries

In the 1960s and 1970s bus ministries were among the key evangelistic methodologies for many churches. Some larger churches purchased entire

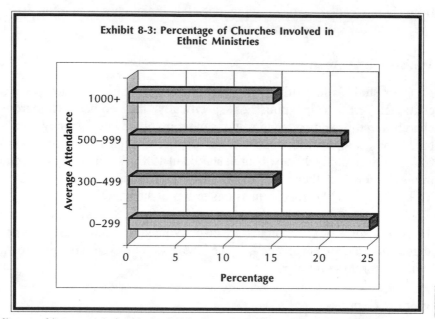

Exhibit 8-3: Percentage of Churches Involved in Ethnic Ministries

fleets of buses to bring lost children and adults to Sunday School and worship services.

As we will see later in this chapter, bus ministries are used infrequently today for specific evangelistic ministries. Several of the churches in this study, however, utilized bus ministries as a community or social ministry.

We were surprised that 165 of the 576 churches still had some type of busing ministry in operation. Church leaders indicated that these ministries were largely social or community-oriented rather than explicitly evangelistic. "We pick up senior adults who have no way to get to church," said an Alabama minister of education. A Georgia pastor commented, "The purpose of our bus ministry is to pick up children and youth at a local children's home. We view these efforts as part of our ministry to the community."

Exhibit 8-4 clearly depicts the more frequent use of busing ministries in the smaller churches. A pastor of a megachurch shared with us that an effective busing ministry would require an expenditure of resources that the church was not prepared to make. "I wish we had the money to send buses to every corner of the city. A small church can make an impact on their church with just one bus going to one place in their community. We wouldn't know where to begin!"

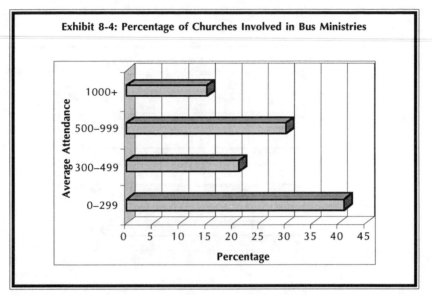

Exhibit 8-4: Percentage of Churches Involved in Bus Ministries

Busing ministries may not be the impact ministry of two and three decades earlier, but they have not completely faded away. Nearly 30 percent of the churches still had some type of busing ministry, with the greatest concentration in the smaller churches.

Family Ministries

Family ministry is a broad term that can refer to a number of different ministries. For some churches family ministry simply refers to a wide range of activities including recreational activities. For other churches the term means in-depth spiritual and emotional resources specifically designed to strengthen the family. Because of the varied ministries that were placed in this category, nearly 90 percent of the churches indicated an involvement in family ministries (see exhibit 8-5).

Beyond the statistical indicators, we heard from these churches that they are committed to helping strengthen the family. "We believe that, as the family goes, so goes the nation," a Maryland pastor said. "In almost everything we do we ask the question: Can this help our members and the community to strengthen the family? We don't automatically eliminate a ministry if the answer is no, but that question is asked quite a bit."

The churches mentioned family ministries more as an avenue to strengthen Christian families rather than to offer a specific evangelistic outreach. Only a small minority of the churches spoke of family ministries as first being evangelistically motivated.

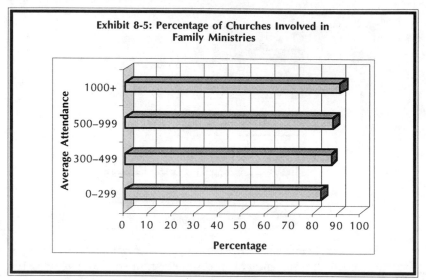

Exhibit 8-5: Percentage of Churches Involved in Family Ministries

Counseling Ministries

Seventy percent of all churches surveyed say that they offer some kind of counseling ministry for the church and the community. Of course, a counseling ministry can range from a meeting with a bivocational pastor to an appointment with a full-time counseling minister on a megachurch's staff. Many of the counseling ministries, especially in the middle-sized churches, were "staffed" by laypersons. Some of the laypersons had received rather extensive training while others were acting as counselors because of their life's experience. As exhibit 8-6 shows, almost 70 percent of churches in every size category say that they have a counseling ministry.

But Are the Ministries Evangelistic?

Our study was designed specifically to ask questions about evangelistic methodologies. As shown in appendix 2, we asked the respondents to evaluate twenty-three methodologies in terms of their evangelistic effectiveness. Before we reveal the perceived evangelistic value of these methodologies, we will share with you three major conclusions about ministries and evangelism.

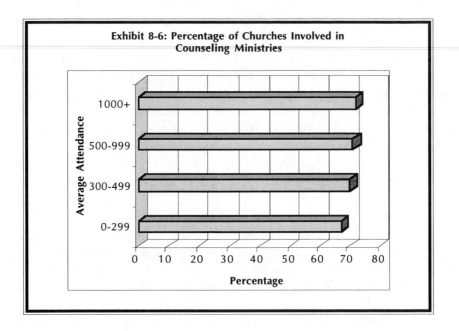

Exhibit 8-6: Percentage of Churches Involved in Counseling Ministries

Ministries Should Be Evangelistic

An overwhelming sentiment we heard in our follow-up interviews is that social and community ministries should be evangelistic. "We have an average of four or five community ministries going on in a particular week," a Texas pastor said. "We make certain that the workers are trained in ways that they can share their faith with the recipients of our ministries."

Since we heard from 576 of the most evangelistic churches in America, we fully expected this sentiment. Because of their evangelistic intentionality and evangelistic attitude, the strong feelings about evangelism in ministries was no surprise. Perhaps the surprise came in our next discovery.

Most of the Ministries Are Not Evangelistically Effective

Later in this chapter we will share with you the perceived evangelistic effectiveness of five broad categories of ministries. As a rule the pastors of the 576 churches were disappointed if not frustrated with anemic evangelistic efforts in most of the social and community ministries. "We are doing everything we know how to do to see evangelistic growth in our ministries," a Texas megachurch associate pastor told us. "We have trained workers, provided evangelistic literature, conducted follow-up visits in the home, attempted to establish relationships, you name it! But very few of our baptisms come as a result of these ministries."

The nature of this study is such that we received many responses that were perceptual. While we did not necessarily believe that the respondents' perceptions and reality were in conflict, we did discern that the leaders evaluated their churches and themselves ruthlessly. The comments we received about ministry ineffectiveness in evangelism was but one example of their vigorous and continuous evaluative process.

Ministry Will Continue Regardless of Evangelistic Effectiveness

Rarely did our research team hear a comment about discontinuing a ministry because of its evangelistic ineffectiveness. Listen to the insightful words of a Kentucky pastor: "Fewer than 2 percent of our baptisms each year come as a direct result of the community ministries we offer. We are not proud of that statistic, and we will do everything we can to make our ministries more intentionally evangelistic." The pastor paused and continued, "But we don't see involvement in helping hurting persons as optional. We are constantly reminded of the One who said 'whatever you did for one of the least of these brothers of mine, you did for me.' That's our source of motivation to be involved in ministry."

Though I cannot predict the future, I believe their social and community ministries will become more evangelistic. Though the church did not participate in our survey, First Baptist Church of Leesburg, Florida, is being highlighted by Southern Baptists as a model for doing ministry with evangelistic effectiveness. Churches like First Baptist, Leesburg, and the churches in our survey indicated that an eagerness to learn and an attitude of evangelistic zeal in ministry will enable them to transform ministries into true opportunities for evangelism.

Evaluating Five Categories of Ministries Evangelistically

We now turn to the churches' own assessment of the evangelistic effectiveness of their social and community ministries. Despite less-than-enthusiastic evaluations of themselves, there were no indications that these ministries would be discontinued. To the contrary, many of the churches were looking for greater ministry involvement with heightened evangelistic efforts.

Weekday Ministries

Exhibit 8-7 is a reminder of the discussion of chapter 2, the ten surprises of this study. Weekday ministries were mostly defined as day care, Christian schools, moms' day out, and similar ministries. Several churches indicated that day care was a financially subsidized ministry for single mothers in the community. As the exhibit shows, only slightly above 10 percent of the churches viewed weekday ministries as evangelistically effective. Most of the leaders saw value in the ministries, but lamented their minimal impact for evangelism.

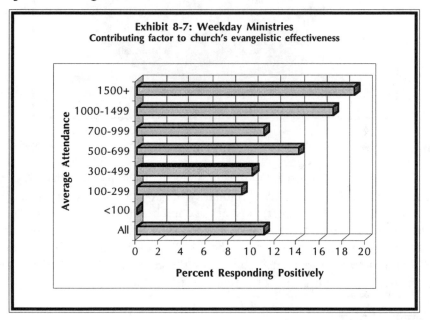

Exhibit 8-7: Weekday Ministries
Contributing factor to church's evangelistic effectiveness

Ethnic Ministries

Only 130 of the 576 churches had any type of involvement in ethnic ministries, less than one-fourth of the total churches in the study. Therefore, we are not surprised that, overall, relatively few churches in the survey considered ethnic ministries to be evangelistic.

Most of the churches that did not view ethnic ministries as a factor in their evangelistic effectiveness were those that did not have such ministries. Forty-five of the 576 churches (7.9 percent) cited ethnic ministries as a main or contributing factor to their evangelistic outreach.

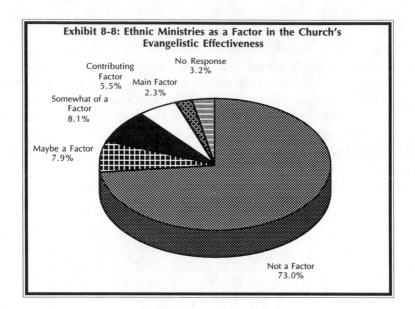

Exhibit 8-8: Ethnic Ministries as a Factor in the Church's Evangelistic Effectiveness

Contributing Factor 5.5%

No Response 3.2%

Main Factor 2.3%

Somewhat of a Factor 8.1%

Maybe a Factor 7.9%

Not a Factor 73.0%

Bus Ministries

Though nearly 30 percent of the churches in this study were involved in busing ministries, most of these ministries did not focus on evangelism. As we saw earlier in the chapter, most of the churches involved in busing ministry viewed it as a way to meet the needs of Christians. Senior citizens were mentioned frequently among those utilizing this ministry. But exhibit 8-9 shows that fewer than 8 percent of the churches considered busing ministries as a contributing or major factor in evangelism.

Family Ministries

Because of the significant number of churches with some kind of family ministry, nearly 40 percent of the respondents indicated that these ministries had an evangelistic thrust. Among the social and community ministries, this factor was among the highest for evangelistic effectiveness. Due to the diversity of these ministries, however, we were unable to identify any specific group of ministries that were more evangelistic than others.

Perhaps more significant, exhibit 8-10 shows that only 11.6 percent of the respondents indicated that family ministries were *not* a factor in their churches' evangelistic effectiveness. We believe that the level of evangelistic activities in the family ministry category warrants future study.

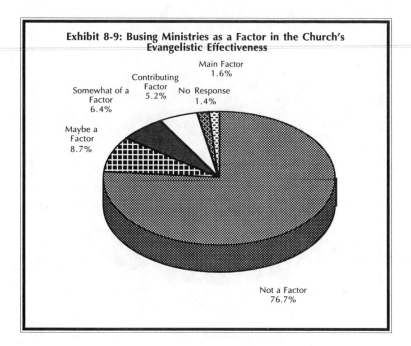

Exhibit 8-9: Busing Ministries as a Factor in the Church's Evangelistic Effectiveness

Main Factor
1.6%

Contributing
Factor
5.2%

Somewhat of a
Factor
6.4%

No Response
1.4%

Maybe a
Factor
8.7%

Not a Factor
76.7%

Counseling Ministries

Counseling ministries included a considerable variety of activities. Still, only 18 percent of the respondents indicated that counseling ministries were a contributing or main factor in their church's evangelistic efforts.

One Florida church had an extensive counseling ministry that was staffed fully by laypersons. The laypersons had received extensive training, but were instructed to refer any difficult assignment to one of nine professional counselors on the church's referral list. The counseling ministry of this church had a strong evangelistic thrust. The associate pastor, who has primary responsibility for the ministry, shared their philosophy: "We believe that a person cannot begin to deal effectively with his or her problems without the presence of Christ. All of our counselors are trained to confront everyone with the claims of Christ. We make no pretense about it. We tell them that they are to go to a secular counselor if they are offended by our confrontational approach. But they have come to us knowing that we are a Christian counseling ministry."

While family ministries were overall more evangelistically effective, counseling ministries apparently could become more evangelistic with

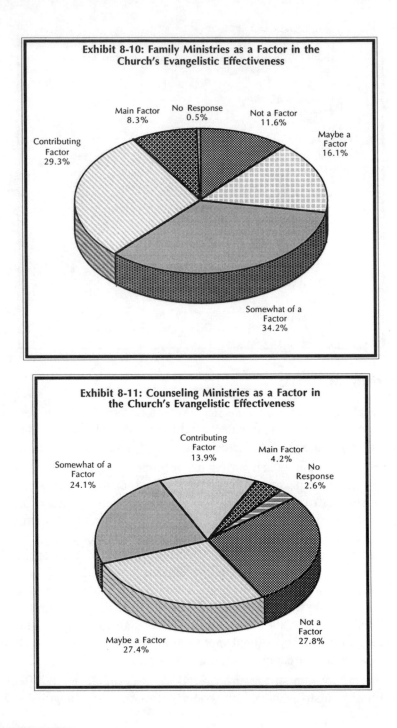

Exhibit 8-10: Family Ministries as a Factor in the Church's Evangelistic Effectiveness

Main Factor 8.3%
No Response 0.5%
Not a Factor 11.6%
Maybe a Factor 16.1%
Contributing Factor 29.3%
Somewhat of a Factor 34.2%

Exhibit 8-11: Counseling Ministries as a Factor in the Church's Evangelistic Effectiveness

Contributing Factor 13.9%
Main Factor 4.2%
No Response 2.6%
Somewhat of a Factor 24.1%
Not a Factor 27.8%
Maybe a Factor 27.4%

greater intentionality. Many church leaders indicated that counseling is the perfect opportunity for witnessing. Said an Illinois pastor, "You have someone who is seeking you out because he or she has a need. You have the ultimate Truth in the person of Jesus Christ. You have the perfect setting to share that Truth with someone. It is the single best opportunity for evangelistic sharing."

Another pastor, this one from Alabama, had similar sentiments. "The problem with most counseling ministries is that they aren't intentionally evangelistic. Nearly one-fourth of our baptisms last year came directly from a counseling session. We have discovered that a large number of counselees referred to us aren't Christians. We would be clearly disobedient if we didn't witness to them."

Conclusion: Ministries Grow in an Atmosphere of Love

More than any programmatic attempt to start community ministries in a church, the most effective ministries are those that develop from an atmosphere of love and concern. The most successful ministries to which we were introduced were not those formed in a committee seeking to justify its existence. To the contrary, the most effective ministries were begun somewhat unexpectedly. Believers in a church saw a need and began to find ways to meet that need. Before long, an entire ministry had developed with an impact far greater than anyone imagined.

The following are additional comments from pastors and other leaders in the leading ministry churches in our study:

- "The attitude of our church is positive, enthusiastic, and loving. We emphasize reaching out to others on a continual basis."
- "We have learned to love people as Christ did—unconditionally. Our Sunday School teachers have first responsibility to let us know of needs in their classes and in the community."
- "Our church tries to let everyone know that they are loved by God within our 'family' of God."
- "We strive to embody the gospel in all that we do through love and concern."
- "We have been told that the environment of our church is loving and accepting."
- "If there is any one factor that makes our church what it is today, it is that we are a church that loves people. We have heard that from

visitors and people who are ministered to by our church many times over."

Love is the common denominator. But how does a church create a loving atmosphere that is conducive to meaningful ministry? We received many responses to this question, but three answers stood out because of their frequency.

One key factor for an atmosphere of love is strong biblical preaching. "You cannot be in the Word very long without hearing about the amazing love and grace of God. Our church began truly to see that love when we received 'meaty' Bible preaching from our new pastor," an Arkansas layperson said.

A second significant factor that engenders an environment of love is a season of prayer and fasting. We heard many testimonies from church leaders about the miraculous work of God after a new corporate prayer emphasis was begun, or after the leadership of the church called the people to an extended time of prayer and fasting. Not only did numerical and evangelistic growth result, but new ministries often began as well. These new ministries were born out of renewed hearts that expressed love and concern.

The third key factor is that these churches demonstrate love and acceptance because the pastor models love and acceptance. "We were a church divided before our pastor came here," a Georgia layperson shared. "His example of unconditional love and acceptance has not only helped us to heal old wounds, it has also been a model for us to emulate."

Evangelistic churches are involved in ministries for their communities. They demonstrate the love and concern of Christ. Not all of their ministries are explicitly evangelistic, but most of their ministries are born out of hearts of love and concern. The love of Christ compels the people of these churches to share the gospel and minister unto the least of these.

CHAPTER NINE

Mission-Minded Churches
Baptize More!

And now, compelled by the Spirit, I am going to Jerusalem, not knowing what will happen to me there. I only know that in every city the Holy Spirit warns me that prison and hardships are facing me. However, I consider my life worth nothing to me, if only I may finish the race and complete the task the Lord Jesus has given me—the task of testifying to the gospel of God's grace.

Apostle Paul (Acts 20:22–24)

A pastor in the Deep South told us of his first attempt to lead his church to start a new church. The staff and deacons had led the church through an entire year of fact-finding, information, and inspiration. Everything appeared to be going smoothly. Within nine months, the pastor thought, a new church would be born. He might have given up had he known it would be two tries and two years later before the church approved a new mission. Yet the leadership persevered, and eventually a new church was started.

"That first business conference was a shocker," the pastor lamented. "I still have bad feelings when I think about it." What he thought would be a time of celebration turned into a night of disaster. Troublemakers in the church had gathered other members, mostly inactive ones. "The presence of several persons I had hardly seen should have been a warning to me," the pastor shared. "I was just too naive. I thought they had come because of the excitement of starting a new church."

Although the subject had been broadly discussed for over a year, several negative issues were raised at that meeting. Instead of affirming the goal of reaching new people, the issues focused on the losses the mother church would experience. "We can't afford to give up members. "We're not even meeting budget now," a disgruntled member argued. "Can you imagine the deficit we'll have when these people leave us?"

Yet another member spoke, one whom the pastor had never met. "We will hurt other churches in the area if we start a new church on the east end. There is not a church in the area that's filled to capacity. We've got no business taking away from their potential growth!"

Then another person spoke in a semi-conciliatory tone, "Look, we all want to reach people for Christ. I don't think anyone here would deny that goal. But, as we can hear from so many at this meeting, we're not really ready for such a major move. I move that we table the motion to start a new church. Perhaps we can come back to this issue at a better time."

The motion carried. Approval to start a new church would not come for two more years.

In another church in a bordering state, a pastor was leading his church to greater missions giving through the Cooperative Program, a Southern Baptist mission-giving conduit. The church was giving 10 percent of their total budget to the Cooperative Program, and the proposal before the people would increase that percentage to twelve.

For weeks the stewardship committee had shared with the people how the funds would be used to send the gospel worldwide. Missionaries had spoken in services, testifying to the work of God in home and foreign fields. Like the previous church, the enthusiasm seemed high; the time seemed right to take this step of faith. But also like the previous church, the naysayers were ready. "We have a $500,000 budget," said one outspoken critic. "We're already giving $50,000 to the Cooperative Program, and now we're proposing adding $6,000 to that total. Folks, we have unmet needs at home. How can we justify sending this much money to other areas of the world?"

The 10 percent level was retained for that year. It increased to only 11 percent the following year.

Increasing a church's mission support by starting new churches or giving more to mission causes is not always an easy task. The objections always seem to make sense, especially if the critic does not trust in a supernatural God with abundant resources. Why do the pastors and leaders of these 576 churches continue striving to lead their churches to new levels of missions commitment? Would it not be easier for them to be content with their local ministry and avoid the battles?

Yet the commitment of these leaders makes as much sense as the Apostle Paul's determination to go to Jerusalem, even though he knew imprisonment, hardships, and persecution awaited him (Acts 20:22–24). These leaders, like Paul, know that God's mission is bigger than any one church. They also know that the Savior commanded them to be witnesses beyond Jerusalem, to Judea, Samaria, and the ends of the earth (Acts 1:8). Focusing all church resources on the local church is nothing less than sinful disobedience.

This chapter focuses on churches that have visionary leaders, leaders who see beyond their own church and their own community. They believe in a God who multiplies resources miraculously. Their attitude anticipates God's miracles rather than lamenting possible losses.

An Attitude of Missions

Consider Bethel Baptist Church in Chesapeake, Virginia, where Houston Roberson is pastor. This church has an attendance of 250 in worship, yet they do missions as if they had unlimited resources. In addition to missions giving, this church makes a conscious effort to obey the Acts 1:8 command of missions. They have a four-pronged approach to missions.

1. Project Jerusalem: The ministry of the local church.

2. Project Judea: Ministry to families in Chesapeake.

3. Project Samaria: Home mission projects, backyard Bible clubs, etc.

4. Project Uttermost: Church sends mission teams to Moldova of the former Soviet Union. Currently going twice each year, mission teams will be going annually hereafter.

Bethel Baptist is representative of many of the churches that participated in this study. The leadership has an attitude of missions that not only sees its local ministry needs, but sees beyond them as well. And these pastors and leaders have discovered that local ministry and global missions do not compete with one another. To the contrary, the churches have learned that God blesses an Acts 1:8 vision. God returns in many ways any "losses" of funds or people.

The "Going" Mindset Means Mission

In chapter 7, we saw that one of the attitudes of the church leaders to whom we spoke was an attitude of "going." Exhibit 9-1 shows the overwhelming response to the statement, "Non-Christians usually will not come to us to find God. We have to go to them." Over 90 percent of the respondents indicated that they agreed with the statement.

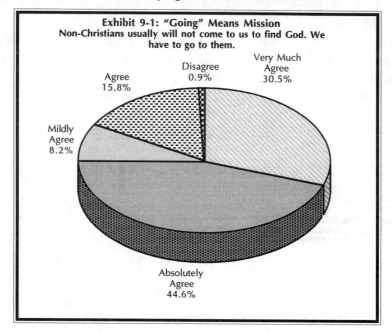

Exhibit 9-1: "Going" Means Mission
Non-Christians usually will not come to us to find God. We have to go to them.

Disagree 0.9%
Very Much Agree 30.5%
Agree 15.8%
Mildly Agree 8.2%
Absolutely Agree 44.6%

When we initially made the statement for our survey, our purpose was to discern if an attitude of intentional *local* outreach was present among the leaders of these churches. But our respondents interpreted the statement more broadly than we intended. "When you said in your statement 'We have to go to them,' I wasn't just thinking of people in our immediate community," a Texas pastor said. "To me, 'going' according to Scripture means that we reach out in our community, but it also means that we have a global missions commitment. Anything less is not reaching out according to the Bible."

A few churches did not indicate a strong mission mindset, but the overwhelming number of churches were baptizing more people *and* giving more to missions *and* being a part of some missions project. While we did not have a control group to compare to these 576 evangelistic churches, the data we collected leaves little doubt about both the evangelistic and missions commitment of these churches.

In the following pages we will look at missions beyond the context of the local church and the immediate community, beyond "Jerusalem" of Acts 1:8. We attempted to discern the mission mindsets of these evangelistic leaders in three different ways. First, we asked leaders to respond to a statement about the "self-preservation" of the local institutional church. Second, we asked them to share their level of missions giving, particularly through the Southern Baptist conduit called the Cooperative Program. Third, we asked them to tell us of any new church starts their churches had implemented in the past twelve months. After receiving this data, I wished that we had asked about church starts over a longer period. I was amazed at the churches' responses for only a one-year period.

As we gathered this data and conducted follow-up interviews, we gleaned some valuable insights about mission attitudes. I will conclude the chapter by framing these attitudes in a section called "Ten Mission Myths."

Self-Preservation of the Church

In a previous book[1] I addressed the issue of "status-quo-itis" that is prevalent in many churches in America today. The primary emphasis is the preservation of the institution rather than an outward focus for the kingdom of God. Organization and structure become ends instead of means. Instead of being vehicles and instruments for the kingdom, budgets, buildings, and programs become a focus unto themselves. God wants us to ask: "What is His will for the church?" However, maintenance churches ask: "How much will it cost us?" They skew their priorities by making decisions for the wrong reasons.

I have served as a consultant with hundreds of churches. In addition, I have been in many more churches in other capacities. Without doubt, many American churches are afflicted with status-quo-itis.

Yet an increasing number of churches are moving beyond the mire of the status quo to a new enthusiasm for extending God's kingdom. These churches want to grow, but their own numerical growth is not an ultimate goal. These churches desire to impact God's kingdom as much as possible. They see their local mission field, but they also see mission fields in other states and other nations.

No other group of churches has ever impressed me with their kingdom mindset to the degree of these 576 churches. Their attitude toward the local church is refreshing. "I used to be concerned about the numbers in our church," a Louisiana pastor admitted. "As a result, I worried when attendance was down on a given week, worried when people did not join the church, worried when offerings were low. I was getting my ego fulfilled by the numerical gains of the church."

The pastor's heart was changed during a time of prayer. "I came under deep conviction about my attitude. God seemed to be telling me that His kingdom was bigger than one church. At that point I repented of my sin of self-centeredness and gave the church to God." The results, said the pastor, had two immediate effects. "First, my entire disposition changed. I learned to relax. Even my wife noticed that I worried a lot less. But the big surprise to me was that the numbers actually improved! They may dip again in the future, but I have given them to God no matter what."

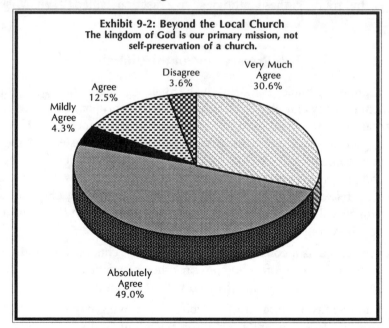

Exhibit 9-2: Beyond the Local Church
The kingdom of God is our primary mission, not self-preservation of a church.

Very Much Agree 30.6%
Disagree 3.6%
Agree 12.5%
Mildly Agree 4.3%
Absolutely Agree 49.0%

Exhibit 9-2 illustrates the attitudes of the leaders of these 576 churches. Nearly 80 percent responded to the statement on the priority of kingdom work in the two most affirmative categories, "very much agree" and "absolutely agree." Few statements of attitude received affirmative responses this high. It is indicative of the commitment of these pastors to see the local church field and beyond.

Giving Pattern to Missions

Twenty/twenty hindsight has shown us some areas that we wished we would have included on the original survey. For mission giving, we simply asked the percentage of the church's annual budget given to the Cooperative Program, Southern Baptist's plan for unified mission giving. As we spoke to the leaders in follow-up interviews, however, we discovered that many of the churches give to the Cooperative Program *plus* other mission organizations and personnel. Still the Cooperative Program level of giving provides some idea of the churches' financial commitment to missions.

These 576 churches give an amazing 9.7 percent to the Cooperative Program, in addition to other mission giving. For the uninitiated, this means that for every one hundred dollars the church receives, it gives to mission causes through the Cooperative Program almost ten dollars. The churches are "tithing" their own budget, plus giving to other mission offerings outside the budget.

As exhibit 9-3 shows, the level of giving does not vary that much according to church size and attendance. No size category of churches averages less than 9 percent to the Cooperative Program. The category with the highest average mission giving is churches with an average attendance ranging from 300 to 499.

In many of our follow-up interviews we asked the pastors to indicate their churches' Cooperative Program giving plans for the future. Without exception we were told that Cooperative Program giving would either increase or remain the same. No respondents indicated that the percentage would decline.

This type of commitment to missions is a further indication of the churches' belief that "giving away" funds does not hurt the church. "We believe in the principle of 'Malachi' giving," said an Ohio pastor. "We preach all the time that Christians should give at least a tithe of their earning to God's church. Why shouldn't the church provide that same example of obedient giving? As a church we corporately tithe our budget (plus 4 percent) to the Cooperative Program. God has always provided for our church financially even though we are giving a large sum to missions."

We have been talking with and about 576 of the most evangelistic churches in America. They have great need for resources to evangelize

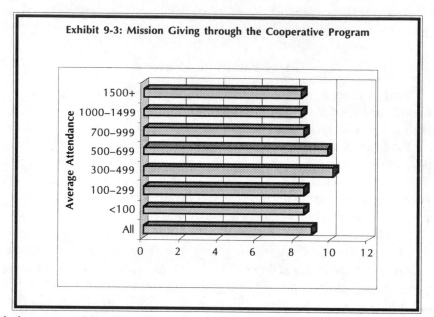

Exhibit 9-3: Mission Giving through the Cooperative Program

their communities. Yet these churches are also committed to reaching the world through their missions giving. They have found that a worldview of missions enhances their commitment to the local community instead of detracting from it.

Evangelistic Churches and Church Planting

In a one-year period, the 576 churches in this study started 140 church-type missions or new churches. In addition, many other types of new starts were reported by these churches. To get a good perspective of this incredible feat, let us look at the track record of the entire Southern Baptist denomination for the past ten years.

From 1984 to 1993 the denomination counted an average of 455 new churches per year. Net change in new churches per year over that same period was an average of 221 churches (see exhibit 9-4). With about 40,000 churches in the denomination, a new church was started each year for every 88 churches. Southern Baptists are among the most aggressive church planters in the nation, so we could assume that 1 new church per year for every 88 churches would be a fairly healthy ratio.

Yet the churches in our survey did much better. The denomination's average is 1 new church for every 88 churches, but this group's average is

Exhibit 9-4: New Southern Baptist Churches

Year	First Time Reporting	Reorganized	Dropped	Net Changed
Source: Strategic Information and Planning Section, The Baptist Sunday School Board, SBC, Nashville, TN.				
1984	450	13	254	209
1985	458	17	236	239
1986	433	10	306	137
1987	404	14	248	170
1988	472	7	198	281
1989	434	9	225	218
1990	445	13	269	189
1991	454	24	231	247
1992	497	17	248	266
1993	499	8	250	257

1 church for every 4 churches! Some of these comments are indicative of the commitment to church planting:

- "Most of our baptisms come from our mission church, rather than the mother church. The new work is our primary source of conversion growth."
- "Don't pour new wine into old wineskins! Start new churches! That's the key to our evangelistic strategy."
- "We have set a goal to start five churches in the next ten years."
- "Church planting is the key to reaching the unchurched. Our mission church is reaching people that our church could never reach!"

The size of the church was not a factor in starting a new church. The smallest and the largest groups of churches were all represented well among the church-planting churches. Exhibit 9-5 shows that more churches were started by mid-sized churches with an attendance of 300 to 499. But thirty-one churches were started by churches with an attendance less than 300.

Post Falls Baptist Church in Post Falls, Idaho, has an attendance of two hundred. But pastor Bill Hohenstreet has not let that size deter the fellowship from starting new works. The church has already started two missions and has a goal of starting a new mission at least every two years.

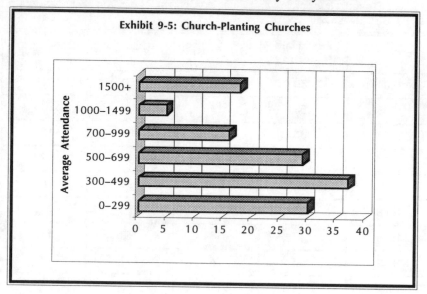

Exhibit 9-5: Church-Planting Churches

Ten "Missions Myths"

Beyond the plethora of statistical data we used to demonstrate the mission mindset of the great majority of these churches, we also heard from the leaders about ten myths their churches had to overcome. In every case where the commitment to missions was made, every myth was proved to be unfounded. They are presented in no particular order.

Myth #1: Missions Giving Takes Away from the Budget

In almost every situation where pastors attempted to lead their churches to greater missions giving, opposition arose because of concerns over the negative impact upon the budget. An Indiana pastor shared these thoughts with us: "We promote individual stewardship with the cliché 'You can't outgive God,' and people believe it. But when we talk about our churches giving away funds to missions, some people begin screaming! 'We can't afford it,' they tell us. It's as if our God can handle our individual financial needs, but He's not big enough to look after the church's needs."

We were given numerous testimonies of how God blessed churches that gave sacrificially to missions. A church treasurer told us, "I didn't see how we could give another 2 percent to the Cooperative Program. We were already giving 11 percent of our budget. But we did it, and we never missed a budget need. It was nothing short of a miracle!"

Several pastors warned us, however, about the possibility of apathy for mission action and outreach when mission giving is strong. "Some Christians like to believe that mission giving is sufficient reason for outreach apathy," said an Arkansas layperson. "They think that they have done their part for the Great Commission by writing a check. We are constantly struggling to communicate that missions means both giving *and* going; it's 'both/and,' not 'either/or.'"

Nevertheless, we were impressed that, despite short-term sacrifices for greater missions giving, all the churches to whom we spoke said that budget needs were met. The leaders believe in a God who will supply *all* their needs.

Myth #2: Starting New Churches Hurts the Mother Church

The second myth is similar to the first. From a human perspective, giving away something means you will have less. But in God's plan of economy, giving for Him means multifold blessings.

It is easy to understand why some people see a newly planted church as a detriment to the mother church. Start-up funds are required. Usually those who go from the mother church to start the mission are among the most faithful givers. An immediate budget impact is felt. Moreover, the people who go are also members in key positions of service. Starting a church *is* a tremendous sacrifice.

Once again God's miraculous plan of economy defies the logic of men and women. A California pastor said, "For almost one year after we started the mission church, we really had to make some adjustments. We didn't have the people or the money that we had become accustomed to." He continued, "But somewhere after that first year, we no longer talked about the great sacrifice. Our ministries were back to full funding, and people were serving. It was as if God had quietly replaced all that we had sacrificed."

Another pain that is often mentioned in starting a new mission is the loss of relationships. Indeed, the families that leave the mother church are often some of the most loved and respected people in the church. Their absence creates a big void. But as we heard repeatedly, God sends new families to the mother church that create new excitement and offer new ministries. Starting a new church is a sacrifice, but it is not a detriment to the mother church. Indeed, we were told, the blessings are usually returned many times over.

Myth #3: Now Is Not a Good Time

If we fallible humans always made decisions on our own sense of timing, we would never have marriages, babies, or houses. The leaders of these evangelistic churches indicated that the timing argument was often used by critics who argued against mission giving or starting new churches.

"There always seems to be reasons why *now* is not the best time to start a church," a Georgia pastor said. "We need additional staff; our building needs renovations; we need to focus on discipleship; and the reasons not to start a mission go on and on. We heard them all, but we eventually moved forward."

Myth #4: We Are Not Large Enough to Start a New Church

One common myth of mission is related to church size. The size issue is typically related to the attendance or to the budget. It is somewhat similar to a recent story I read about the incomes of individuals. According to the story, over three-fourths of Americans feel that their financial needs could be met if they earned an additional ten thousand dollars. Thus the person with the twenty-thousand-dollar income desires thirty thousand dollars, but the person with the thirty-thousand-dollar income requires forty thousand dollars; and so the story goes with each new income level. No one ever feels he has enough income.

Many who object to starting new churches do so because their church is "not quite large enough" to handle such an endeavor. "We need about twenty thousand dollars more in our budget" or "Another fifty in attendance will put us to the point of starting a new work." Interestingly, these excuses occur in all size churches. Refer back to exhibit 9-5. Note that the three smallest categories of churches started the most new works.

One pastor told of a well-meaning friend who criticized the plans to start a new church. The critic brought the pastor extensive statistical data, charts, and graphs showing him how the church could easily start a new church when a new level of growth was realized. The pastor decided to follow his friend's advice. One year later all the key statistical points had been realized. But the friendly critic came back with new data showing that a slightly higher level of growth was needed!

Myth #5: We've Already Done Our Part

Almost every church leader has heard a church member, when he or she is asked to serve in a position of ministry, give the excuse: "I've already done my time for this church!" The words sound like the person has served a few years of prison time.

Some church members think in those terms for the corporate church, especially if the church has started a mission in the past, or has given sacrificially to missions. Their attitude is that the past is sufficient for all ministry and service in the future. Contrast this with Paul's resolve to keep "pressing on toward the goal."

Myth #6: A New Church Will Hurt Other Churches in the Area

"I live near the area where we are planning to start a new church," the troubled church member exclaimed. "Within two miles of the location I counted seven other churches, and none of them are filled to capacity. All that we'll do with our church is hurt the churches in the area."

That voice of protest is registered in similar ways whenever a church prepares to multiply itself. It is perhaps the most common objection raised by Christians who are concerned about new churches. Is this a valid objection? Do we really need new churches? Can we be better stewards of people, time, and money by stimulating growth in existing churches rather than starting new ones?

Rarely does a new church adversely affect other churches in the area. Usually the new church will reach people whom the existing church has not and will not be able to reach. And a new church engenders excitement in the community that benefits all the churches.

Each church in a community has its own identity and niche, an identity which draws certain people that other churches will not draw. The new church adds another identity and niche which can be used to reach new people for the kingdom.

Myth #7: The Community Is Fully Churched

A common argument against starting churches is that an area is "fully churched." This argument carries a twofold meaning: (1) enough churches are already present in the community; (2) the unchurched population is negligible in size. Are such perceptions reality?

In 1820, our nation's population was 9.6 million. With nearly eleven thousand congregations, the new nation had one church for every 875 residents.[2] By 1860, these eleven thousand churches had multiplied to fifty-four thousand, but population had increased to 31.6 million, or one church for every 600 residents.

Unfortunately the trend toward more churches per capita stopped in 1860, and in 1990 the ratio of church to population was still 1:600, the same as in 1860.

A more important consideration than the ratio of churches to the population is the number of Americans who do not attend church at all. In the last quarter of a century our nation has become a true mission field as a growing percentage of the population dropped out of church involvement. Consequently, as many as 85 percent of all churches in America are either plateaued or declining.[3] In 1988, church growth expert Win Arn declared that 71 percent of the total U.S. population is either unaffiliated with any religion or are Christians "in name only."[4] George Gallup's study in the same year showed that 44 percent of the population is solidly unchurched.[5] C. Peter Wagner estimates that the unchurched population in America may be as high as 55 percent.[6]

Our nation does *not* have enough churches. We need tens of thousands of new churches to reach people who have not responded to existing churches. Rarely, if ever, is a part of our population, or any one community, fully churched. A new work may reach those people so that they will become devoted followers of Christ.

Myth #8: International Missions Is Not Our Calling

Some churches will argue that missions giving to areas beyond America is not their specific calling. They see their churches as ministries and missions for the local community.

"I pray that our church will never have that limited vision," a Florida pastor said. "Some of our members question our large giving to foreign missions. When they do, I remind them of Acts 1:8. Whenever we give to foreign missions, we are responding to Christ's call to be witnesses beyond our 'Jerusalem.'"

Myth #9: Boomers and Busters Will Not Contribute to Mission Causes

The much-discussed and sometimes maligned generations called the baby boomers and baby busters are often scapegoats for anemic mission giving. The argument typically goes that these two generations are unwilling to give to causes that they cannot experience themselves. The argument has two major flaws.

First, any attempt to stereotype an entire generation (or two) is an exercise in futility. The boomers alone have 76 million in their generation. It is absurd to believe that this huge group thinks and acts monolithically. Within this generation are some of the most generous givers to missions anywhere. Many are just waiting to be asked. Millions of baby boomers and baby busters have the potential to be the largest financial supporters of missions in history.

A second flaw in the argument is the assumption that missions giving and the experiencing of missions cannot be congruent. Many churches in this study shared with us exciting mission trips in which laypersons experienced firsthand God's work in other nations and people groups.

The oldest baby boomers turned fifty in 1996. As this generation of 76 million continues to mature, we may well see the most significant level of giving to missions ever. The churches in this study refused to accept the conventional wisdom that boomers and busters are anemic mission supporters. To the contrary, many of the churches see some of their highest contributions ever from two generations that others had declared terminally selfish.

Myth #10: Our Small Contribution Really Does Not Make a Difference

A final myth is the idea that one church's contribution to a foreign or home mission cause is almost insignificant in light of the total giving of all churches to such a cause. Why not "keep the funds at home" where they will really make a difference? If every church acted on that logic, no one would give and there would be no missions.

Conclusion: An Attitude of Missions

Lakeview Baptist Church in Auburn, Alabama, is a model church for missions. Pastor Al Jackson has been with the church for over fifteen years. During these years he has led the church from an attendance of approximately 200 to a worship attendance today exceeding 1,200.

Auburn is not a large city. Most of the population is concentrated in the state university located in the town, Auburn University.

Because of the large number of college students in the church, per capita giving is relatively low. Still, in recent years, the church has purchased property and built a beautiful new facility. They have yet to sell their former location. With such a scenario, one might expect that the church could not support mission causes to any significant extent. After all, per capita giving is low and expenses for a new facility are high.

The church has not abandoned local missions. It is consistently one of the leading baptismal churches in the state. But in addition to its local missions effort, Lakeview is known throughout the denomination as one of the great supporters of missions around the world. Here are a few of the evidences of Lakeview's commitment under the leadership of Al Jackson.

- The church is a significant giver to the Cooperative Program, to special missions funds, and to individual missionaries.
- Dozens of missionaries around the nation and around the world have come from Lakeview.
- Missionaries are frequent speakers in the pulpit of Lakeview.
- Pastor Al Jackson prays for individual missionaries by name every day.
- The church's prayer ministry remembers the missionaries continuously.
- Numbers of persons from Lakeview are currently training in seminaries; many will one day be missionaries.
- Numerous persons go on short-term mission trips each year.

Lakeview Baptist Church, in the providence of God, has been able to baptize hundreds locally, build new facilities, give abundantly to missions causes, and keep an outstanding ministerial staff, all on a budget that is lower than a typical church of Lakeview's size. God has truly blessed the ministry of the church; and He has shown the people of Lakeview that they need not choose between Jerusalem, Judea, Samaria, or the ends of the earth. They can have missions and evangelism taking place in all parts of Auburn without compromising their commitment to be a mission supporter around the world.

Many churches in this study demonstrated that God honors the commitment to missions. Local evangelistic efforts need not conflict or compete with missions giving for causes around the world. This study has shown that local evangelism and worldwide missions can be "both/and" instead of "either/or." Mission-minded churches in this study truly do baptize more!

CHAPTER TEN

Evangelism and Discipleship: "Both/And," Not "Either/Or"

There is considerable evidence which suggests at least one-third and perhaps as many as one-half of all Protestant church members do not feel a sense of belonging to the congregation of which they are members. They have been received into membership, but have never felt they have been accepted into the fellowship circle.

Lyle Schaller

The most significant contribution of the Church Growth Movement has been its insistence that evangelism and discipleship cannot be compartmentalized into two separate disciplines with different emphases. Donald McGavran, the father of the church growth movement, was a missionary to India in the 1930s and 1940s. He lamented that so much activity was taking place in the name of evangelism but that very few disciples were being made. His frustration led him to begin using a new phrase for evangelism, a phrase that was simply named "church growth."

He coined the phrase "church growth" because he saw that the *process* of evangelism, if it is truly effective, must result in the *product* of church growth. In other words, effective evangelism results in fruit-bearing disciples in the local church—church growth. Evangelism that results in "free-floating converts" with no visible commitment to a local church is ineffective evangelism. Effective evangelism is the Great Commission evangelism of Matthew 28:19, evangelism that makes disciples. And disciples are clearly committed followers of Jesus Christ, followers whose commitments are always manifest through the ministry of a local church.

Perhaps one of the most impressive aspects of the churches in this study is their commitment to make disciples. None of the churches indicated that their work was done after a decision was made by a person to receive Christ. Incorporation and active discipleship in the local body were seen as essential.

In the vernacular of some church growth literature, the concern is for both the "front door" and the "back door." A church does not choose to be an evangelistic *or* a discipleship church. Separating evangelism from discipleship has no New Testament foundation. Early believers were always disciples, or else they were not really a part of the church.

Like most church leaders who have a heart for New Testament evangelism, the leaders of these 576 evangelistic churches struggle with the discipleship or assimilation of new believers and new members. We found this to be the most-discussed of all subjects we addressed in the study. In the hundreds of pages of comments we received, comments on discipleship and assimilation easily surpassed all others in number. Nearly one thousand comments about the topic were registered, many of them unsolicited.

An Affirmation of Observations

For two years prior to this study, I held extensive conversations with churches around America. In these churches I discerned nine major emerging trends. One of those trends was the renewal of the Sunday School. In my book *Giant Awakenings,* I note that some of the most dynamic churches in our nation are returning to the basics of what has been perceived to be a traditional methodology—the Sunday School.[1] The study of evangelistic churches confirmed these earlier observations. If anything, the earlier observations were understated, particularly in the area of assimilation.

Please hear and heed the following statement: By an overwhelming response, these evangelistic churches told us that *Sunday School is the key assimilation tool in their churches.* Nothing else was close. Over 90 percent of the churches shared this insight with us. The following are some of their responses to our question, "What specific measures do you take to insure that the people baptized remain involved in the church?"

> "New converts are assigned into discipleship groups for a period of ten to twelve weeks, and then assimilated into Sunday School classes." Gene Swinson, pastor, GraceWay Baptist Church, Augusta, Georgia

"Sunday School is the best way to assimilate new converts. In that setting they build small group relationships." Bill Skaar, pastor, Central Baptist Church, Livingston, Texas

"We plug the new converts into a small group relationship through the Sunday School as quickly as possible. The key is to build relationships." Robert Jackson, pastor, Peninsula Baptist Church, Mooresville, North Carolina

"'Care leaders are assigned to individuals who have the responsibility of getting new converts involved in Sunday School as quickly as possible." Lewis McLean, pastor, Stewartsville Baptist Church, Laurinburg, North Carolina

"Emphasis is placed on small group fellowships in the Sunday School for each age group." Houston Roberson, pastor, Bethel Baptist Church, Chesapeake, Virginia

"We emphasize relationships in the Sunday School." Dennis Tabor, pastor, Tenth Street Baptist Church, Palmetto, Florida

"New converts and new members are assimilated into the church through Sunday School small groups and their fellowships." Johnny Williams, minister of music, Morningside Baptist Church, Valdosta, Georgia

"Our approach is threefold. We have new member classes, one-on-one discipleship, and we plug them into Sunday School as soon as possible." Leslie Williams, minister of education, Wayside Baptist Church, Miami, Florida

"New converts are best assimilated through small groups in the Sunday School." Randall Reeves, minister of music, First Baptist Church of Saks, Anniston, Alabama

"Our assimilation process is pretty basic: a new members class and the Sunday School." Sammie Daniels, pastor, Park City Baptist Church, Park City, Montana

These quotes are only a sample of the overwhelming response we received affirming Sunday School as the primary assimilation arm of these evangelistic churches. Later in this chapter we will examine the reasons behind this phenomenon. For now, however, we will attempt to evaluate the effectiveness of assimilation in these churches.

How Effective Is Assimilation and Discipleship in the Churches?

We asked church leaders this question: "What percent of those baptized in the last two years continue to be active in the church?" We recognized that their responses would imperfectly indicate assimilation effectiveness for two reasons. First, some new Christians would move to another community—especially military personnel. Second, our study does not have a control group with which to compare assimilation percentages. We can make only subjective assessments about the effectiveness of our study group. Nevertheless, most persons who have been in leadership roles in churches have some insight into "good" assimilation ratios. We will approach the data with that discernment.

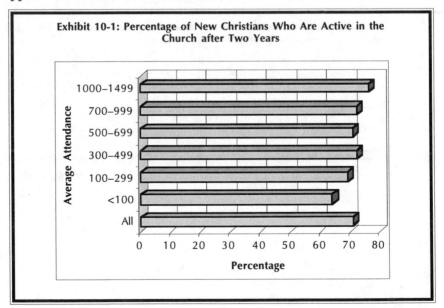

Exhibit 10-1: Percentage of New Christians Who Are Active in the Church after Two Years

Over 71 percent of the new Christians remained active in the church two years after their conversion and baptism. Though we cannot make dogmatic statements about the effectiveness of assimilation, the percentages shown in exhibit 10-1 are very good. I believe this for two reasons. First, simple demographic turnover in two years should result in 15 to 20 percent of the new believers moving to another location. Second, the percentages shown above are for new Christians only, not total new members. These churches have been given the opportunity by God to win people to Christ and bring them into the local fellowship of believers. Because nearly three-fourths of the newly baptized are still in the churches two years later, it appears that the churches responded to the challenges well.

The assimilation rates of larger churches were pleasantly surprising. In fact the best assimilation percentage was for churches with an attendance between 1,000 and 1,499. Though the rate dropped ten points for churches with an attendance over 1,500, the assimilation rate for these largest churches was about the same as churches with an attendance of 100 to 299.

Major Principles of Assimilation and Discipleship

Numerous methodologies for assimilation and discipleship emerged in this study. As we will see shortly, the Sunday School methodology was the overwhelming choice for discipleship among the 576 churches. Yet before we discuss methods, let us examine three major principles the leaders shared with us.

Though the methodologies were many, we found that the most effective assimilation took place where churches were developing disciples through three key foundational elements: expectations, relationships and involvement. Exhibit 10-2 illustrates this reality as a pyramid. The foundation has three corners (expectations, relationships, and involvement). The apex represents assimilation.

Where only one or two of these elements were present, assimilation was the least effective. Churches that were truly making lasting disciples nurtured relationships, raised expectations, and opened doors to involvement in ministry.

Expectations

One church in our study implemented the following requirements for membership:

1. A ten-week membership class.

2. A four-hour session on understanding and discovering spiritual gifts.

3. Placement in some level of ministry.

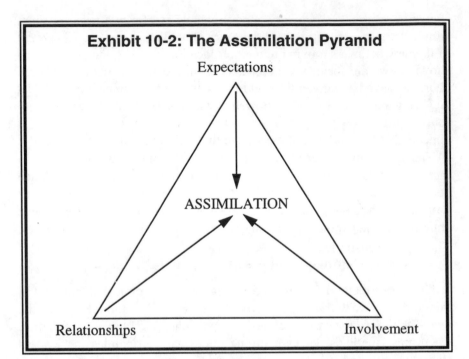

Exhibit 10-2: The Assimilation Pyramid

Expectations

ASSIMILATION

Relationships   Involvement

Repeatedly we heard from church leaders who were tired of low expectations that resulted in weak commitment among church members. A Michigan pastor said, "I've been in churches all my life where church membership means no more than a group of people yelling 'Amen' after someone walks the aisle. That is nothing like the New Testament pattern of total commitment and discipleship. We have weak churches with apathetic members because we place no biblical expectations on them!"

One pattern that emerged from this study was that an increasing number of churches were making membership more difficult. A Tennessee minister of education said that this new paradigm has not come painlessly: "Many of our church members do not like our new membership requirements. They feel that any Christian has a right to be a member of our church. We are making the transition, but it is difficult."

Indeed, some church leaders noticed a decline in membership additions when expectations were raised. "We were adding about seventy new members a year before we raised the membership standards," an Alabama associate pastor told us. "The numbers were cut in half for about eighteen months after we required membership classes and ministry placement. But now we're almost back to seventy each year, and our back door is almost completely closed!"

The most successful assimilation churches addressed the issues of expectations, relationships, and involvement. When even one of these three aspects was missing, assimilation was much less effective. And the foundation that was most likely to be missing was expectations. Church leaders told us that it was the most difficult to implement and the most painful during transition.

Relationships

Almost every book that has been written on assimilation and discipleship stresses the importance of new members developing relationships. These evangelistic leaders agreed. Relationship building was a key concern in their assimilation processes.

Most pundits on assimilation stress that a new member must establish from two to seven "meaningful relationships" within a short period, usually less than one year after becoming a part of the fellowship. Respondents to our survey indicated that assimilation was much easier if relationships already existed between a current member and a new member before the new member joined the church.

Willow Creek Community Church has taught this same lesson. In the formative years of the church, the young members were inviting their friends and co-workers to the church's exciting seeker services. Relationships had already been established before a new person came to the church. A sense of belonging was natural as friends enjoyed the fellowship of one another. As the fame of the church grew, however, the unchurched Harrys and Sallys started attending based on the reputation of Willow Creek alone. The natural relationship pattern was no longer in place for a large number of people. In the early nineties, attendance began dropping a bit as the back door opened wider.

In 1993 Willow Creek began restructuring their small group ministry. They recognized the need for new believers to begin relating to other Christians. Once the church enhanced the small group ministry, attendance again began to increase.[2]

Relationship building is key. Though Sunday School is the primary relational ministry of these evangelistic churches, other effective methodologies will be explained later in this chapter.

Involvement

The third requisite for effective assimilation in these churches was ministry involvement. Some churches required ministry involvement; others strongly encouraged it. Most congregations resisted this, but it was the most effective approach for assimilation.

Most of the churches, however, simply encouraged ministry involvement. Membership would be granted regardless of any ministry commitment, though the church expected some level of ministry involvement.

In the area of ministry involvement, the most noticeable trend was the emphasis placed on spiritual gifts. Many of these churches offered (a few required) training sessions for persons to learn about spiritual gifts and to discover their own gifts. These sessions often included a time to take a spiritual gift inventory. Once a person knew his or her spiritual gifts, he or she would be given the opportunity to become involved in a ministry that best "fits" the gift mix.

What Are the Assimilation Methodologies?

All assimilation methodologies of the 576 evangelistic churches were implemented to address one or more of the three major principles: expectations, relationships, and involvement. Sunday School was the only methodology used to address all three principles. And only a minority of the churches said that their Sunday School was effective in all three areas.

Sunday School as the Assimilation Arm

Relationships do not develop in large groups; they grow in one-on-one settings and in small groups. These Southern Baptist evangelistic churches told us clearly that their primary small group methodology is the Sunday School. How did the Sunday School fare in the three major principles of assimilation?

Relationship Building. The strength of Sunday School for assimilation was building relationships. Leaders knew that worship services were the front door, but they also knew the Sunday School was important to close the back door. We were amazed at the sheer volume of responses we received about Sunday School and its assimilation opportunities.

A pastor and worship leader spoke with us about the relationship between these "two doors": worship and Sunday School. The worship leader was grateful for the new emphasis on worship in American churches. "There is definitely a worship renewal taking place in our nation's churches. It's exciting to see the exciting changes taking place. I am not surprised that worship has become the front door. I can easily see how an unbeliever can really sense the presence of God in many churches. When authentic worship took place in the early church, the non-believers on the outside were amazed. And many were won to Christ."

The worship leader, however, pleaded for balance. "We must always realize that biblical growth is both authentic worship and disciple-making community in small groups. A church with an overemphasis of one aspect over another is out of balance."

The pastor added, "In many churches outside Southern Baptist circles, a small group renewal *is* taking place, and it's getting a lot of publicity. The idea of building community in a small group is a hot topic today. But we Southern Baptists need to realize that we have always had a community- and disciple-making small group. It's called Sunday School. That is our small group. And I know I am biased, but I believe that Sunday School is the best small group approach yesterday or today!"

Raising Expectations. Leaders also saw Sunday School as a means to increase expectations of members. We were told that a healthy Sunday School nurtures a high level of accountability and expectations. In a healthy Sunday School class, strong biblical teachings are taking place. Nothing can engender a sense of our Christian responsibility better than the clear teachings of God's Word.

A healthy Sunday School class expects its members to be present for weekly teachings, for ministry involvement within the group, and for out-reach beyond the group. Of course, none of the leaders of these churches claimed to have the perfect Sunday School, but many spoke excitedly about particular classes.

"We hold up the 'Adult 5 Ladies Class' as a model for the church," a Texas pastor told us. "This class is for ladies, primarily widows, over age seventy. Now most people would think that a group this age would be in an idle gear. Not these women!" He shared with us that the key to the class's success is its expectations. "The teacher of the class is seventy-four years old, and she has a motto for the class: 'Don't come if you won't work.' Everybody does something in that class, from outreach visits to cooking for others to making telephone calls. The class has defied all demographic trends and increased in attendance 100 percent in three years!"

Involvement. Perhaps the greatest struggle for many Sunday School organizations has been the third principle or foundation of the pyramid—involvement. By involvement we mean serving in a place of meaningful ministry. Sitting in a pew or attending a Sunday School class alone does not constitute involvement as we have defined it.

Leaders of these churches told us that most Sunday School class members, even active members, are not involved in ministry. For many churches this issue is the "missing piece of the puzzle" necessary for significant assimilation to take place.

Sunday School *does* have the potential, however, to be that missing piece. In the older ladies' Sunday School class just mentioned, almost three-fourths of the class are involved in meaningful ministry. They have discovered that Sunday School offers many ways to be involved. In a healthy, functioning Sunday school class, every class member sees himself or herself as a minister.

New Members' Class

The second most frequently mentioned methodology for assimilation and discipleship was a new members' class. We heard of classes that were completed in one afternoon to those that went for several months consecutively. The variety of approaches to these classes can be gleaned from the respondents' own words:

> "We have a six-week new members' class that takes place during the Sunday School hour."

> "Our new members' class goes for twelve weeks and stresses the basic doctrines of the faith."

> "The purpose of our new members' class is to help people discover and utilize their spiritual gifts."

> "I [the pastor] lead a membership class for four hours on Sunday afternoon."

> "Our three-week new members' class is followed by deacons' visits in the homes to see if further help is needed or if questions are unanswered."

"The pastor leads a six-week class called 'New Horizons.'"

"We have a ten-week study class for new Christians. For new members who are already Christians, we ask them to attend a four-week training session for involvement in ministry."

"Our new members have an orientation session where they learn about our church and Baptist beliefs."

"The pastor teaches a thirteen-week new members' class followed by a quarterly fellowship meal."

We received over three hundred comments about new members' classes. The responses were diverse but they focused on *expectations*. (See again the assimilation triangle in exhibit 10-2.) Whereas Sunday School has at least two or three strong foundations, the new members' class rarely engenders lasting relationships, and few persons in these classes get involved in ministry. The classes focus on the expectations of a Christian or the expectations of new members. Several examples are noteworthy.

- *Doctrinal instructions*: These are the truths of God's Word. Expectations are that you will be obedient to His call.
- *Church orientation*: Here are some basic facts about our church. We want you to be informed because you are expected to be a contributing member in service and money.
- *Ministry opportunities awareness*: There are many places of service in our church. Where would you like to serve?
- *Learning the purpose or vision of the church*: God has called our church for a specific purpose at a specific time. How will you contribute to this purpose?

A new members' class, we were told, is effective to a point. It can contribute significantly to the "expectations" foundation of assimilation. Its role in strengthening relationships and engendering involvement in ministry, however, is minimal.

"Assigned" Relationships

Some churches assigned a person or persons to a new member in order to help that person establish relationships in the church. The most common example was the assignment of a deacon and spouse to a new member, where the deacon's family would be involved in varied activities to get to know the new member.

Rarely did we hear of this approach as the only way a church was attempting to assimilate new members. Indeed we rarely heard that this approach was the lone method used to help establish relationships.

A Tennessee pastor explained, "The 'buddy system,' as we call it, has limited benefit. If it is well done, the new member will have a greater appreciation for the church and the person who initiates the relationship. It is even possible that a healthy, long-term relationship could develop between the two members." Most of the time, the pastor said, the impact is negligible. "The downside of this approach is that you are attempting to create relationships artificially. We have seen a few cases of severe personality conflicts. The church would have done better in those examples to do nothing."

One-on-One Discipleship

One-on-one discipling carries the same warnings as assigned relationships if the discipler and disciple are not free to choose each other. In most churches, however, discipling relationships develop more naturally. A good one-on-one discipling situation will help build relationships and increase expectations of the new member or new Christian. Most of the respondents indicated very limited success in this approach's leading to greater ministry involvement of the new member.

While this is one of the better assimilation or discipleship approaches, no church reported complete satisfaction with this methodology. The primary problem, we were told, was finding enough committed disciplers who were willing to give the hours necessary to such a labor-intensive responsibility. And usually the ones who offered their services as discipler were some of the busiest church members.

Ministry-Discovery Classes

About one-third of the respondents indicated that their churches offer ongoing classes to help place people into ministry. Some merely give people information about what they can do in a church, but others are much more intense.

The most common of the ministry-discovery classes was mentioned earlier: spiritual-gift classes. Though no two churches do these classes in an identical fashion, many of the respondents indicated some common approaches:

- Biblical teachings on the types of spiritual gifts, the purpose of spiritual gifts, and the use of spiritual gifts.
- Some means, often a spiritual gifts inventory, to help Christians discover their own spiritual gifts.
- Assistance to learn how one's spiritual gifts may be used in real-life ministry, particularly in the ministry opportunities within the church.
- Placement in ministry.

These classes fill a void that other assimilation methodologies have had difficulty filling. They are specifically designed to contribute to the "involvement" foundation of the assimilation pyramid. The classes are rarely designed to engender relationships, though they can contribute to increasing expectations for ministry, the third foundation of the pyramid.

Covenant Agreements

A few churches reported using covenant agreements as an assimilation approach. Because those who mentioned it were so excited about it, we will take a few moments to explain.

In churches with a covenant agreement, persons receive membership rights, privileges, and responsibilities after agreeing to certain expectations and stipulations. Some of the different expectations that were mentioned included:

- An agreement to be involved in some ministry of the church.
- A pledge to give 10 percent or more of one's income to the ministry of the church.
- A promise not to be involved in malicious talk against the church, its leadership, and its members.
- A commitment to attend on a regular basis as much as it is physically possible.
- A commitment to prayer, regular Bible study, and sharing of one's faith.

Of course, not all of the covenant-agreement churches included all of these stipulations. But some of the churches included more. Again, several pastors indicated that they would like to implement more demanding membership requirements. "We've come to think of church membership as nothing more than being on a roll. I can't believe that we even use the phrase 'inactive members.' That should be a contradiction in terminology!"

Why then are not more churches implementing such covenants? "Quite honestly," an Alabama pastor admitted, "it's a matter of survival. Our church is just not ready for such a radical change. In time, maybe, but not now."

The *Experiencing God* Factor

Experiencing God is a Southern Baptist-originated study about discerning the will of God. Specifically, it is an approach that asks what God is doing in this world so that we might be a part of His blessings. The impact of this study on churches and Christians across this nation has been incalculable. There may be no other discipleship instrument used today that is changing lives to the extent of *Experiencing God*. Over 62 percent of the churches in this survey (362 of the 576 churches) have used the discipleship study in their churches. Most of them use it on a continuous basis. We heard from many church leaders about its life-changing impact on members. Exhibit 10-3 shows the percentage of churches by size that use *Experiencing God* as a discipleship instrument.

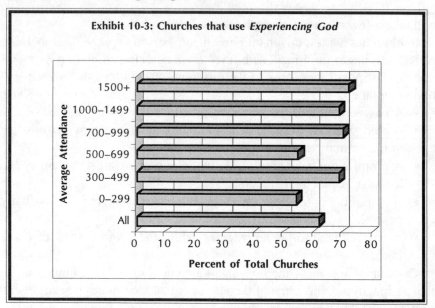

Exhibit 10-3: Churches that use *Experiencing God*

Among the churches that use *Experiencing God*, 16.5 percent of resident membership had been through the program at the time of our survey. If our study group is representative of the entire denomination, over

1.5 million Southern Baptists would have gone through the program. The impact of *Experiencing God* upon churches and Christians is difficult to measure, but it is undoubtedly a major development of the past few years.

Assimilation and Discipleship Methodologies on the Assimilation Pyramid

Perhaps the most insightful information we received from the churches regarding assimilation is: three key elements are necessary for effective assimilation to take place—expectations, relationships, and involvements. Exhibit 10-4 shows the methodologies we just discussed on the assimilation pyramid with the three foundational principles.

The pyramid shows that these churches have developed or utilized various methods to disciple and assimilate new members and new Christians. The emphasis of these methodologies is largely upon expectations and relationships. The greatest need is to develop other methods or create new ways to get more people involved in ministry.

Conclusion: Disciples, Not Converts

Most of the 576 churches in this study are making disciples, not just making converts. They are reaching persons with the gospel of Jesus Christ, but they are seeing them mature into fruit-bearing disciples in a local church. They are truly seeking to be obedient to the Great Commission of Matthew 28:19.

But while these churches have made significant strides toward becoming disciple-making churches, their leaders confess that assimilation is an ongoing struggle and challenge. A California pastor expressed it well when he said, "Losing a member or seeing a member become less and less active is one of my greatest pains. It just makes me sick!"

Some data we shared with you relate to methodologies that have been used for many years. But some represent emerging trends. I make no claim to foresee the future, but I will share some projections based on the information we received from these churches.

1. *Sunday School will continue to grow in importance.* A worship renewal has been underway for almost three decades. I think a Sunday School renewal is imminent. Perhaps it has already begun. Certainly the importance of Sunday School as an assimilation arm of the church is clearly recognized by outstanding churches.

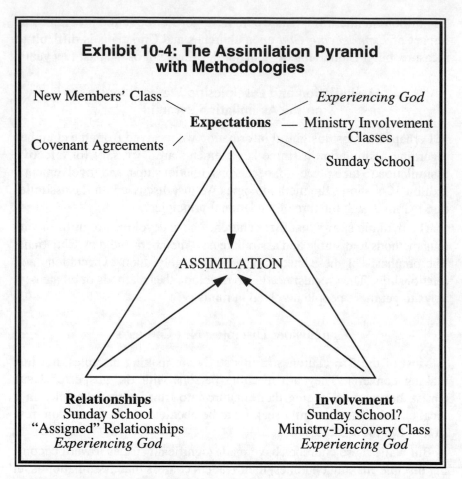

Exhibit 10-4: The Assimilation Pyramid with Methodologies

New Members' Class

Experiencing God

Expectations — Ministry Involvement Classes

Covenant Agreements

Sunday School

ASSIMILATION

Relationships
Sunday School
"Assigned" Relationships
Experiencing God

Involvement
Sunday School?
Ministry-Discovery Class
Experiencing God

2. *Interest will increase in spiritual gifts for assimilation purposes.* Interest in spiritual gifts has been strong for twenty years, but it has not yet peaked. Improved and comprehensive spiritual gift inventories may prove to be one of the hottest-selling products to churches.

3. *Some churches will seek to make membership more meaningful and more difficult.* One reason the back door of many churches is so wide open is because front door issues were not properly addressed. Most Rotary Clubs require higher levels of commitment than most churches! It is little wonder that the drop-out rate in churches across our nation is so high.

High-expectation churches may become more common in the twenty-first century. The demands of discipleship may be expressed more clearly through the expectations of church members.

I do not think we have fully comprehended the impact of *Experiencing God* upon churches. Such an understanding is a study needed greatly for the future. We can safely say that the impact of the program has been phenomenal, but the future impact may even be greater. Keep in mind that over 60 percent of the churches in this study had an ongoing program of *Experiencing God*. But only 16.5 percent of the resident members in the participating churches had been through the program. The greatest impact is yet to come.

4. *Churches across the land will achieve a greater balance in ministry.* That balance will be evident in emphases on evangelism, missions, social ministries, teaching, and discipleship. Evangelism and missions will continue to be the priority, but greater commitment will be made to ministries that are not specifically evangelistic.

I have been called an "obnoxious optimist" by those who hear of my great hope for the church in America. This study has caused me to be more obnoxiously hopeful than ever before. And our research on churches' assimilation and discipleship efforts has convinced me that the back door is beginning to close.

CHAPTER ELEVEN

Miscellaneous Matters and Important Lessons

You sure do ask a lot of questions!
Pastor of a church in this study, commenting
to the author after two hours of interviews

Every time I look at the statistical data, the returned surveys, the lengthy quotes and interviews typed by my secretary and doctoral students, I seem to find new information. I have attempted to communicate most of this information, to you but, undoubtedly, I will uncover something new after this book is published.

A significant portion of the survey was not communicated in previous chapters, so I am using this chapter to catch up a bit. Therefore, this material may seem a bit disjointed, but the data is interesting. I will reserve most of my comments for the twelve summary lessons at the conclusion of the chapter.

Miscellaneous Material and Matters

Most of the information which follows will give you an idea of the type of churches in this study. Thus far you have seen the churches identified by denomination, age, location, and size. Now you will see the further identity marks of setting, racial composition, socioeconomic composition, and educational level of the pastor, to name a few.

Setting of the Churches

Most but by no means all of the churches surveyed were suburban. Sufficient setting diversity allowed us to assess different kinds of churches.

We were gratified to learn that 53 of the 576 churches (9.3 percent of the total) were in transition neighborhoods and still were experiencing evangelistic growth.

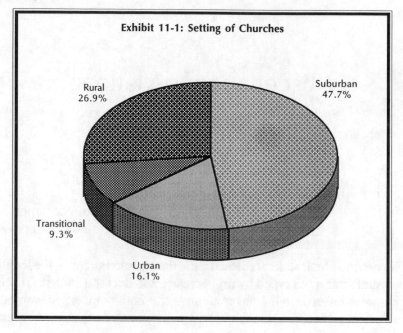

Exhibit 11-1: Setting of Churches

Rural 26.9%

Suburban 47.7%

Transitional 9.3%

Urban 16.1%

Racial and Ethnic Composition of Churches

Most of the 576 churches provided us with a racial composition of their memberships. As exhibit 11-2 indicates, most of the churches are predominantly white. In every size category, the percentage of whites was never lower than 87 percent.

The largest churches (1,500 and above) were the most racially diverse. These churches were 87 percent white, 9 percent black, and 4 percent Asian and Hispanic. The smaller churches tended to be the most predominantly white.

Socioeconomic Composition of Church

Nearly 60 percent of the resident membership was classified as middle class. Some persons may be surprised that over 23 percent of the membership of these churches is lower class socioeconomically (lower and upper-lower). Only 2.4 percent of the churches' membership is upper class.

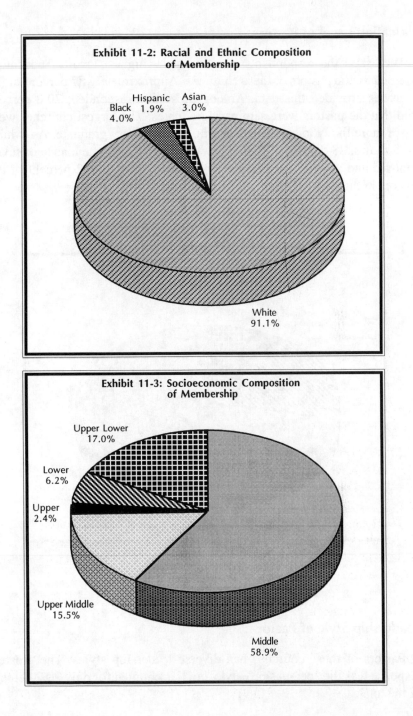

Exhibit 11-2: Racial and Ethnic Composition
of Membership

Hispanic 1.9%
Asian 3.0%
Black 4.0%
White 91.1%

Exhibit 11-3: Socioeconomic Composition
of Membership

Upper Lower 17.0%
Lower 6.2%
Upper 2.4%
Upper Middle 15.5%
Middle 58.9%

Education Level of Pastors

We asked the respondents to give us the highest level of education attained by the pastors of these churches. Approximately 87 percent of the churches provided this data. Among those that responded, 70.8 percent said that the pastors were seminary graduates. The largest churches were much more likely to have a pastor who is a seminary graduate. As exhibit 11-5 shows, 88 percent of pastors in churches with an attendance of seven hundred and above were seminary graduates. Less than 2 percent of the pastors in these larger churches had less than a college degree.

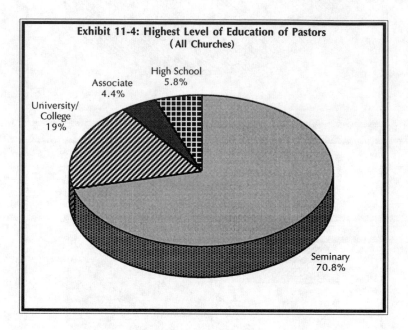

Exhibit 11-4: Highest Level of Education of Pastors (All Churches)

High School 5.8%
Associate 4.4%
University/College 19%
Seminary 70.8%

Leadership Style of Pastor

Pastors of these churches had diverse leadership styles. The greatest response was the "persuasion" style, but it accounted for only 30.2 percent of the total.

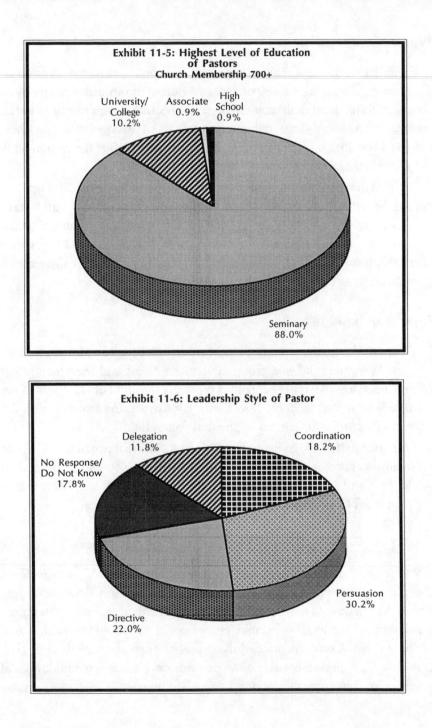

Exhibit 11-5: Highest Level of Education of Pastors
Church Membership 700+

University/College 10.2%
Associate 0.9%
High School 0.9%
Seminary 88.0%

Exhibit 11-6: Leadership Style of Pastor

Delegation 11.8%
Coordination 18.2%
No Response/Do Not Know 17.8%
Persuasion 30.2%
Directive 22.0%

Type of Congregation

Exhibit 11-7 defines four different orientations toward the mission of the church. We asked the respondents to rank them in order of the most dominant to the least dominant. We were expecting a high response to the "outreach" mission since our study was about evangelistic churches. Exhibit 11-8 does indeed show that well over one-half of the respondents did say that their church was outreach-oriented first.

Perhaps the surprising aspect of this response was that *only* 57.6 percent ranked the outreach orientation first. Almost one-fourth of the church leaders categorized their churches as "fellowship" oriented, a view that the church is a sanctuary from the secular world. We did not ask questions about this issue in follow-up interviews to determine possible differences of philosophy.

Sources of Baptisms

The new Christians in these 576 churches can be grouped into two categories. We called the one group "inner" baptisms and the other group "outer" baptisms. An inner baptism is typically the child of members of the church. We wanted to know how many baptisms came from outside the church—as one pastor termed it "the real pagan field."

Well over half of all the baptisms came from "the real pagan field." These evangelistic churches are having an impact in the hard-to-reach unchurched world. Exhibit 11-9 shows that evangelistic churches of all sizes were reaching people for Christ beyond the members of church families.

Twelve Lessons from Evangelistic Churches

My research team and I learned a great deal from these 576 evangelistic churches. Any attempt to summarize these lessons simply does not do justice to the wisdom of these church leaders. Nevertheless, I have attempted the assignment, realizing that much more could and should be said. A few of these lessons were mentioned in an earlier chapter on methodologies. But now I am presenting these lessons not only from a methodological perspective, but from the totality of methodology, theology, and principles.

Exhibit 11-7
Type of Congregation

The following are four different orientations toward the mission of the church. Most congregations are a mixture of the four, but typically one of them is dominant. The first two orientations are "this-worldly" in focus; the latter two are more "other-worldly" in focus. Rank the four in the order of the most dominant to the least for your congregation, one through four.

Activist - This world is the arena of God's redemptive activity and, therefore, the arena in which God calls the congregation to speak out on issues and engage in corporate action, working for social change and transformation toward a more just and loving society.

Civic - This world is the arena in which God calls Christians to act and to take responsibility for public life; however, the civic orientation is more comfortable with existing social and economic institutions. This congregation will use service to the community to reach people for Christ. It is important to be an example of Christ-likeness to the community by showing the love of God in action/service.

Outreach - This congregation will focus on a formal soul-winning program and inviting the unchurched to participate in worship. Members are encouraged to witness to their faith, sharing the message of salvation with those outside the fellowship and lead them to membership in the church.

Fellowship - This orientation encourages the view that the church exists as a sanctuary for the members from the secular world. Nurturing and support are the key focus for the programming of the church. The task is to resist the temptation of contemporary pleasures and lifestyles. These people believe their deepest loyalty belongs to God. Their motivation for witnessing is providing a solution for sin and corruption.

Lesson #1: Evangelism Is Hard Work

An ever-present tension is apparent in the Book of Acts as Luke describes the dynamic evangelistic growth of the early church. Believers were pouring out their lives planting churches, proclaiming the gospel, and defending the faith. But only Jesus saves people. Only the Holy Spirit convicts persons. Only God draws people unto Himself. Still, believers

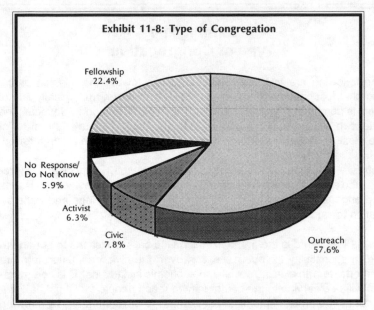

Exhibit 11-8: Type of Congregation

Fellowship
22.4%

No Response/
Do Not Know
5.9%

Activist
6.3%

Civic
7.8%

Outreach
57.6%

worked and worked, some literally giving their own lives, to be God's instruments to spread the gospel.

Laziness could not in any way describe the leaders of these evangelistic churches. The level of commitment necessary for a church to have an evangelistic impact is considerable. There are really no shortcuts.

We spoke with church leaders who had been "pressing on" for the gospel at the same church for ten, fifteen, and twenty years. Sometimes they feel as if they are on a treadmill with little or no progress being made. Many expressed that they had experienced frustrations, aggravations, and discouragement. But they pressed on. They persisted. And now many are seeing the fruit of their labor and the blessings of God.

Some pastors, staff, and laypersons look at successful evangelistic churches and try to imitate them. They desire to know the "secret" of their success so that they might emulate it for quick results.

Yet none of these pastors viewed their evangelistic churches as a quick-fix model. They had labored in prayer. They had rejoiced in successes and wept in failures. They learned from their failures so that they might make a difference for the Kingdom. And the people in these churches worked; they toiled for hours a day, seven days a week. They viewed evangelism as the most urgent task of the church so they kept pressing on. Make no mistake about it. Evangelism is hard work.

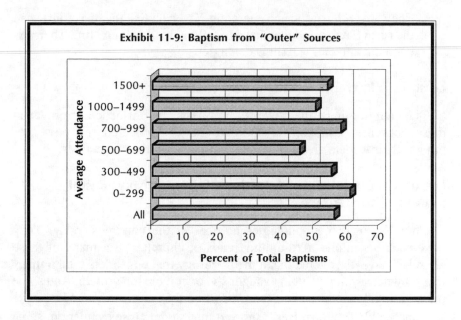

Exhibit 11-9: Baptism from "Outer" Sources

Lesson #2: Leadership's Attitude Is Critical

From these churches we learned that effective evangelism, humanly speaking, is the result of leadership. And the attitude of the leadership is perhaps one of the most critical factors in the growth of the church. What do we mean by leadership's attitude? Perhaps a profile of the leaders will give some insight to this question. Most of these evangelistic leaders exhibited the following attitudes:

- They believe in a supernatural God who is still working in His churches today. They communicate often to the people of the church that "all things are possible through God." They are optimistic, not because they hold some name-it-and-claim-it theology, but because they believe miracles still happen.

- They communicate love, sincere love. They do more than teach that "God so loved the world"; they model God's love in their own lives. Their members know that their pastors love them. And that love is contagious.

- They are happy leaders. Their piety does not make their faces look like freshly eaten lemons. They truly have learned how to "rejoice in the Lord always."

- They are enthusiastic and energetic. They act like they have just seen the risen Savior, and they have to tell the world about Him. Their excitement and enthusiasm is contagious.

Lesson #3: Prayer Is Foundational

One cannot escape the powerful and pervasive influence of prayer in these churches. Evangelistic churches have discovered the power of prayer; their leaders are discovering that power in their own lives.

Lesson #4: Church Growth Methods Do Not Always Result in Evangelistic Growth

Church growth methodologies number in the hundreds today. They have been tested and tried by thousands of churches. But many of these churches have discovered that a methodology that engenders total numerical growth may not result in evangelistic or conversion growth. And some methodologies produce short-term growth only.

Chapter 2 ("Ten Surprises") showed that, under close evaluation, some highly acclaimed methodologies may not be evangelistic, whereas some of the methodologies that have been written off may be still some of the best ways to reach people for Christ. If evangelistic growth is the measuring rod, we may very well see a change in emphasis. Conversion growth is a better measurement for effectiveness than total growth. These church leaders are first concerned about Kingdom growth.

Lesson #5: The Bible Is the Best Book on Evangelism and Church Growth

The strong emphases on expository preaching and Sunday School (or other small groups) has shown us the incredible hunger for biblical teaching. Most of these churches are making disciples because they are helping Christians mature in the "meaty" teachings of Scripture. And the believers who are firmly grounded in the Word, we discovered, were more likely to be evangelistic and outreach-oriented.

Lesson #6 Evangelism Is the Priority but Balance Is Important

We learned from these churches that evangelism was their priority ministry. An Arizona layleader told us, "Nothing is more important than the eternal destiny of a person. Evangelism must ever be at the forefront of our priorities."

But the evangelistic priority did not mean that these churches were one-dimensional in their ministries. We found churches with extraordinary emphasis on missions, discipleship, and social ministries. Evangelistic emphasis seems to enhance these other ministries. The churches are well balanced in their ministries, but many reminded us repeatedly that evangelism comes first.

Lesson #7: Pastoral Tenure Is Important

A long pastorate at one church does not guarantee evangelistic growth, but it is almost a prerequisite for sustained evangelistic growth. After speaking to pastors who had been at churches for many years, we discerned a pattern common in their tenure. Roughly speaking, it went something like this.

Years 0–2: Honeymoon. The members see the pastor as omnipotent and inerrant. Everything he does is lauded and praised. Excitement abounds and enthusiasm grows.

Years 3–6: Trial and testing. Church members see the pastor as anemic and errant. Questions begin to rise about his leadership abilities, his preaching, his pastoral care skills, his wife, and the color of his ties. Most divorces in marriages occur after a "honeymoon period" of two to three years. Most pastors leave frustrated, or they are force-terminated during that time period.

Years 7–12: Ministry and growth. Members now call him "pastor" and mean it. He has survived the trial and testing period. He has withstood the criticisms, and many of his critics have left the church (especially after his seven-week sermon series on Ananias and Sapphira). These can be among the most fruitful years of a pastor's ministry.

Years 13–15: Reevaluation. The pastor is considering whether this church will be a lifetime ministry, or if he will move on. Few pastors continue beyond this length of tenure.

Years 16 and on: Renewed ministry and growth. If the pastor stays to this point, he is probably committed to a lifetime ministry at the church. The length of productivity of this period is largely dependent upon the pastor's attitude. If he begins to act like retirement is near, the productivity of ministry and growth is over.

Most Southern Baptist pastors leave their churches during the trial and testing period. They have not even entered into the ministry and growth period. However, the average tenure of pastors in this study was 7.3 years, and many of the leaders had longevity far beyond the average.

Lesson #8: Effective Evangelism Is Both Relational and "Going"

Contemporary church growth and evangelism literature favors the relational aspects of evangelism over the confrontational. We learned from these churches that effective evangelism is both relational and confrontational. The churches stress the importance of developing relationships with the nonbeliever so that lifestyle witness can be effective. But they also insist that evangelism is "going," moving beyond the comfort zones of home or work and confronting persons with the claims of Jesus Christ. We were told that an overemphasis of one approach at the expense of the other creates an unhealthy imbalance and environment.

Lesson #9: Effective Discipleship Has Three Foundations: Expectation, Relationship, and Involvement

One of the more valuable lessons we learned was that an effective discipleship and assimilation ministry must have *all* of three foundations. First, the church should have high expectations of its members, particularly new members. A direct correlation exists between the depth of commitment expected and communicated to a church member, and the likelihood of that member staying active in the church.

Second, relationships must be developed for a person to remain in a church. Churches approach this need in varied ways.

Finally, churches should have different ways to involve people in ministry. Mere attendance, even if it is faithful and regular, is not enough to retain people. Involvement is mandatory.

Lesson #10: Evangelistic Churches Give Sacrificially

These churches taught us a valuable lesson on stewardship. We most often relate giving and biblical stewardship to the individual. But stewardship principles also apply to the corporate body. Many of these evangelistic churches are sacrificial givers. They give money to missions, but they also "give away" people and other resources to start new churches. They give their time to mission needs in the community, in home missions, and even in missions around the world.

Most church leaders fret about losing money and people, but leaders of these churches believe God will bless churches that give joyously and abundantly.

A recent article on "megashifts" in the church stated that people in the church today have a myopic perspective. Global thinking is giving way to local thinking only. Missionary forces are declining, the article said, and giving to foreign missions is down.[1] This may indeed be a trend but not among our 576 churches. These churches believed in "both/and" obedience to Acts 1:8.

Lesson #11: Theology Is Related to Evangelistic Growth

Two theological issues were clearly important in these churches. The first issue preceded the second.

First, a high view of Scripture does not guarantee evangelistic growth, but a more liberal approach to the Bible virtually guarantees evangelistic apathy, as Dean Kelley has shown. Why? The second issue will explain.

Second, these church leaders had a literal understanding of hell and heaven. They believed saved persons go to heaven and lost persons suffer eternally in hell. Their methodologies emanated from their theology. Those evangelistic methodologies reflected the great urgency of their ministry to share the gospel of Jesus Christ.

Lesson #12: The Basics Are Important

New emphases were evident on biblical literacy and depth; on sharing the gospel in the community; on prayer; on discipleship; on preaching; and on worship. The churches did not necessarily reject new and innovative methodologies, but they continued to focus on the basics.

Evangelism for a New Millennium: With Gratitude to These Churches

As we enter a third millennium since the birth of Christ, the challenges for the church are great. To read some of the Christian prognostications, however, one might wonder if the church has a chance. From my perspective, many churches, especially those in this study, are taking on more and more characteristics of first-century churches. And our world is taking on more and more characteristics of Graeco-Roman society. The church flourished in those early years. I am naive enough to believe that God's Spirit can send another first-century revival in the twenty-first century.

The church will continue to reach out to those often-discussed generations called the baby boomers and baby busters in the next century. I'm a boomer. Some boomers are over fifty. Before we know it, AARP will be full of boomers! Next are the skeptical busters. But then another generation, seventy-two million strong, will become adults early in the twenty-first century. I have named this new generation, those born between the years 1976 and 1994, the "bridgers" since they will bridge two millennia. In a later book I want to address the challenges of reaching the bridgers.

Can the churches of the twenty-first century reach the aging boomers, the skeptical busters, and the growing bridgers? After spending nearly two years with some of the most evangelistic churches in America, my level of optimism is running high. It has been my prayer that the messages from these churches would be communicated clearly to Christians through this book. We have seen churches in every conceivable geographical location, of every size, in every socioeconomic position, of all ages, and of a multitude of styles and approaches, reach people for Christ. Their message is loud and clear. God is blessing these churches, and He can bless yours.

I thank God for the men and women of these 576 churches. They have been a source of great encouragement and inspiration to me.

And I especially want to thank you, the reader, for listening to the messages of these churches. You may not have agreed with everything that you heard, but you were willing to listen. I pray that, somewhere in the pages, charts, and graphs of this book, you heard a quiet voice. And that voice was neither that of the author nor of the leaders of these churches. That voice was the voice of God. Perhaps He gave you a word of encouragement. Perhaps a word of instruction. Or exhortation. Or edification. I pray that somehow you heard His voice.

Since it is His voice we desire to hear above all others, I invite you to join me in my own heartfelt prayer for me and my church. Perhaps the prayer could be your own.

*D*ear Father. Thank You for allowing me to get a glimpse of Your work in these churches. Thank You for the leaders You have given the churches and the wisdom You have given the leaders. Lord, show me how I might learn from these churches. Help me to see the world through Your eyes. Show me how to share the good news of Your Son in a difficult world today. And give me the wisdom to know how best to be obedient to the Great Commission. May it all bring glory to Your name. In the name of Your Son Jesus I pray.
   Amen.

APPENDIX 1

Participating Churches

STATE	CITY	CHURCH	PASTOR
Alabama	Alexandria	Mount Zion Baptist Church	Garry Ragsdale
	Andalusia	Harmony Baptist Church	Denny Couturie
	Anniston	Gladeview Baptist Church	William E. Rice
	Anniston	Greenbrier Road Baptist Church	Bill Wilks
	Anniston	Hill Crest Baptist Church	Rick Reaves
	Anniston	First Baptist Church of Saks	Charles L. Owens
	Athens	Lindsay Lane Baptist Church	Dusty McLemore
	Athens	Round Island Baptist Church	William E. Bailey
	Auburn	Lakeview Baptist Church	Al Jackson
	Cropwell	Cropwell Baptist Church	Kenneth Bullard
	Demopolis	Fairhaven Baptist Church	Joseph H. Guthrie
	Dothan	Calvary Baptist Church	Van Gauthe
	Dothan	Heritage Baptist Church	Sidney W. Nichols
	Dothan	Memphis Baptist Church	Ernest C. O'Neal
	Dothan	Ridgecrest Baptist Church	Jerry L. Spencer
	Elmore	Mt. Hebron West Baptist Church	Kenneth R. Clement
	Gadsden	East Gadsden Baptist Church	Gary Rivers
	Grant	First Baptist Church	Anthony M. Barnes
	Headland	Trinity Baptist Church	Donald Moore
	Lacey's Spring	Union Grove Baptist Church	Kenneth Galyean
	Lanett	Happy Valley Baptist Church	Floyd E. Aikens

STATE	CITY	CHURCH	PASTOR
Alabama	Logan	Logan Baptist Church	Stanley A. Graves
	Loxley	Maranatha Baptist Church	Web MacCartee
	Madison	Wall Highway Baptist Church	Sonny Kirk
	Mobile	First Baptist Church, Tillman's Corner	Andy Hepburn
	Montgomery	Taylor Road Baptist Church	Joseph C. Godfrey
	Moody	First Baptist Church	Scott W. Stokes
	Muscle Shoals	First Baptist Church	Jeff L. Noblit
	Oxford	Grace Baptist Church	Clyde N. Roberts
	Phenix City	Grace Baptist Church	Joseph Appiah
	Salem	Concord Baptist Church	Lewis N. Passmore
	Southside	First Baptist Church	William E. Kirkpatrick
	Wetumpka	Santuck Baptist Church	Morgan Bailey
Alaska	Anchorage	Faith Baptist Church	Walter E. Davidson
	Anchorage	Grandview Baptist Church	Robert E. Jones
	Anchorage	Muldoon Road Baptist Church	James Hamilton
	Anchorage	University Baptist Church	Tim Miller
	Eagle River	First Baptist Church	Bob L. Buster
	Kenai	First Baptist Church	Alan D. Nichols
Arizona	Glendale	West Glendale Baptist Church	William Ray
	Green Valley	Green Valley Baptist Church	Glenn D. Lawson
	Mesa	Hi-Way Baptist Church	Woody G. Lewis
	Tucson	First Southern Baptist Church	Ronald L. Hart
	Tucson	Mountain View Baptist Church	Barry Jude
	Yuma	Foothills Southern Baptist Church	Mitchell A. McDonald
Arkansas	Alma	First Baptist Church	Bob Shelton
	Alpena	Osage Baptist Church	Lannie Younger
	Beebe	First Baptist Church	Ronnie L. Mayes
	Camden	Calvary Baptist Church	Don B. Phillips
	Clinton	First Baptist Church	Tommy W. Shaw
	Conway	Friendship Baptist Church	Ken J. Jordan

STATE	CITY	CHURCH	PASTOR
Arkansas	Conway	Oak Bowery Baptist Church	Jack Ruble
	De Queen	First Baptist Church	Faron Rogers
	Forrest City	Good Hope Baptist Church	John D. Webb
	Fort Smith	East Side Baptist Church	Pastorless
	Greenbrier	First Baptist Church	Gary Kirkendoll
	Hampton	First Baptist Church	Dwain Miller
	Hot Springs	Lakeside Baptist Church	Ronnie W. Rogers
	Jonesboro	Nettleton Baptist Church	Stanley H. Ballard
	Marmaduke	First Baptist Church	Roger G. Duffel
	Pangburn	First Baptist Church	Charles Christie
	Paragould	West View Baptist Church	Bengy S. Massey
	Rogers	Charity Southern Baptist Church	John A. Nauman
	Rogers	Immanuel Baptist Church	Thomas E. Hatley
	Springdale	Elmdale Baptist Church	Mark W. Brooks
	Springdale	First Baptist Church	Ronnie W. Floyd
	Texarkana	Trinity Baptist Church	Wallace Edgar
California	Bakersfield	Panama Baptist Church	Larry L. Dotson
	Bakersfield	Valley Baptist Church	Phil A. Neighbors and Roger Spradlin
	Barstow	First Baptist Church	Scott Williamson
	Clovis	Clovis Hills Community Church	Steve Davidson
	Compton	New Brighter Day Baptist Church	Ernest C. Bowdry
	Corona	Olive Branch Community Church	Dewight Riddle
	Fairfield	Temple Baptist Church	Robert D. Lewis
	Fremont	Fremont Bible Fellowship	Horacio Jones
	La Grange	Lake Don Pedro Baptist Church	Hans Frei
	La Puente	Cornerstone International Church	Paul T. Lacanilao
	Lake Forest	El Toro Baptist Church	Ira F. Day
	Lake Isabella	Mountain View Southern Baptist Church	Deryl Lackey
	Lakeside	Lakeside Baptist Church	Robert Walton

STATE	CITY	CHURCH	PASTOR
California	Livermore	Trinity Baptist Church	James A. Meek
	Lompoc	First Southern Baptist Church	J. T. Reed
	Northridge	Mandarin Baptist Church	Daniel C. Hsu
	Oakland	Berkland Baptist Church	Andrew Lee
	Patterson	First Southern Baptist Church	Philip A. Ensley
	Porterville	First Southern Baptist Church	Mike McGuffee
	Redding	Bonnyview Baptist Church	Dennis J. McGowan
	Roseville	West Roseville Baptist Church	Pastorless
	Salinas	North Salinas Baptist Church	W. Bryan Harris
	San Bernardino	Immanuel Baptist Church	Rob Zinn
	San Francisco	Western Hills Church	Karl Sarpalius
	San Mateo	San Francisco Mandarin Baptist	Luke Chu
	Tehachapi	Country Oaks Baptist Church	K. A. Walker
	Turlock	Berkley Avenue Baptist Church	James L. Wilson
	Tustin	First Baptist Church of Irvine	Dudley Briston
	Twentynine Palms	Palms Southern Baptist Church	Lance Baldwin
	Vacaville	First Baptist Church	Leroy Gainey
	Vallejo	Castlewood Baptist Church	Frank D. Ward
	Victorville	Faith Baptist Church	Ron Hogue
	Visalia	Visalia Lahu Baptist Church	Sadudee Harichaikol
Colorado	Arvada	Foothills Community Church	Bryan D. Day
	Colorado Springs	Chapel Hills Baptist Church	William C. Lighty
	Colorado Springs	Pikes Peak Park Baptist Church	Douglas B. Lohrey
	Florence	First Southern Baptist Church	James W. Royal
	Monte Vista	Calvary Baptist Church	Richard M. Nettles
	Northglenn	First Southern Baptist Church	John D. Talbert
	Westminster	First Southern Baptist Church	Ed Gatlin
Connect-icut	Groton	Pleasant Valley Baptist Church	James E. Schneider
	Hartford	Old Ship of Zion Baptist Church	M. Robert McKnight

STATE	CITY	CHURCH	PASTOR
Florida	Carol City	New Life Baptist Church	Joshua M. Garvin
	Clearwater	Countryside Baptist Church	Bruce Crawford
	Cocoa	Clearlake First Baptist Church	Richard L. Miller
	Crestview	Live Oak Baptist Church	Billy W. White
	Daytona Beach	First Baptist Church	Bobby H. Welch
	Dover	First Baptist Church	Steve Bingham
	Eagle Lake	First Baptist Church	David Drake
	Eustis	First Baptist Church	James W. Watt
	Fort Lauderdale	Riverland Baptist Church	Ronald Mensinger
	Fort Myers	McGregor Baptist Church	James Holbrook
	Fort Pierce	Orange Avenue Baptist Church	David Hart
	Fort Pierce	Westside Baptist Church	Dale K. Ingersoll
	Geneva	First Baptist Church	Daryl G. Permenter
	Groveland	First Baptist Church	Charles Dick
	Hernando	Riverside Baptist Church	Charles Brennan
	Highland City	First Baptist Church	Greg L. Douglas
	High Springs	Fellowship Baptist Church	Charles R. Pinkerton
	Holiday	Calvary Baptist Church	Terry McKenzie
	Interlachen	First Baptist Church	James A. Roberson
	Jacksonville	Crown Point Baptist Church	Steven E. Thompson
	Jacksonville	Fort Caroline Baptist Church	Jimmy D. Patterson
	Jacksonville	San Jose Baptist Church	William E. Kirkland
	Jacksonville	Shindler Drive Baptist Church	Jay Huddleston
	Jacksonville	St. Augustine Road Baptist Church	Harper Bumpers
	La Crosse	Lacrosse Baptist Church	Sebby L. Volpe
	Lake City	Hopeful Baptist Church	Rick McCall
	Lake Butler	Providence Village Baptist Church	Alan D. Hammock
	Lakeland	Scott Lake Baptist Church	Stephen B. Henderson
	Lynn Haven	Cook Memorial Baptist Church	Morris W. Denman
	Mary Esther	First Baptist Church	Joe H. Plott

STATE	CITY	CHURCH	PASTOR
Florida	Melbourne	Harbor City Baptist Church	James L. Leftwich
	Miami	Chinese Baptist Church	K. W. Lan
	Miami	Trinity Baptist Church	Victor Reyes-Sotolongo
	Miami	Wayside Baptist Church	Pastorless
	Miami Lakes	Miami Lakes Baptist Church	Brian D. Pipping
	Newberry	Union Baptist Church	Donald J. Knight
	Niceville	Northbay Baptist Church	Warren Fox
	Ocala	Maranatha Baptist Church	Thomas W. Fortune
	Okeechobee	Treasure Island Baptist Church	John Giddens
	Orlando	First Baptist Church of Central Florida	Gene Pritchard
	Palatka	Peniel Baptist Church	Dannie Williams
	Palmetto	Tenth Street Baptist Church	Dennis Tabor
	Panama City	Hiland Park Baptist Church	Donald Pickerill
	Plant City	Shiloh Baptist Church	Joseph A. Bowles
	Sarasota	Sarasota Baptist Church	David E. Clippard
	Sarasota	Southside Baptist Church	R. W. Briant
	Seminole	First Baptist Church	Craig Price
	St. Augustine	Calvary Baptist Church	David E. Beauchamp
	Tampa	Manhattan Baptist Church	Preston T. Bailey
	Tampa	Town 'n' Country Baptist Church	Daniel E. Wade
	Tequesta	First Baptist Church	Kenneth Babrick
	Trenton	First Baptist Church	Ricky R. Lawrence
	Waldo	First Baptist Church	Larry D. Law
	Windermere	First Baptist Church	Mark E. Matheson
	Winter Park	Goldenrod Baptist Church	Ronald N. Potter
Georgia	Adel	Massee Baptist Church	Philip Badley
	Atlanta	Christian Fellowship Baptist Church	Emmanuel L. McCall
	Augusta	GraceWay Church	Gene R. Swinson
	Augusta	Windsor Spring Baptist Church	Steven P. Hartman
	Austell	Friendship Baptist Church	J. R. Shattles

STATE	CITY	CHURCH	PASTOR
	Bowersville	Flat Shoals Baptist Church	Eddy R. Mattison
	Calhoun	Trinity Baptist Church	Ronnie McBrayer
	Canton	Hopewell Baptist Church	Norman R. Hunt
	Carrollton	New Vision Baptist Church	Kenneth Rooks
	Clarkesville	Hollywood Baptist Church	A. Lane Fordham
	Clermont	Concord Baptist Church	Glen E. Cox
	Columbus	Oates Avenue Baptist Church	Doug Grubbs
	Columbus	Southside Baptist Church	John A. Whaley
	Cumming	North Lanier Baptist Church	Rushton S. Ricketson
	Dacula	Hebron Baptist Church	Larry W. Wynn
	Dalton	Macedonia Baptist Church	Steve Flockhart
	Dalton	Mount Rachel Baptist Church	Shane W. Craven
	Douglas	Eastside Baptist Church	John W. Dobbins
	Duluth	Pleasant Hill Baptist Church	D. Franklin Cox
Georgia	Evans	Grace Baptist Church	Bill Hilley
	Evans	West Acres Baptist Church	Larry C. Harmon
	Flowery Branch	Blackshear Place Baptist Church	James W. Austin
	Griffin	Oak Hill Baptist Church	Steve Stewart
	Hampton	First Baptist Church	Terry L. Quick
	Hephzibah	Miracle Baptist Church	John T. Raborn
	Hinesville	South Main Baptist Church	Billy R. Massey
	Kingsland	First Baptist Church	Vernon G. Dillingham
	Leesburg	First Baptist Church	Bobby Harrell
	Lizella	Lizella Baptist Church	M. Allen Hughes
	Loganville	Center Hill Baptist Church	David A. Dills
	Marietta	Johnson Ferry Baptist Church	Bryant Wright
	Marietta	Sewell Mill Baptist Church	John Moody
	McDonough	Eagle's Landing First Baptist Church	Timothy P. Dowdy
	Midway	First Baptist Church	William T. Horstmeyer
	Milledgeville	Victory Baptist Church	Kenneth A. Walker

STATE	CITY	CHURCH	PASTOR
Georgia	Mount Airy	Antioch Baptist Church	Pastorless
	Perry	Houston Lake Baptist Church	A. C. Truluck
	Red Oak	First Baptist Church	William N. Freeman
	Rome	Calvary Baptist Church	Frank G. Wood
	Savannah	Calvary Baptist Temple	Len B. Turner
	Savannah	Chevis Oaks Baptist Church	James Eddy Davis
	Savannah	Immanuel Baptist Church	Stephen E. Batts
	Smarr	New Providence Baptist Church	Stephen R. Darnell
	Snellville	First Baptist Church	James G. Merritt
	Stone Mountain	Rockbridge Road Baptist Church	Floyd Tharp
	Swainsboro	Hillcrest Baptist Church	John R. Strickland
	Tate	Cool Springs Baptist Church	David L. Chancey
	Thomasville	Newark Baptist Church	James C. Bryson
	Toccoa	Hill Street Baptist Church	Paul E. Garrison
	Valdosta	Morningside Baptist Church	Wayne Robertson
	Valdosta	Perimeter Road Baptist Church	Craig Bailey
	Woodstock	First Baptist Church	Johnny Hunt
Hawaii	Kaneohe	Pali View Baptist Church	Stephen D. Murphy
	Mililani	Mililani Baptist Church	C. Eugene Phillips
Idaho	Coeur D' Alene	Emmanuel Baptist Church	Dan R. Brandel
	Post Falls	Post Falls Baptist Church	William J. Hohenstreet
Illinois	Chicago	Sweet Holy Spirit Baptist Church	Larry D. Trotter
	Chicago	Uptown Baptist Church	Tom Maluga
	Chicago Heights	Fellowship Baptist Church	Ron Long
	Christopher	First Baptist Church	Timothy J. Cowin
	Decatur	Tabernacle Baptist Church	Patrick M. Pajak
	Mulkeytown	Cleburne Baptist Church	Bill Gilmore
	New Baden	First Baptist Church	Billy P. Cecil

STATE	CITY	CHURCH	PASTOR
Indiana	Clay City	Faith Southern Baptist Church	Ray Deeter
	Crown Point	Eastlake Baptist Church	John N. Rogers
	Greenwood	Calvary Baptist Church	Kenny E. Townsend
	Osceola	New Life Baptist Church	Michael A. Cramer
Kansas	Belle Plaine	First Baptist Church	Richard L. Schmidt
	Coffeyville	First Southern Baptist Church	Scott Palmer
	Garden City	First Southern Baptist Church	Randy Caddell
	Lawrence	Cornerstone Southern Baptist Church	Timothy A. Folds
	Overland Park	Emmanuel Baptist Church	Carl W. Garrett
Kentucky	Berea	Bethel Baptist Church	Randy McPheron
	Bowling Green	Living Hope Baptist Church	Brad S. Johnson
	Cecila	Franklin Crossroads Baptist Church	Ron Davis
	Covington	Immanuel Baptist Church	Charles E. Owens
	Crofton	Crofton Baptist Church	Calvin L. Bryant
	Danville	Immanuel Baptist Church	Barry M. Jeffries
	Elizabethtown	Valley Creek Baptist Church	Steven R. Hill
	Frankfort	Buck Run Baptist Church	Robert H. Jackson
	Frankfort	North Frankfort Baptist Church	David A. Smith
	Lewisburg	Green Ridge Baptist Church	Chris C. Butler
	Louisville	Springdale Church	David A. Butler
	Madisonville	Liberty Baptist Church	Doyle Eddings
	Oak Grove	First Baptist Church	Ron G. Wells
	Sebree	First Baptist Church	Bob Hardison
	Shepherdsville	Cedar Grove Baptist Church	Don Cox
	Shepherdsville	Eastern Gate Baptist Church	Pastorless
	Shepherdsville	Mt. Elmira Baptist Church	Brian Campbell
Louisiana	Coushatta	First Baptist Church	Benny Alford
	De Quincy	New Hope Baptist Church	Charles K. Gibbs
	Dry Prong	New Prospect Baptist Church	Leonard Free
	Eunice	Emmanuel Baptist Church	Darryl J. Hoychick

STATE	CITY	CHURCH	PASTOR
Louisiana	Eunice	First Baptist Church	Clark L. Palmer
	Greenwell Springs	Greenwell Springs Baptist Church	Barry Wilkinson
	Hammond	Ebenezer Baptist Church	Kenneth Allen
	Haughton	Haughton Baptist Church	H. M. Prothro
	Haynesville	First Baptist Church	Mickey L. Hawkins
	Houma	First Baptist Church	Glen Wentworth
	Jennings	Bethel Baptist Church	Chris Stephens
	Jennings	First Baptist Church	Lindsay Burns
	La Place	First Baptist Church	Major C. Speights
	Lafayette	East Bayou Baptist Church	Mike Walker
	Lake Charles	Emmanuel Baptist Church	Pastorless
	Lake Charles	Trinity Baptist Church	David E. Hankins
	Livingston	Colyell Baptist Church	Glen Douglas
	Marrero	First Baptist Church	Dino J. Senesi
	Metairie	Celebration Church	Dennis Watson
	New Orleans	Coliseum Place Baptist Church	John Curtis
	New Orleans	First Baptist Church	Pastorless
	New Orleans	Oak Park Baptist Church	Gail W. Debord
	Pineville	Donahue Baptist Church	James Greer
	Prairieville	Dutchtown Baptist Church	Melvin Daniel
	Ruston	Cook Baptist Church	Gilbert G. Arthur
	Shreveport	Northwoods Baptist Church	Freddie R. Harper
	Shreveport	Western Hills Baptist Church	H. D. Smith
	West Monroe	Highland Baptist Church	Gordon E. Dean
Maine	Brunswick	Maine Street Baptist Church	Dale T. Morell
Maryland	Baltimore	First Baptist Church	Richard H. Peoples
	Columbia	Covenant Baptist Church	Dana W. Collett
	Mount Airy	Mount Airy Baptist Church	Michael L. Trammell
	Port Deposit	Pleasant View Baptist Church	Harold M. Phillips

STATE	CITY	CHURCH	PASTOR
Michigan	Lake	Bethany Baptist Church	Latt H. Edwards
	New Baltimore	First Baptist Church	Joseph P. Berna
	Rochester Hills	Korean First Baptist Church	Daniel S. Kim
Mississippi	Booneville	East Booneville Baptist Church	Jim Holcomb
	Booneville	Thrasher Baptist Church	Charles E. Smith
	Brandon	Crossgates Baptist Church	Barry Clingan
	Brandon	Park Place Baptist Church	Bobby Williamson
	Byhalia	Barton First Baptist Church	John McMullen
	Columbus	Fairview Baptist Church	Mickey Dalrymple
	Crystal Springs	New Zion Baptist Church	Leroy J. Brewer
	Escatawpa	Four Mile Creek Baptist Church	Thomas Brill
	Greenville	Emmanuel Baptist Church	John Noble
	Laurel	Indian Springs Baptist Church	Robert D. Keyes
	Long Beach	Sharon Baptist Church	W. Lynn Chapuis
	Louisville	South Louisville Baptist Church	Andre W. Dobson
	Meridian	Northcrest Baptist Church	Malcolm R. Lewis
	Nesbit	First Baptist Church	Mike Montalbano
	Olive Branch	First Baptist Church	P. J. Scott
	Purvis	Okahola Baptist Church	Eugene Haden
	Ripley	West Ripley Baptist Church	Billy W. Baker
	Tupelo	East Heights Baptist Church	Steven F. Bain
	Tupelo	Harrisburg Baptist Church	Forrest Sheffield
	Tupelo	West Jackson Street Baptist Church	Bert Harper
	Verona	First Baptist Church	David E. Hamilton
Missouri	Arnold	First Baptist Church	Gerald R. Davidson
	Branson	Skyline Southern Baptist Church	Gaylen Bohrer
	Carl Junction	First Baptist Church	Ted E. Wilkins
	Dittmer	Morse Mill Baptist Church	James A. Johnston
	Holt	Northern Hills Baptist Church	Richard D. Hubbard
	Independence	Birchwood Baptist Church	Lindell Reed

STATE	CITY	CHURCH	PASTOR
Missouri	Knob Noster	First Baptist Church	Timothy VanBebber
	Mountain View	First Baptist Church	James A. McCullen
	Mount Vernon	Covenant Baptist Church	Mark A. Killingsworth
	Nixa	First Baptist Church	Richard L. Eakins
	Ozark	Eastern Gate Baptist Church	Mike Howell
	O'Fallon	First Baptist Church	Gary N. Taylor
	Patterson	Patterson Baptist Church	William H. Bond
	Republic	Calvary Baptist Church	Michael L. Green
	Springfield	South Gate Baptist Church	Nolan Carrier
	St. Joseph	McCarthy Baptist Church	John P. Swadley
	St. Louis	First Baptist Church of Affton	Ronald D. Wilcoxson
	St. Peters	First Baptist Church	David D. Spriggs
	Warrenton	Warrenton Baptist Church	Charles R. Stillwell
	Warsaw	Cedar Grove Baptist Church	Bill Hix
	Washington	First Baptist Church	Charles T. Williams
	Waynesville	Westside Baptist Church	Lee Schaffer
Montana	Billings	Rimrock Baptist Church	John F. Hunn
	Park City	Park City Baptist Church	Sammie Daniels
Nebraska	Omaha	Harrison Street Baptist Church	Roger Criser
	Omaha	Westside Baptist Church	Anthony W. Lambert
Nevada	Henderson	Highland Hills Baptist Church	John M. Simmons
New Mexico	Bloomfield	First Baptist Church	Joseph L. Bunce
	Silver City	First Baptist Church	Jesse R. Liles
New York	Rome	One Heart Church	David Pope
	Schenectady	Trinity Baptist Church	James M. Guenther

STATE	CITY	CHURCH	PASTOR
North Carolina	Charlotte	McKee Road Baptist Church	Rick K. Blackwood
	Charlotte	Sunset Road Baptist Church	Stephen M. Bass
	Clemmons	Center Grove Baptist Church	Mark E. Harris
	Creedmoor	First Baptist Church	Robert Brown
	Durham	Bethesda Baptist Church	John M. Butler
	Ellenboro	Liberty Baptist Church	Owen Duncan
	Fayetteville	Arran Lake Baptist Church	Jeff Isenhour
	Fayetteville	Cumberland Baptist Church	David M. Odom
	Fayetteville	Village Drive Baptist Church	Bruce O. Martin
	Goldsboro	Adamsville Baptist Church	Alfred R. Wright
	Greensboro	Willomore Baptist Church	Donald Shelton
	Grover	Patterson Springs Baptist Church	Steven J. Waters
	Huntersville	First Baptist Church	Johnson G. Dorn
	Icard	First Baptist Church	Bobby D. Earls
	Jacksonville	Blue Creek Baptist Church	Lamar F. Sutton
	Kannapolis	Blackwelder Park Baptist Church	Stanley J. Welch
	Kings Mountain	Bethlehem Baptist Church	Harold Beam
	Kitty Hawk	First Baptist Church	Clinton Hardee
	Laurinburg	Stewartsville Baptist Church	Lewis F. McLean
	Monroe	Corinth Baptist Church	Jeffrey L. Smith
	Mooresville	Peninsula Baptist Church	Robert H. Jackson
	Morganton	Hartland Baptist Church	Steve Parker
	Pleasant Garden	Pleasant Garden Baptist Church	Michael J. Barrett
	Raleigh	Ephesus Baptist Church	Leslie H. Giles
	Rocky Mount	Memorial Baptist Church	Joe Price
	Shelby	Christopher Road Baptist Church	Mickey G. Heyward
	Wilmington	College Acres Baptist Church	Jeff Nichols
	Wilmington	Northside Baptist Church	Kenneth Chinn
	Wilmington	Scotts Hill Baptist Church	Eddie Davis
Ohio	Batavia	Batavia Heights Baptist Church	Pastorless

STATE	CITY	CHURCH	PASTOR
Ohio	Chilo	Light of the World Church	Michael A. Marriott
	Columbus	Lane Avenue Baptist Church	Wayne I. Nicholson
	Dayton	Airway Baptist Church	Vernon Ware
	Dayton	Miami Valley Community Church	Tim Cox
	Dayton	North Central Baptist Church	Bobby R. Hall
	Fairfield	River Road Baptist Church	Dennis W. Lewis
	Granville	Spring Hills Baptist Church	Jeffrey J. Pound
	Grove City	First Baptist Church	Jerry L. Neal
	Huber Heights	First Baptist Church	Ronald Mitchell
	Norwood	New Bethel Baptist Church	Kirk P. Pike
	Vermilion	Lakeview Baptist Church	Guy Morton
Oklahoma	Altus	First Baptist Church	Keith Wiginton
	Arcadia	First Southern Baptist Church	Ronnie L. Ogle
	Atoka	First Baptist Church	Jeff Holland
	Bixby	Riverview Baptist Church	L. M. Woodson
	Broken Arrow	Arrow Heights Baptist Church	Robert H. Green
	Claremore	Faith Baptist Church	Wayne Keely
	Collinsville	First Baptist Church	Wana T. Archer
	Cushing	Oak Grove Missionary Baptist Church	Jackie Allen
	Edmond	Emmanuel Southern Baptist Church	David R. Goff
	Edmond	First Baptist Church	Alan Day
	Edmond	Waterloo Road Baptist Church	Timothy C. Richardson
	Eufaula	Lindsey Chapel Baptist Church	Timothy J. Turner
	Hennessey	First Baptist Church	Ernie D. Rogers
	Hugo	Oak Grove Baptist Church	Hershel Reed
	Inola	First Baptist Church	Michael A. Butler
	Kingfisher	First Southern Baptist Church	Fred W. King
	Lawton	Trinity Baptist Church	Eddie K. Coast
	McLoud	First Baptist Church	Dan Weaver
	Miami	First Baptist Church	David B. Whitlock

STATE	CITY	CHURCH	PASTOR
Oklahoma	Muskogee	Timothy Baptist Church	Greg Cox
Oklahoma	Mustang	First Baptist Church	Bill Langley
Oklahoma	Oklahoma City	Knob Hill Baptist Church	Rick E. Goodman
Oklahoma	Wagoner	Twin Oaks Baptist Church	Wesley L. Graver
Oregon	Glendale	Glendale Baptist Church	Tillman R. Crownover
Pennsylvania	Bedford	Colonial Hills Baptist Church	John I. Morris
Pennsylvania	Indiana	Bryan Hill Baptist Church	Charles W. Morris
Pennsylvania	Mechanicsburg	Country and Town Baptist Church	Charles M. Teague
Pennsylvania	New Freedom	Mason Dixon Baptist Church	Pastorless
Rhode Island	Warwick	Faith Baptist Church	Richard Wright
South Dakota	Rapid City	Calvary Baptist Church	Benjamin F. Woods
South Carolina	Anderson	Northside Baptist Church	Robert H. White
South Carolina	Bluffton	First Baptist Church	Ronald Gregory
South Carolina	Chapin	Chapin Baptist Church	Kenneth W. Kelly
South Carolina	Clinton	Calvary Baptist Church	Philip D. Bryson
South Carolina	Easley	Powdersville First Baptist Church	Jack W. Hester
South Carolina	Easley	Westwood Baptist Church	William G. Thornhill
South Carolina	Fountain Inn	Pleasant Grove Baptist Church	Tony L. Beam
South Carolina	Gloverville	First Baptist Church	Joe T. Youngblood
South Carolina	Greenville	Forestville Baptist Church	Marshall Fagg
South Carolina	Hartsville	Lakeview Baptist Church	Donald C. Purvis
South Carolina	Lugoff	Lugoff Friendship Baptist Church	Bruce Watford
South Carolina	Saluda	Saluda Baptist Church	Timothy C. Tomlinson
South Carolina	Spartanburg	North Spartanburg First Baptist Church	Michael S. Hamlet
South Carolina	Spartanburg	Saxon Baptist Church	Monty King
South Carolina	Sumter	Shaw Heights Baptist Church	Victor L. Cheek

STATE	CITY	CHURCH	PASTOR
South Carolina	Swansea	Sardis Baptist Church	Donald T. Satterwhite
	Taylors	Lee Road Baptist Church	Eddie Leopard
	Townville	Oakdale Baptist Church	David P. Blizzard
	West Columbia	Agape Baptist Church	Bill H. Howard
Tennessee	Brighton	Beaver Baptist Church	Wade Wallace
	Bristol	Tennessee Avenue Baptist Church	Joseph W. Hudson
	Celina	First Baptist Church	Doug Plumlee
	Chattanooga	Morris Hill Baptist Church	Bill Mason
	Chattanooga	Silverdale Baptist Church	Bobby Atkins
	Clarksville	Hilldale Baptist Church	Verlon W. Moore
	Clarksville	New Providence Baptist Church	Philip J. Dougan
	Cookeville	Stevens Street Baptist Church	Jimmy Arms
	Cookeville	Washington Avenue Baptist Church	Robert M. Ward
	Germantown	Immanuel Baptist Church	Scott Payne
	Gladeville	Gladeville Baptist Church	Bruce D. Grubbs
	Gleason	Beech Springs Baptist Church	Bob Copeland
	Hermitage	Hermitage Hills Baptist Church	H. D. Haun
	Hixson	Central Baptist Church	Ron Phillips
	Hohenwald	First Baptist Church	Timothy E. Miller
	Jackson	Poplar Heights Baptist Church	Joe McIntire
	Jackson	Woodland Baptist Church	Robert D. Ervin
	Johnson City	Mountain View Baptist Church	James Cambron
	Kingsport	Higher Ground Baptist Church	Phil Hoskins
	Knoxville	Sevier Heights Baptist Church	Hollie S. Miller
	La Vergne	First Baptist Church	Milton L. Hicks
	Lawrenceburg	Mars Hill Baptist Church	Mickey D. Brackin
	Lebanon	Immanuel Baptist Church	Donald Owens
	Millington	Second Baptist Church	Scott T. Walker
	Mount Juliet	Green Hill Baptist Church	W. D. Thomason

STATE	CITY	CHURCH	PASTOR
Tennessee	Oak Ridge	Calvary Baptist Church	Steve McDonald
	Pikeville	First Baptist Church	Lonnie P. Cummings
	Ripley	Eastland Baptist Church	Roy W. Harkness
	Saint Bethlehem	First Baptist Church	John M. Thomas
	Spring City	First Baptist Church	Steven H. Pearson
	Talbott	Talbott Baptist Church	Jerry Utsman
	Tullahoma	Grace Baptist Church	Mike Grass
	Union City	Calvary Baptist Church	Melvin Poe
	Waynesboro	Green River Baptist Church	Pastorless
	Westmoreland	Twin Hills Baptist Church	Albert L. Crouch
Texas	Abilene	Holiday Hills Baptist Church	Gary E. Bender
	Adkins	Salem Sayers Baptist Church	Tony Romans
	Amarillo	Coulter Road Baptist Church	Larry A. Payne
	Amarillo	San Jacinto Baptist Church	Stan Coffey
	Andrews	Calvary Baptist Church	Mike Henson
	Arlington	Lake Arlington Baptist Church	David George
	Atlanta	West Side Baptist Church	Jim Howard
	Austin	Marshall Ford Baptist Church	Gene Smith
	Baytown	Second Baptist Church	Bruce L. Baker
	Belton	First Baptist Church	Andy Davis
	Bryan	Hillcrest Baptist Church	Joe D. Loftis
	Burleson	Cana Baptist Church	Mike Lowery
	Carrollton	Woodlake Baptist Church	Ed Ethridge
	Chandler	West Lake Baptist Church	Robert Sexton
	Channelview	Memorial Baptist Church	Novice Northington
	Copperas Cove	Robertson Avenue Baptist Church	John H. Hooser
	Corpus Christi	Gardendale Baptist Church	Terry G. Fox
	Corpus Christi	Southcrest Baptist Church	Buddy Murphrey
	Corpus Christi	Yorktown Baptist Church	Samuel K. Douglass
	Dayton	Calvary Baptist Church	Wayne Hardin

STATE	CITY	CHURCH	PASTOR
Texas	Dayton	Midway Baptist Church	Steve A. Cartin
	El Paso	El Paso Chinese Baptist Church	James Vang
	Elm Mott	First Baptist Church	Walter Crouch
	Emory	Emory Baptist Church	Rodney Williams
	Fort Stockton	First Baptist Church	David McFadden
	Garland	Sweethome Missionary Baptist Church	Lewis W. Wilson
	Garrison	First Baptist Church	John N. McGuire
	Gladewater	Friendship Baptist Church	Paul Rucker
	Glen Rose	Emmanuel Baptist Church	Pastorless
	Granbury	Lakeside Baptist Church	John D. Duncan
	Greenville	Dixon Baptist Church	Kelly F. Carr
	Hamshire	First Baptist Church	Joseph W. Constantine
	Houston	Bear Creek Baptist Church	Stephen L. Peace
	Houston	Cornerstone Baptist Church	Ken Shuman
	Houston	Forest Oaks Baptist Church	Zane D. Chambers
	Houston	Second Baptist Church	Edwin H. Young
	Houston	Sterling Wood Baptist Church	A. Dale Jones
	Houston	Wilcrest Baptist Church	Rodney M. Woo
	Iowa Park	Faith Baptist Church	Gregory L. Ammons
	Irving	Fellowship of Las Colinas	Ed Young
	Katy	Kingsland Baptist Church	Pastorless
	Keller	Mount Gilead Baptist Church	Daniel B. Forshee
	Killeen	Memorial Baptist Church	Joe D. Rich
	Kingwood	Forest Cove Baptist Church	David L. Lino
	La Marque	Highlands Baptist Church	Leo Smith
	La Porte	Bayshore Baptist Church	Stanley Jordan
	La Porte	Second Baptist Church	Bobbye L. Worsham
	Livingston	Central Baptist Church	Bill Skaar
	Malakoff	First Baptist Church	Casey Perry
	McAllen	Baptist Temple	Randy McDonald

STATE	CITY	CHURCH	PASTOR
	McAllen	Emmanuel Baptist Church	Roland Lopez
	McAllen	First Baptist Church	Bill Sutton
	Midland	Alamo Heights Baptist Church	Ben G. Condray
	Midland	Greenwood Baptist Church	Wayman Swopes
	Mount Pleasant	Trinity Baptist Church	Pastorless
	North Richland Hills	Northwood Baptist Church	Bob Roberts
	Palestine	Westwood Baptist Church	Robert Rachuig
	Peaster	First Baptist Church	John Anderson
	Port Neches	Central Baptist Church	David Broussard
	Rosanky	Rosanky Baptist Church	Y. J. Jimenez
	Rowlett	First Baptist Church	Stephen P. Leatherwood
	Rusk	Eastside Baptist Church	Newton R. Hambrick
	San Antonio	Valley Hi First Baptist Church	Curtis R. Hallford
Texas	Santa Fe	First Baptist Church of Arcadia	Thomas S. Brewer
	Santa Fe	First Baptist Church of Ata Loma	Alan R. Splawn
	Schertz	First Baptist Church	Don W. Jeffreys
	Silsbee	Fletcher Emanuel Church Alive	Richard Vaughan
	Silsbee	Pinecrest Baptist Church	Robert Carter
	Slaton	Westview Baptist Church	Chris Seidlitz
	Spring	Klein First Baptist Church	H. R. Onarecker
	Spring	Spring Memorial Baptist Church	J. Kevin Basham
	Sugar Land	Sugar Creek Baptist Church	Fenton Moorhead
	Sunnyvale	First Baptist Church	Charles L. Wilson
	The Colony	Lakeway Baptist Church	Michael Weaver
	Tomball	Graceview Baptist Church	Bryan Donahoo
	Universal City	First Baptist Church	Tommy R. Grozier
	Waskom	First Baptist Church	Jim Walsh
	Watauga	Harvest Baptist Church	Ollin Collins
	West Columbia	First Baptist Church	Larry W. Craig

STATE	CITY	CHURCH	PASTOR
Utah	Brigham City	First Baptist Church	James H. Herod
	Salt Lake City	Southeast Baptist Church	R. Michael Gray
	West Valley City	First Baptist Church	Warren Osburn
Virginia	Chesapeake	Bethel Baptist Church	Houston F. Roberson
	Fairfax Station	Virgnia Korean Baptist Church	Se Won Suh
	Fancy Gap	Skyview Baptist Church	Elmon O. Thompson
	Fredericksburg	Spotswood Baptist Church	Bob R. Melvin
	Gloucester	Ebenezer Baptist Church	Michael L. Adams
	Norfolk	First Baptist Church	Robert E. Reccord
	Norfolk	Ocean View Baptist Church	David N. Clay
	Palmyra	Effort Baptist Church	John P. Chandler
	Ridgeway	Hillcrest Baptist Church	Douglas T. Ramsey
	Stafford	Mount Ararat Baptist Church	Aubrey D. Whitten
	Stafford	Victory Baptist Church	Clive E. Beer
	Swords Creek	Swords Creek Baptist Church	Les Richie
	Vinton	Mineral Springs Baptist Church	A. S. Corbin
	Williamsburg	York River Baptist Church	William C. Cashman
	Woodbridge	Grace Baptist Church	Charles A. Chilton
	Yorktown	Bethel Baptist Church	Franklin D. Hall
	Yorktown	Grafton Baptist Church	James D. Moynihan
Washington	Airway Heights	First Baptist Church	Bob Cassels
	Bothell	First Baptist Church	Sam Friend
	East Wenatchee	Eastmont Baptist Church	Bob Bauer
	Lynnwood	First Baptist Church	Reginald D. Corns
	Tacoma	First Baptist Church	Walter V. Kellcy
	Tacoma	Parkland First Baptist Church	Buddy Ellis
	Yakima	First Southern Baptist Church	Johnny W. Lay

STATE	CITY	CHURCH	PASTOR
West Virginia	Charleston	North Charleston Baptist Church	Richard Bowden
West Virginia	Shepherdstown	Covenant Baptist Church	Ronald L. Larson
Wyoming	Cheyenne	Sunnyside Baptist Church	James H. Stiles

The Survey Instrument

A STUDY OF THE CHARACTERISTICS OF HIGH-BAPTISMAL CHURCHES IN THE SOUTHERN BAPTIST CONVENTION
The Southern Baptist Theological Seminary
Billy Graham School of Missions, Evangelism, and Church Growth
Thom S. Rainer, Dean

QUESTIONNAIRE SURVEY

The purpose of this survey is to glean a better understanding of the characteristics of churches which have high-baptismal rates. High-baptismal churches are churches that have a ratio of one baptism for every nineteen resident members or less. Your willingness to take time to complete these questions will be a tremendous help in preparing ministers for the future and for informing today's church. Please take time now to fill out the questionnaire. Thank you. *(Please note questions on front and back of pages)*

Section A: Evangelistic Methods

Respond to each of the following statements in terms of which one or more of these activities or situations best interprets the reasons for your church having a good baptismal ratio.

1=Not a factor   2=May be a factor 3=Somewhat a factor
4=Contributing factor 5=Main factor

_____ Preaching
_____ Revival/Renewal Activities
_____ Sunday School Program
_____ Bus Ministry

_____ Feeder and Receptor Patterns from Other Churches
_____ Intentional Positioning That Targets a Specific Population
_____ Music Ministry
_____ Pulpit Teaching
_____ Unchurched Relationships with Church Members
_____ Weekday Ministries, Day Care, Christian School
_____ Next to the Right Institution, University, Hospital, etc.
_____ High-Visibility and High-Profile Speakers, Musicians, Major Events, etc.
_____ Seeker Services
_____ Multiple and Gifted Staff
_____ Ethnic Ministry
_____ Women's Ministry
_____ Youth Ministry
_____ Weekly Outreach Ministry
_____ Evangelism Training Programs
_____ Relational Witness of Members
_____ Prayer Ministry
_____ Family Ministries
_____ Counseling Ministries
_____ Others that would be a "4" or "5"

Section B: Attitudes Toward Evangelism

Select the response which best describes your attitude toward the following statements of assumption.

1=Do not agree   2=Somewhat Agree   3=Agree
4=Very Much Agree   5=Absolutely Agree, Most Important

_____ Evangelism is not concerned with numbers, but with meeting the spiritual needs of people.
_____ Evangelism occurs when people are given a wide variety of choices.
_____ Evangelism occurs when people are matched with their skills and gifts.
_____ Evangelism provides a wider outreach to people in need.
_____ Deep down, non-Christians really want to know and obey God.
_____ Non-Christians typically have five or more significant encounters with the gospel before coming into a relationship with Jesus.

_____ Non-Christians usually will not come to us to find God. We have to go to them.

_____ Evangelism is the easiest and most natural of the church's ministries.

_____ Effective evangelism requires little training.

_____ Friendly, openhearted people make the best evangelists.

_____ Church life, spent nurturing the fellowship only, produces saints who are neither friendly nor openhearted to outsiders.

_____ The kingdom of God is the primary mission and issue of our shared life as Christians, not self-preservation or the perpetuation of a church.

_____ The primary foundation of all our evangelism is love.

_____ Placing expectations upon someone we are evangelizing is always injurious and works against that person coming to Christ.

_____ We become holy and righteous by identifying with Jesus and surrendering to His will for us rather than trying to obey the law.

_____ Each person in relationship with Jesus is primarily responsible for his or her own follow-up and fellowship needs.

_____ Prayer is foundational to effective evangelism.

_____ The Holy Spirit is the only true evangelist who has ever existed, as well as the only disciple-maker.

_____ It is normal for everyone who loves Jesus to have a heart for the poor, sick, lost, widowed, and homeless.

_____ We are committed to prayer as an essential element of any successful outreach venture.

_____ Non-Christians may not remember what they have been told regarding God's love, but they always remember what they have experienced as God's love.

_____ None of us can manufacture the Holy Spirit's genuine working.

_____ The Holy Spirit is able, willing, and free to break in and carry on His work in unspectacular, non-manipulative, and surprising ways.

_____ An atmosphere of strength, freshness, and vitality comes upon believers when they spend time with non-Christians.

_____ Because of irrational fears, the average Southern Baptist today has no plans to participate actively in evangelism.

_____ Most Christians are so far out of touch with the world around them that they know little of its fears, problems, concerns, or issues.

_____ Because God is highly committed to the lost, almost any evangelistic approach will work given enough time and commitment to sharing the good news.

_____ Effective evangelism is more a mindset than a program outcome.

_____ The value of evangelism will regularly conflict with the typical programs of church life.

_____ Because they are central to the mission of the local church, funding for evangelism ought to be seen as a part of the regular church budget rather than the areas to be financed by special offerings.

_____ Our evangelism is really an overflow of our relationship with God and our relationship with people.

Section C: Worship Style

Choose the description which best captures the design of your services.

_____ Sunday Morning, main or primary_____

_____ Sunday Morning, early or other, not applicable _____

_____ Sunday Evening, not applicable _____

_____ Wednesday, not applicable _____

_____ Other Service times _____

1 - Liturgical

Mood: formal, solemn, majestic. Music: pipe organ, traditional hymns, classical anthems. Purpose: "To lead the church to give corporate recognition to the transcendent glory of God." Favors reverence over relevance. It runs counter to the cultural obsession with contemporary entertainment. Biblical model: Isaiah 6.

2 - Traditional

Mood: orderly, majestic, contemplative. Music: organ and piano, traditional and gospel hymns, traditional and contemporary anthems. Purpose: "To lead the congregation to praise and thank God for His goodness and to hear Him speak through His Word." Geared for people from a religious culture and background. The most frequent Southern Baptist format. Biblical model: Col. 3:16–17.

3 - Revivalist

Mood: exuberant, celebrative, informal. Music: organ, piano, and taped music, gospel hymns, contemporary Christian songs and anthems.

Purpose: "To save the lost and encourage believers to witness." More evangelistic than contemplative worship. Biblical model: Acts 2–3.

4 - Contemporary

Mood: expressive, celebrative, contemporary, informal. Music: keyboard, piano and taped music, praise choruses and contemporary Christian songs. Purpose: "To offer a sacrifice of praise to the Lord in a spirit of joyful adoration." This is contemporary worship for believers, but does attract some non-Christians and un-churched. Biblical model: Psalm 150.

5 - Seeker

Mood: celebrative, contemporary, informal. Music: Piano, taped music, synthesizer and band, scriptural music and contemporary Christian music, little congregational singing in the traditional sense. Purpose: "Present the gospel in clear non-God talk terms and modern forms." An upbeat, non-threatening evangelistic service for non-Christians seeking God. Biblical model: Acts 17:16–34.

6 - Blended

Combinations of elements in both traditional and contemporary.

7 - Other style(s)

Section D: Composition of Congregation

The following are four different orientations toward the mission of the church. Most congregations are a mixture of the four, but typically one of them is dominant. The first two orientations are "this-worldly" in focus; the latter two are more "other-worldly" in focus. Rank the four in the order of the most dominant to the least for your congregation, one through four.

_____ **Activist** - This world is the arena of God's redemptive activity and, therefore, the arena in which God calls the congregation to speak out on issues and engage in corporate action, working for social change and transformation toward a more just and loving society.

_____ **Civic** - This world is the arena in which God calls Christians to act and to take responsibility for public life; however, the civic orientation is more comfortable with existing social and economic institutions. This congregation will use service to the community to reach people for Christ. It is important to be an example of Christ-likeness to the community by showing the love of God in action/service.

_____ **Outreach** - This congregation will focus on a formal soul-winning program and inviting the unchurched to participate in worship. Members are encouraged to witness to their faith, sharing the message of salvation with those outside the fellowship and leading them to membership in the church.

_____ **Fellowship** - This orientation encourages the view that the church exists as a sanctuary for the members from the secular world. Nurturing and support are the key focus for the programming of the church. The task is to resist the temptation of contemporary pleasures and lifestyles. These people believe their deepest loyalty belongs to God. Their motivation for witnessing is providing a solution for sin and corruption.

Section E: Personal Beliefs

_____ 1. Which of the following best expresses your belief about God?

(A) God is the creator of an orderly world, but does not now guide it or intervene in its course or affairs of the lives of individuals; (B) Although God has and can act in history and communicate with persons directly, it is not something that happens very often; (C) God is constantly at work in the world directing people, nations, and events; (D) God is the world and is potentially in every person, thing, and event.

_____ 2. Which one of the following best expresses your view of the Bible?

(A) The Bible is the record of many different people's responses to God. Because of this, persons and churches today are often forced to interpret for themselves the Bible's basic moral and spiritual teachings; (B) The Bible is the inspired Word of God and its basic moral spiritual teachings are clear and true, even if it does contain some human error; (C) The Bible is the actual Word of God and is to be taken literally and completely.

_____ 3. Which of the following best expresses your belief about sin and salvation?

(A) I believe all people are inherently good, and to the extent sin and salvation have meaning to all, it has to do with people realizing or not realizing their human potential for good; (B) Although people are sinful, all people participate in God's salvation regardless of how they live their life, even if they do not believe in God; (C) All people are sinful but need only to believe in and ask for God's forgiveness to be saved; (D) All people are sinful and if they are to be saved must earn it through living a good life, devoted to God.

Section F: Preaching Model

Which of these models for preaching do you find to be the most influential in helping individuals receive Christ as their personal Savior? Rank them showing a one (1) for the model that you feel is most productive, to the model that you feel is least helpful with a number five (5).

_____ **Expository** - An expository sermon contains a clear statement of the biblical idea that is legitimately derived from a passage or passages.

_____ **Textual** - The textual sermons tend to be of shorter texts than expository sermons and lean toward topical styles, but they are focused on a biblical text and the message of that text.

_____ **Topical** - The model is hard to identify clearly. The best understanding seems to be that this approach is driven by a subject and the subject matched to Scripture. Usually used when it does not appear that there is text that speaks directly to the subject.

_____ **Thematic** - The purpose of this sermon is to identify the principles that help the Christians understand God and their faith. The better use of this model will carefully show how the listeners could apply the message of the text in their own walk of faith.

_____ **Narrative** - The narrative sermon is a story that, from the outset to conclusion, binds the entire message to a single plot as theme. This is a sermon-as-story understanding of the text.

_____ **Alternate** - Anything that does not fit into the above models.

_____

_____

_____

Section G: Other Helpful Information

What percent of those baptized in the last two years continue to be active in the church? _____

What specific measures do you take to ensure that the people baptized remain involved in the church? _____

Size of church: (check one in each column)

	Resident membership	Attendance (Highest of worship or Sunday School)
Under 100	_____	_____
100–299	_____	_____
300–499	_____	_____
500–699	_____	_____
700–999	_____	_____
1000–1499	_____	_____
Over 1500	_____	_____

Setting of church:

Urban	_____	Rural	_____
Suburban	_____	Transitional	_____

Age of church: _____

How long have you been at this church? _____

Racial, ethnic, and socioeconomic composition of resident members.

White	_____%	Upper Class	_____%
Black	_____%	Upper Middle	_____%
Asian	_____%	Middle	_____%
Hispanic	_____%	Upper Lower	_____%
		Lower	_____%

Cooperative program giving. Percent of annual budget: _____%

New church starts in last year: _____

Your highest level of education:

High School	_____	Seminary	_____
Associate	_____	University/college	_____

Seminary Attended: _____

Inner and outer sources of baptisms - family or relative of a church member?

_____ Percent of baptisms last year from people not in family of or relative to church members.

Which leadership orientation do you most often use?

_____ Directive		_____ Coordination	
_____ Persuasion		_____ Delegation	

Staff composition. List full- and part-time staff positions by title.

_____

_____

_____

_____

List the use of CWT/EE, Experiencing God, Masterlife, or other programs and the participation level in percent of resident membership in the last year:

CWT/EE   _____   _____%

Experiencing God   _____   _____%

Masterlife Part 1   _____   _____%

Masterlife Part 2   _____   _____%

Other   _____   _____%

       _____   _____%

Section H: Anything else you would like to suggest, which has affected the good ratio of baptisms that your church has experienced, that has not been covered in this survey?

_____

_____

_____

_____

_____

Thank you for your time.

Your name_____

Are you the pastor? _____. If no, please give position_____

Church name_____

City, state _____

Notes

Chapter 1

1. C. Peter Wagner, *Church Growth and the Whole Gospel: A Biblical Mandate* (San Francisco: Harper and Row, 1981), 77.

2. George G. Hunter III, *The Contagious Congregation: Frontiers in Evangelism and Church Growth* (Nashville: Abingdon, 1979), 104.

3. See Bobb Biehl, *Stop Setting Goals If You Would Rather Solve Problems* (New York: Moorings, 1995).

Chapter 2

1. See Thom S. Rainer, *Giant Awakenings* (Nashville: Broadman and Holman, 1995), chapter 3, "Teach These Things . . . The Renewal of Sunday School."

2. See Lyle E. Schaller, *The Seven-Day-A-Week Church* (Nashville: Abingdon, 1992), especially chapters 2 and 3.

Chapter 3

1. See, for example C. Peter Wagner, *Leading Your Church to Growth* (Ventura, Calif.: Regal, 1984), 215–18. Wagner stated, on 215, that "I am looking forward to much more research on this [preaching and church growth] in the future." After twelve years he is still waiting!

2. Dean Kelley, *Why Conservative Churches Are Growing*, rev. ed. (Macon, Ga.: Mercer University, 1986).

3. This study is cited in David F. Wells, *No Place for Truth or Whatever Happened to Evangelical Theology?* (Grand Rapids, Mich.: Eerdmans, 1993), 251–52. The journals mentioned are *Pulpit Digest* and *Preaching*, covering the years 1981 to 1991.

4. See Thom S. Rainer, *Giant Awakenings* (Nashville: Broadman & Holman, 1995), especially 46–47 and 113–19.

Chapter 4

1. See Thom S. Rainer, *Giant Awakenings* (Nashville: Broadman & Holman, 1995), 18–19.

2. C. Peter Wagner, *Churches That Pray* (Ventura, Calif.: Regal, 1993), 81.

3. Ibid., 96–97.

4. Ibid., 98.

5. Ibid., 99.

6. Ibid., 65.

7. Ibid.

Chapter 5

1. R. Wayne Jones, *Overcoming Barriers to Sunday School Growth* (Nashville: Broadman, 1987), 173–74.

2. See Thom S. Rainer, *Giant Awakenings* (Nashville: Broadman & Holman, 1995), chapter 3. The study cited is Dean R. Hoge, Benton Johnson, and Donald A. Luidens, *Vanishing Boundaries: The Religion of Mainline Protestant Baby Boomers* (Louisville: Westminster/John Knox, 1994).

Chapter 6

1. See Thom S. Rainer, *Giant Awakenings* (Nashville: Broadman & Holman, 1995), chapter 9.
2. Interview with Brian Saylor, vice-president of Church Growth Institute, Forest, Va., 20 November 1995.

Chapter 7

1. George Barna, *Evangelism That Works* (Ventura, Calif.: Regal, 1995), 90.
2. Ibid.
3. Michael Green, *Evangelism in the Early Church* (Grand Rapids: Eerdmans, 1970), 249.
4. Ibid., 251.
5. The Engel scale can be found in many evangelism and church growth books. The best discussion of the tool is found in C. Peter Wagner, *Strategies for Church Growth* (Ventura, Caif.: Regal, 1987), 124.
6. Lynne and Bill Hybels, *Rediscovering Church* (Grand Rapids, Mich.: Zondervan, 1995).
7. Ibid., 137.
8. Ibid.
9. See Dean M. Kelley, *Why Conservative Churches Are Growing*, rev. ed. (Macon, Ga.: Mercer University, 1986).

Chapter 8

1. C. Kirk Hadaway, *Church Growth Principles: Separating Fact from Fiction* (Nashville: Broadman, 1991), 169.
2. Ibid.
3. Ibid.
4. Ibid.
5. Lausanne Covenant, see article 5, "Christian Social Responsibility."

Chapter 9

1. See Thom S. Rainer, *Eating the Elephant* (Nashville: Broadman & Holman, 1994).
2. Lyle E. Schaller, *44 Questions for Church Planters* (Nashville: Abingdon, 1991), 15. Schaller's book has a wealth of information about the American historical data on church planting.
3. Aubrey Malphurs, *Planting Growing Churches for the 21st Century* (Grand Rapids: Baker, 1992), 13.
4. Cited in Malphurs, 14.
5. Ibid.
6. Ibid., 35.

Chapter 10

1. See Thom S. Rainer, *Giant Awakenings* (Nashville: Broadman & Holman, 1995), chapter 3: "The Renewal of the Sunday School."
2. See Lynne and Bill Hybels, *Rediscovering Church* (Grand Rapids: Zondervan, 1995).

Chapter 11

1. David Goetz and Kevin Miller. "Megashifts" *Leadership*, Vol. 16, no. 4 (Fall 1995): 111–13.

Index